Network Type/Feature	Description	Page
Wireless Hotspots — Wireless NIC	**Wireless hotspots**—Go wireless at hotels, airports, coffee shops, etc.	182
Wireless NIC — Wireless Router — Broadband Modem — Internet — STOP	**Network security**—Protect the computers on your network from intruders, viruses, spam, and other threats.	206, 224, 242
XXX — STOP — Internet	**Child safety**—Add parental controls to your network to keep your kids safe on the Internet and limit usage to times that you determine.	252
Wireless NIC — Wireless Print Server	**Wireless printers**—Set up a wireless print server so printers can be located anywhere in your house.	271
Wireless Video Camera	**Video surveillance**—Set up a wireless video camera at home, which allows you to keep an eye on your house from afar or check in on latchkey kids from work.	287
555-1212 — Internet Phone Adapter — Wireless Router — Broadband Modem — Internet — Public Telephone System	**Internet phone service**—Make telephone calls by using the Internet, saving you money and adding flexibility.	324

Home Networking Simplified

An illustrated home networking handbook for the everyday user

Jim Doherty

Neil Anderson

Illustrations by Nathan Clement

Cisco Press
800 East 96th Street
Indianapolis, IN 46240

Home Networking Simplified

Jim Doherty

Neil Anderson

Copyright© 2005 Cisco Systems, Inc.

Published by:
Cisco Press
800 East 96th Street
Indianapolis, IN 46240 USA

Printed in the United States of America 1 2 3 4 5 6 7 8 9 0

First Printing June 2005

Library of Congress Cataloging-in-Publication Number: 2004109285

ISBN: 1-58720-136-4

Warning and Disclaimer

This book is designed to provide information about home networking. Every effort has been made to make this book as complete and as accurate as possible, but no warranty or fitness is implied.

The information is provided on an "as is" basis. The author, Cisco Press, and Cisco Systems, Inc. shall have neither liability nor responsibility to any person or entity with respect to any loss or damages arising from the information contained in this book or from the use of the discs or programs that may accompany it.

The opinions expressed in this book belong to the author and are not necessarily those of Cisco Systems, Inc.

Trademark Acknowledgments

All terms mentioned in this book that are known to be trademarks or service marks have been appropriately capitalized. Cisco Press or Cisco Systems, Inc. cannot attest to the accuracy of this information. Use of a term in this book should not be regarded as affecting the validity of any trademark or service mark.

Corporate and Government Sales

Cisco Press offers excellent discounts on this book when ordered in quantity for bulk purchases or special sales.

For more information please contact: U.S. Corporate and Government Sales: 1-800-382-3419 corpsales@pearsontechgroup.com

For sales outside the U.S. please contact: International Sales international@pearsoned.com

Feedback Information

At Cisco Press, our goal is to create in-depth technical books of the highest quality and value. Each book is crafted with care and precision, undergoing rigorous development that involves the unique expertise of members from the professional technical community.

Readers' feedback is a natural continuation of this process. If you have any comments regarding how we could improve the quality of this book, or otherwise alter it to better suit your needs, you can contact us through e-mail at feedback@ciscopress.com. Please make sure to include the book title and ISBN in your message.

We greatly appreciate your assistance.

CISCO SYSTEMS

Corporate Headquarters
Cisco Systems, Inc.
170 West Tasman Drive
San Jose, CA 95134-1706
USA
www.cisco.com
Tel: 408 526-4000
    800 553-NETS (6387)
Fax: 408 526-4100

European Headquarters
Cisco Systems International BV
Haarlerbergpark
Haarlerbergweg 13-19
1101 CH Amsterdam
The Netherlands
www-europe.cisco.com
Tel: 31 0 20 357 1000
Fax: 31 0 20 357 1100

Americas Headquarters
Cisco Systems, Inc.
170 West Tasman Drive
San Jose, CA 95134-1706
USA
www.cisco.com
Tel: 408 526-7660
Fax: 408 527-0883

Asia Pacific Headquarters
Cisco Systems, Inc.
Capital Tower
168 Robinson Road
#22-01 to #29-01
Singapore 068912
www.cisco.com
Tel: +65 6317 7777
Fax: +65 6317 7799

Cisco Systems has more than 200 offices in the following countries and regions. Addresses, phone numbers, and fax numbers are listed on the Cisco.com Web site at www.cisco.com/go/offices.

Argentina • Australia • Austria • Belgium • Brazil • Bulgaria • Canada • Chile • China PRC • Colombia • Costa Rica • Croatia • Czech Republic Denmark • Dubai, UAE • Finland • France • Germany • Greece • Hong Kong SAR • Hungary • India • Indonesia • Ireland • Israel • Italy Japan • Korea • Luxembourg • Malaysia • Mexico • The Netherlands • New Zealand • Norway • Peru • Philippines • Poland • Portugal Puerto Rico • Romania • Russia • Saudi Arabia • Scotland • Singapore • Slovakia • Slovenia • South Africa • Spain • Sweden Switzerland • Taiwan • Thailand • Turkey • Ukraine • United Kingdom • United States • Venezuela • Vietnam • Zimbabwe

Publisher
John Wait

Editor-in-Chief
John Kane

Cisco Representative
Anthony Wolfenden

Cisco Press Program Manager
Jeff Brady

Production Manager
Patrick Kanouse

Development Editor
Sheri Cain

Copy Editor
Katherin Bidwell

Technical Editors
Bill Adams
Jonathan Donaldson
Bradley Mitchell

Team Coordinator
Tammi Barnett

Book Designer and Compositor
Mark Shirar

Cover Designer
Louisa Adair

Indexer
WordWise

About the Authors

Jim Doherty is currently a director of strategic marketing with Symbol Technologies, responsible for marketing industry-based solutions. Prior to joining Symbol, Jim worked at Cisco Systems, where he led marketing campaigns for IP telephony, and routing and switching. Over the past several years, he has taught professionals in both academic and industry settings on a broad range of topics, including networking, electric circuits, statistics, and wireless communication methods. Jim is the coauthor of *Cisco Networking Simplified* and wrote the Study Notes section of the *Cisco CCNA Flash Cards and Exam Practice Kit*. Jim holds a B.S. in electrical engineering from N.C. State University and an MBA from Duke University. Jim also served in the United States Marine Corps, where he earned the rank of sergeant, before leaving to pursue an education.

Neil Anderson is a manager in Enterprise Systems Engineering at Cisco Systems, currently responsible for IP network systems architectures for global Enterprise customers. Neil has 20 years of diverse telecom experience, including public telephone systems, mobile telephone systems, IP networks, wireless networking, and home networks. Neil has held roles in research and development, systems engineering, and technical marketing. At Cisco Systems, Neil has worked with virtual private network (VPN), voice over IP (VoIP), and wireless LAN (WLAN) technologies, focusing on networking solutions for enterprise and small business customers. Neil holds a B.S. in computer science.

About the Technical Editors

Bill Adams is a senior staff engineer wireless data testing technical lead at Sony Ericsson Mobile Communications. He joined Ericsson in July 1998. Prior to then he was a software engineer at IBM's Network Computing Software Division, RTP, NC. Bill holds a bachelor of science in industrial relations from the University of North Carolina at Chapel Hill.

Jonathan Donaldson joined Cisco in 1998 and is currently working as a technical lead engineer in the new Cisco Commercial Voice and Video Business Unit. Jonathan has held a wide range of positions while at Cisco, starting as a systems engineer focused on U.S. military customers in Europe. Since that time, Jonathan has been a testing engineer and a technical marketing engineer. Through these positions, Jonathan has had a strong thirst for mastering new technologies. He enjoys spending time with his wife, Janie, and his boys Grant, Evan, and Soon-to-be-#-3.

Bradley Mitchell serves as writer and editor for the Wireless/Networking site at About.com. He has developed online tutorials and reference content on computer networking topics for five years there. Bradley is also a senior software engineer at Intel Corporation. Over the past 11 years at Intel, he has developed, validated, and administered a wide range of network hardware/software systems, published research papers, and developed patents. Bradley obtained his master's degree in computer science from the University of Illinois and his bachelor's degree from M.I.T.

Dedication

A special dedication of this book is given to Karen King, whose courageous battle with ALS continues to teach us the strength of the human spirit. A computer helps Karen to communicate, and through the use of a wireless video camera, her husband monitors her well being. If we bring just one family the knowledge to make such inspiring uses of their home network, all the efforts put into this book will have been worth it.

Acknowledgments

The authors would like to thank the following people:

The fine folks at Cisco Systems and Linksys Networks who provided us with lots of gear, technical assistance, and support: Ann McArtor, Charlie Giancarlo, Michael Wagner, and Stuart Hamilton.

Some really smart folks at Cisco Systems who put up with our technical questions: Joel King, Steve Ochmanski, Lou Ronnau, Brian Cox, Bruce McMurdo, and Ted Hannock.

Our publication team whose patience we tried and tried; John Kane, Sheri Cain (who took the brunt of our abuse), Patrick Kanouse, Tammi Barnett, and the entire Cisco Press staff.

The talented, knowledgeable, and highly entertaining Geek Squad team who protected our readers and will try their best not to make fun of us when they troubleshoot our designs; Chief Inspector Robert Stephens, Agent Michael Sherwood, Agent Ryan Davies, Agent Gavin McKay, Agent Trent Kannenberg, Agent Andrew Douglas, Agent Nathan Bauer, Agent Lee Rocchio, Agent Melinda Cortez, and Stephanie Bothof.

Our illustrator Nathan Clement, who is somehow able to figure out exactly what we want, even when it is not what we ask for.

A very special thanks to our technical reviewers Bill Adams, Jonathan Donaldson, and Bradley Mitchell. It's no small task chasing down our mistakes and misprints. You guys all earned your stripes on this one.

Jim Doherty would like to thank:

Neil Anderson, my coauthor and friend who I stuck with all the hard parts of this book. Never has such a reluctant participant created such outstanding work.

Paul Della Maggiora who helped come up with the idea for this book a long time ago.

My wonderful family who continues to support me in all these time-consuming exercises of self actualization. This book is dedicated to Katie, Samantha, and Conor.

Neil Anderson would like to thank:

Jim Doherty, my coauthor and friend who continues to astound me with his drive and creativity. You have come along way from PFC Momma's Boy.

To my daughters who continue to show me the world through their eyes, my wife who holds down the hard job at home so I get to play with computers and stuff, and my friends who keep me whole. This book is dedicated to Karen, Courtney, and Jillian.

Contents

Contents

Icons Used in This Book

Table I-1 shows the icons that are used in this book.

Table I-1   **Icon List**

Device	Photo	Icon Used
Router		
Wireless Router		
Wired Network Interface Card (NIC)		
Wireless Network Interface Card (NIC)		
Broadband Modem		

Foreword

In 2003, Cisco Systems, Inc., the leader in Internet technologies, acquired Linksys, the leader in home networking technologies. This was a surprising move to some observers at the time but it signaled the recognition by Cisco of home networking as a major growth market and of Linksys as a powerful brand.

One of the things that sets Linksys apart in the market and attracted the notice of Cisco is how easily its products can be set up and used. The average buyer can take a product out of the box, follow the quick setup guide, and immediately begin enjoying the productivity or entertainment advantages of that device.

However, as easy as it is to set up and use Linksys products, consumers are becoming increasingly interested in developing more complex configurations of their home networking equipment, creating the need for a guide that takes a "systems approach" to home networking.

A quick survey of the networking section of your local or online bookstore will turn up dozens of books on the topic of home networking. These books typically fall into two broad categories: how-it-works and how-to-build-it. Many books that take a how-it-works approach either dive too deep or remain too abstract to be very useful to the nontechnical reader. Others attempt to explain basic home networking concepts by oversimplifying the subject and talking down to the reader. Lacking the practical application that most readers are looking for, this type of book is of limited value.

On the other hand, many how-to-build-it books read like a set of stereo instructions. They're hard to follow and rarely account for setup variations. With this kind of guide, the reader ends up with the same setup as the author and is no smarter about the topic at the end of the book than at the beginning.

Home Networking Simplified achieves a happy balance between a how-it-works reader for the average person and a how-to-build-it guide. That alone would place it near the top of the list for home networking books. But this book also does something that's unique in the marketplace: It teaches you how to go "off script." You'll not only learn how to do a given step, but why to do it, how it works, and what happens if you choose to do something else. The result is that when you want to make a modification to your network, whether by implementing additional security, or adding something new, you'll be well equipped to plan, set up, and use new features and new devices.

If you're tired of owing favors to the computer engineer in your family or neighborhood, this is the book for you.

Charles H. Giancarlo
Chief Technology Officer, Cisco Systems, Inc.
President, Cisco-Linksys, LLC

Introduction

Our aim for this book is simple. We want to make the benefits of creating a home network available to all those people out there who are not network engineers or computer science majors. We also want to help explain basic networking concepts so that you have some idea of why things are done, rather than just how things are done (which is where most how-to books leave you at the end of the day).

The primary reason computer networks exist is to enable the sharing of resources and information. In the home, this includes things as basic as sharing an Internet connection among several users. Sharing, however, can also include slightly more complicated feats, such as printer sharing, file sharing, music sharing, and even head-to-head or online gaming.

Any person with multiple home computers can build a network that allows those computers to share resources. How, and to what extent, you do this is really a matter of preference (and cost), but most people are pleasantly surprised by the features available to the consumer today and the ease with which they can be deployed. Better still is that prices have fallen quite a bit in the last few years so you can accomplish much of this while staying on a pretty tight budget.

This book walks you through the important technologies and gives you the practical information you need to build a home network. This stuff does not have to be hard to understand and, while we may not make a network engineer out of you, we can provide you with some basic, useful information about networking.

Most chapters follow a pattern of "What, why, and how-to." The second reason we provide you with more than just a series of step-by-step scripts is that we want—and expect—you to go "off plan." We give detailed instructions on how to build a network, but the one we build is only one of several dozens of possibilities. If you know why we took certain steps, and made certain assumptions, you can go back and make changes as you see fit. This knowledge should help you maintain and grow your network well into the future.

Here is what we propose to do: We start you off with a straightforward primer on networking. Without going into too much detail, we provide you with some very basic, but critical, information on networks and networking technology. After we provide this foundation, we will jump right in with a basic network design that connects one computer to the Internet. From there, will we add more features that provide you with the ability to

- Share files between computers
- Share a printer
- Share a high-speed Internet connection with multiple users
- Create individual e-mail accounts for all users in a home
- Create a wireless network
- Secure your network from external threats
- Make the Internet safe for your kids
- Set up your computer to work in Internet cafes, airports, or other hotspots
- Make telephone calls across the Internet

- Create a "virtual jukebox" and other entertainment systems

- Create home security and surveillance systems

- Set up an online gaming system

If you follow all the steps in this book, you will end up with a really cool, high functioning, secure network. If you read this entire book, you should be able to modify your network to suit future needs, new technologies, or changing preferences.

NOTE This book contains instructions for installing components in computers. Static electric charges can harm such electronic components. Therefore, take precautions not to zap your components. This includes not shuffling your wooly Sponge Bob socks across your orange shag carpet, and stay away from all balloons. We do not recommend spraying your computer (or body) down with antistatic sprays or wrapping your shoe soles in aluminum foil. Just use some common sense, such as touching a metal doorframe, to discharge potential high voltage before touching the components. Jim and Neil have such electric personalities that it is constantly a problem for us.

Before You Begin

Before we jump in, we would like to recommend that you do two things. First, read through the entire book (or at least do a fast read through) before you start building your network. This will help you plan what equipment to buy and will also help you avoid replicating any "dual designs" that we develop in this book. For example, we will create a wired network and then convert it over to a wireless network. If you know you will go wireless, you should not go out and buy the equipment for a wired network. You still need to read the wired section though as that is where we cover file sharing and other features that work the same on both wired and wireless networks.

Our second recommendation is that you create a worksheet and design notebook where you keep your network and PC names, drawings, passwords, and notes. Early on, this may seem unnecessary, but as we move further along, these notes and drawings can and most likely will save you hours of frustration. This is really where most non-professionals get into trouble. Keeping notes while designing your network has a couple of key benefits:

- The simple act of drawing a diagram and writing your thoughts down will help you stay organized and avoid common mistakes before they even happen.

- If you want to make changes later (like a year from now when you forgot why you did the things you did), you can reference your notes and make your life easier.

- If something goes wrong later and you have to call someone for help, you can give them a head start to work from.

Now, for those of you who like to read the last page of a book first, the illustrations on the next pages detail the progression of networks we build throughout this book.

We also include a "how to build it" map on the inside front cover, which serves a quick reference for all the "how-to" sections in the book and their page numbers.

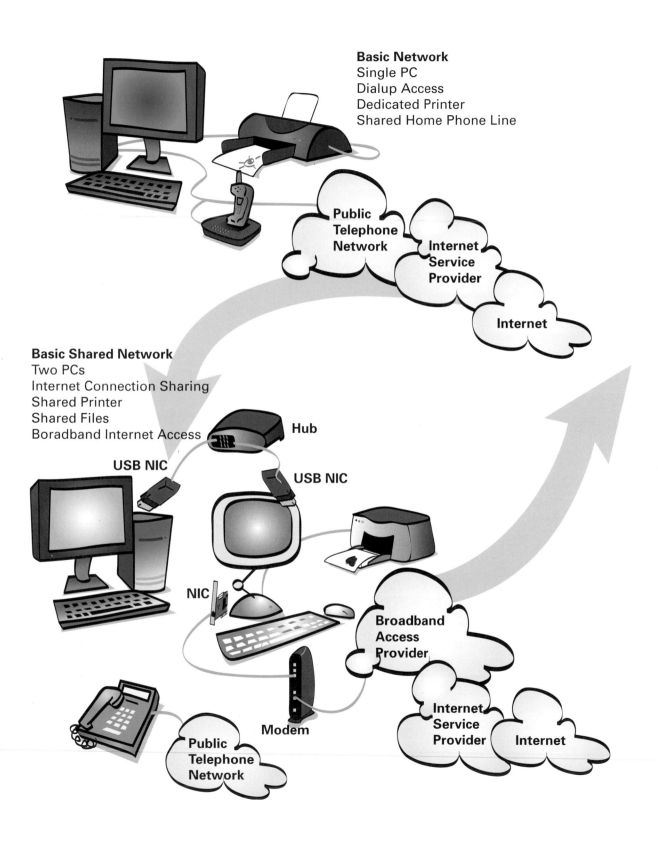

Basic Network
Single PC
Dialup Access
Dedicated Printer
Shared Home Phone Line

Public Telephone Network

Internet Service Provider

Internet

Basic Shared Network
Two PCs
Internet Connection Sharing
Shared Printer
Shared Files
Boradband Internet Access

USB NIC

Hub

USB NIC

NIC

Broadband Access Provider

Modem

Public Telephone Network

Internet Service Provider

Internet

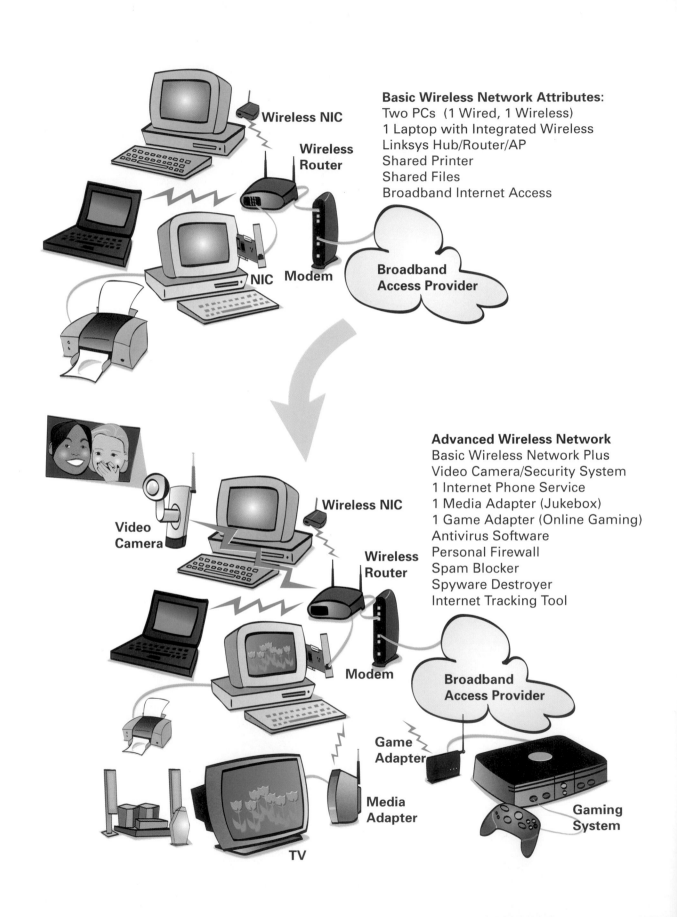

Basic Wireless Network Attributes:
Two PCs (1 Wired, 1 Wireless)
1 Laptop with Integrated Wireless
Linksys Hub/Router/AP
Shared Printer
Shared Files
Broadband Internet Access

Wireless NIC

Wireless Router

NIC   Modem

Broadband Access Provider

Advanced Wireless Network
Basic Wireless Network Plus
Video Camera/Security System
1 Internet Phone Service
1 Media Adapter (Jukebox)
1 Game Adapter (Online Gaming)
Antivirus Software
Personal Firewall
Spam Blocker
Spyware Destroyer
Internet Tracking Tool

Wireless NIC

Video Camera

Wireless Router

Modem

Broadband Access Provider

Game Adapter

Media Adapter

Gaming System

TV

We Can't Cover Everything!

As with any book that simplifies a technical subject, we have to make some trade-offs between accessibility and depth. This section describes some of the assumptions and trade-offs we had to make.

Wireless Versus Wired

Within the home, networks fall into two basic categories: wired and wireless. Wired networks are typically cheaper and faster, but we focus mostly on wireless in this book because of its great flexibility and growing popularity.

Microsoft Windows

For all PC setups used in this book, we only reference Windows 98, Windows 2000, and Windows XP because they are the most common operating systems in use today. If you use a different operating system, the configurations, instructions, and screenshots may not directly apply to you, but the underlying principles and tasks (such as naming a PC) will be common across most operating systems in use today.

Mostly Linksys

Nearly all the equipment used in this book comes from the Linksys catalog. We would be remiss if we failed to mention that our (current and former) employer Cisco Systems, Inc. (Neil and Jim, respectively) is the parent company of Linksys. That said, we really do believe that Linksys has the most comprehensive and easy-to-use/install home networking product suite.

Tips from the Geek Squad

At the end of each part of this book, you can find a chapter written by our good friends from the Geek Squad. For those of you not familiar with the Geek Squad (http://www.geeksquad.com), they are a 24-hour computer support task force established to protect society from the assault of computerized technology. They save your ass and protect you from the evil forces of inefficient networks, crashing hard drives, and corrupt files. They can and will

- Restrain misbehaving hard drives and recover recalcitrant data.

- Rehabilitate disobedient operating systems.

- Make non-printing printers print, non-scanning scanners scan, and non-connecting connections connect.

- Isolate, quarantine, and destroy computer and software viruses.

- Resuscitate dead laptops, PDAs, and desktops.

- End unruly computer activity, reestablishing humanity's dominance over technology.

- Secure networks from intruders, keeping them buttoned down and for your eyes only.

These fine folks have agreed to help us with our goal of helping non-computer geeks understand and deploy basic home networks. To that end, they have been kind enough to read, review, and debug our notes and design plans. Throughout this book, you will see tips from the Geek Squad when a common issue or important point warrants a separate callout.

Happy Networking

What follows is what we hope will be an informative and useful guide to home networking:

- Part I provides a background on networking fundamentals. Even if you have some experience with networks, you may want to glance through this section as some of the key concepts will be put into practice later in the book.

- Part II is where we really jump in and design and build a home network. Key topics here will be file sharing and multiple computer access to the Internet.

- In Part III, we will take an in-depth look at wireless technology. We rebuild the network built in the previous section into a wireless network. We will also show you how to secure your wireless network, and show you how to connect to and safely use public wireless networks and hotspots.

- Part IV deals primarily with network and Internet security. We will show you how to protect your network, files, and devices from malicious or commercial intrusion.

- Part V shows you how to do some really cool stuff, including setting up home video surveillance, using the Internet as your phone system, creating entertainment systems such as music libraries and virtual jukeboxes, and setting up online gaming systems.

 "Too Much of a Good Thing…" To keep the size of this book manageable, we had to limit the number of topics we discussed. All the topics we felt were important are in this book, but some topics that are interesting, but not necessarily critical, did not make the cut. Rather than drop them completely, we created online appendixes for you extra-credit types, which include topics such as binary numbers, how networking will change in the future, how to lock your MAC addresses, and Linksys products. We have noted when a topic is continued in an online appendix. They can be found at this location: http://www.ciscopress.com/1587201364. To access the files, click the **Appendix** link in the More Information box on the book product page.

One of the reasons computers and home networking can be confusing is the number of options, features, and products available. Whenever possible, we cut through the many possibilities and give you clear step-by-step instructions that will work. It's not the only way to set it up, for sure, but it's a way that will work for most people. We hope you enjoy this book and find it to be a useful tool. Good luck, and happy networking. Here we go.

What's a Network?

For our purposes a *network* can simply be defined as a series of *devices* interconnected over a *communication path*. Within this definition devices usually means computers, and the communication path can be wires or airwaves.

Before we dive into connecting computers together, we thought we would spend at least one chapter discussing some basic computer "stuff" and covering some of the terms you are likely to encounter after you start purchasing networking gear or talking to others about it. This chapter briefly reviews PC hardware and discusses network interface cards, which are commonly called NICs. If you are sure that your PC already has a NIC and feel comfortable with your PC or laptop and what each part does, feel free to skip to Chapter 2, "Networking Fundamentals."

PC Hardware and Network Interface Cards

Table 1-1 lists common PC/laptop components and describes each component's job. Although not exhaustive, Table 1-1 covers most of your computer's components. (The Glossary covers all the computer and network terms used throughout the book.)

Table 1-1   Common PC/Laptop Components

Component	Function
CD-ROM drive	Compact Disk Read-Only Memory
DVD/CD writer	Most PCs today have a built-in DVD player that plays movies and other CDs. Many of these devices also allow you to write onto blank CDs.
Central processing unit (CPU)	The computer's "brain" where nearly all calculations are performed.
Printed circuit board (PCB)	A thin plate on which integrated circuits are placed.
Expansion card	A PCB that can be inserted for additional functionality.
Expansion slot	An opening in the computer for expansion cards.
Hard disk drive	This device reads and writes data to hard disk.
Floppy disk drive	These are becoming pretty rare, but some PCs still use 3.5" floppy disks for program or data storage.
Microprocessor	A silicon chip that contains a CPU.

Table 1-1 **Common PC/Laptop Components**

Component	Function
Motherboard	This is the main circuit board of the computer. Everything else in a computer plugs into the motherboard and is controlled by it.
Memory	Internal storage.
Random access memory (RAM)	This is a temporary storage place for data while programs are in use. If the computer loses power, all data in RAM that was not saved is lost.
Read-only memory (ROM)	Pre-recorded or "start up" memory.
Erasable programmable read-only memory (EPROM)	Computer memory not available to the user. This usually contains very basic instructions for the computer's operation.
Socket	A connector for expansion cards.
Interface	A device that connects to pieces of equipment (a mouse and computer, for example).
Network interface card (NIC)	A PCB that provides network access.
Parallel port	An interface that communicates more than one bit of information at a time. Usually used to connect devices such as printers.
Personal Computer Memory Card International Association (PCMCIA) card	This card fits into an expansion slot on a laptop. Many different PCMCIA cards can be purchased for different functions including, but not limited to, extra storage (hard drive), NICs, and cellular modems.
Serial port	An interface that can communicate on 1 bit at a time: usually used to connect external drives and modems.
Universal Serial Bus (USB)	An interface that allows other devices to be connected and disconnected without resetting the system.

Installing Devices in Computers

Different devices are available that extend your computer to do different functions, such as talk to the Internet or other computers. Throughout this book, we give you instructions on how to install such devices to connect computers to printers, to other computers, to networks, and to the Internet.

With all the terms flying around such as serial cable, parallel cable, USB cable, network cable, PCI, PCMCIA, installing devices to your computer can be intimidating. So let's start by sorting through some of that and making it simple. To extend a computer, you can add "cards" inside a computer, or "boxes" and cables outside a computer. Almost everything you can imagine adding to a computer is offered either way, so which one you choose is up to you. Table 1-2 is here to help by giving you some easy-to-remember guidelines.

Table 1-2   Where to Plug Stuff In

Device	What Does It Look Like?	Where Does It Plug Into?
PCI Card—Commonly used to add devices inside desktop PCs, such as sound cards, modems, and network cards	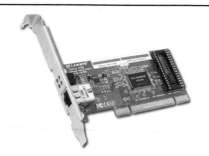	
PCMCIA Card—Commonly used to add devices to laptops, such as wireless network cards.		
Serial Cable—Commonly used to add older devices externally, such as external modems.		
Parallel Cable—Almost exclusively used for printers and some tape drives.		

Table 1-2   Where to Plug Stuff In

Device	What Does It Look Like?	Where Does It Plug Into?
USB—Commonly used to add newer devices externally, such as network ports and video cameras.		
Network or Ethernet Cable—Connects computers to networks (looks like a phone cable but wider).		
Telephone Cable—Connects dialup modems to the telephone system. Also connects DSL modems to the telephone system.		
Coax Cable—Connects broadband cable modems to the cable system.		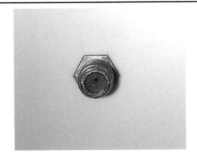

Configuring New Devices in Microsoft Windows

When the Microsoft Windows (98, Me, 2000, and XP) operating system boots, it automatically looks for new devices that have been installed since the last time it was booted. In general, this procedure applies just about every time we go through an installation in this book (in the "How to Build It" sections), so it's good to understand the basics of what's happening.

 GEEK SQUAD If you are reading this book, we're assuming that you are interested in networking. Consequently, if you are using Windows 98 or Me, we strongly urge you to consider moving to Windows XP. If you are running with a lot of processing memory (256 MB of RAM or more), XP will not only make networking easier but will also likely improve your overall computer's performance.

The various Microsoft Windows operating systems contain hundreds (probably thousands) of "drivers" for different kinds of devices and cards. A *driver* is simply a piece of software that lets Windows "talk to" the device, kind of like a language translator at the United Nations. The newer the Windows version, the more drivers are already included; for example, Windows XP has many more drivers "pre-loaded" than Windows 98.

When Windows boots, it searches for new devices (see Figure 1-1). If one is found, it helps find the right driver. If it can't find one, it needs you to supply one by inserting the CD provided with the device you purchased. The latest versions give you the option of looking for the driver on the Internet. After the driver is located, Windows adds the new driver to its library of drivers. You only need to do this one time per new device; after that, Windows can directly "talk to" that device.

Figure 1-1 Windows Searches for a New Device

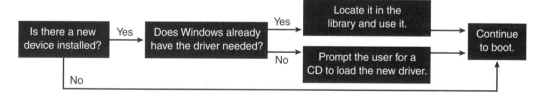

Most of the time, having Windows automatically install the device works just fine. There are occasions where the manufacturer chooses not to have Windows install its device and instead provides an alternate install procedure. The best thing to do is read the install sheet that comes with the device you buy, just to make sure.

 GEEK SQUAD When in doubt, call an expert. Be careful who you call. If you are thinking about calling an in-law to fix it, make sure he knows what he is doing. More family feuds have been started by well-intentioned relatives messing up other family members' computers. If you are looking for free help, it never hurts to make friends with the teenagers first.

Networking Fundamentals

This chapter covers the most basic part of networking; connecting computers and end devices together. We start with a short section on data speeds to familiarize you with terms you will see throughout this book. We will then cover basic cabling so you know what connects all the devices together. We will end the chapter with a primer on IP addressing, which enables computers to know where to send information, and how to know an incoming message is intended for them.

Please read on; it's not as horrible as it sounds. The information provided in this chapter will help you as you start to build your network and make purchase decisions.

Bits and Bytes

We are often impressed with what computers can do, or more correctly, what engineers and software developers get them to do. What most people do not realize, however, is that although computers are capable of making millions of complicated calculations per second, the brains of the computer (a microprocessor) is only able to give and receive simple instructions comprised of electronic signals that represent 1s and 0s. That's it. No complicated instructions, no scripts, not even words. Just a gazillion or so switches that are either on (1) or off (0). (Yes, "gazillion" is an official computer term.)

A system with only two states is called a *binary system.* A single one of these states (a single 1 or a single 0) is called a *bit.* Think of this a single letter. A grouping of 8 bits is called a *byte,* which is analogous to a word.

Bits and bytes are the foundation of computer language, and the number of bits and bytes a computer can process or move per second is a foundation of networking, and the standard by which devices are compared. Table 2-1 shows the common units.

Table 2-1   Common Units

Unit	Bytes	Bits	*Notes*
Bit (b)	1/8 bytes	1 bit	*One "letter."*
Byte (B)	1 byte	8 bits	*One "word."*
Kilobit (Kb)	N/A	1000 bits	*This is a standard unit for dialup modems.*
Kilobyte (KB)	1024 bytes	8000 or so bits	*This should be an even 1000 but it's not. We are as baffled as you are.*

Table 2-1   Common Units

Unit	Bytes	Bits	*Notes*
Megabit (Mb)	N/A	1.024 million bits	*This is a standard unit for high-speed modems.*
Megabyte (MB)	1.024 million bytes	8 million or so bits	*Commonly used to measure storage, such as hard disk drives.*
Gigabit (Gb)	N/A	1.024 billion bits	*This is a standard unit for high-speed routers and switches.*
Gigabyte (GB)	*1.024 billion bytes*	*8 billion or so bits*	*Commonly used to measure storage, such as hard disk drives.*

GEEK SQUAD Gigabyte, schmigabyte. Think this nomenclature is hard to understand? Blame the Greeks, not the Geeks! We are always being given a hard time by civilians for the language of computers. Look at it this way: Instead of a naming system based on Greek prefixes, would you prefer terms like fast, super fast, really super duper fast, and...get my point? It always seems complicated until you try an inferior method. Remember: No amount of storage will ever be enough. Give a cat an inch.

Network Media Types

The first step to creating a computer network is figuring out what to connect the various devices with. This is referred to as network media. *Network media* refers to the physical path that signals take across a network, which pretty much means "using cables." If you go with a wireless network, however, much of your media is air, but even then, you will have some cables in your network. Knowing something about the types of cables used in networks might keep you from using—or worse, from buying—the wrong cable. This section discusses the most common types of media.

Twisted-Pair Cable

A twisted-pair cable is the most common cable used for telephone and computer networks. Within a twisted-pair cable, there are eight smaller wires, which are paired off. Each pair makes up a circuit that is used to send and receive signals. This can cause problems, however, as signals from one pair (or circuit) might cause interference on another pair (for example, two people trying to speak on the phone to each other hear someone else's converstaion). This interfernce is greatly mitigated by twisting the wire pairs together, which ultimately gave the name to the larger cable that contained the pairs. Twisted-pair cables come in two categories:

- **Unshielded twisted-pair (UTP) cables** offer no additional shielding to the wire pairs within the cable and are therefore more prone to electrical interference (from other pairs within the wire, and from external sources). On the plus side, UTP cables tend to be cheaper, have a smaller diameter, and are more pliable than STP cables. UTP is the most common type of cable used in home networks.

- **Shielded twisted-pair (STP) cables** have a protective sheathing (or shield) around each wire pair, and around the entire wire bundle. This shield provides much better protection against electric noise and interference than UTP cables. On the downside, all this extra shielding makes STP thicker, more expensive, and more rigid than UTP.

There are several different types of UTP and STP cables. The type used almost exclusively in home networking is called Category 5 (Cat 5). It is not important to get into what the other types are or how they are different. Cat 5 is the way to go.

This might all be a bit confusing, but there is good news. In the majority of cases, you will use a UTP, Cat 5 straight-through cable with RJ-45 connectors. This cable is widely known as a "Cat 5" cable, so if you need one, just ask for a Cat 5 cable and the folks at the computer store will know exactly what to give you. Oh, and don't worry too much about the difference between Cat 5 and Cat 5e. The "e" just means that it is certified for some very high-speed applications. For home networks, Cat 5 or Cat 5e are both just fine.

 GEEK SQUAD In the event that the person at the store does not know what a Cat 5 cable is, it's perfectly fine to say "the one with the wide telephone thingy on the ends" or "the one with the telephone wire plugging-in thingy." They should be able to find what you want. Don't be too smug about it though; the computer-network gods punish hubris.

Coaxial Cable

Houses most often use *coaxial cable* (coax) for cable-TV applications. The cable-TV signal is carried through a coaxial cable, which contains a copper conductor that is protected by a tube of plastic insulation. That plastic insulation is then covered with a braided copper shielding. These insulation layers provide excellent protection to the transmitted signal, allowing a very broad range of frequencies to be transmitted over relatively long distances.

Coax is relatively inexpensive (but it does cost more per foot than UTP), and it has a much greater reach than Cat 5. There is only one wire inside a coaxial cable, and there is only one standardized connector.

Know Your Media!

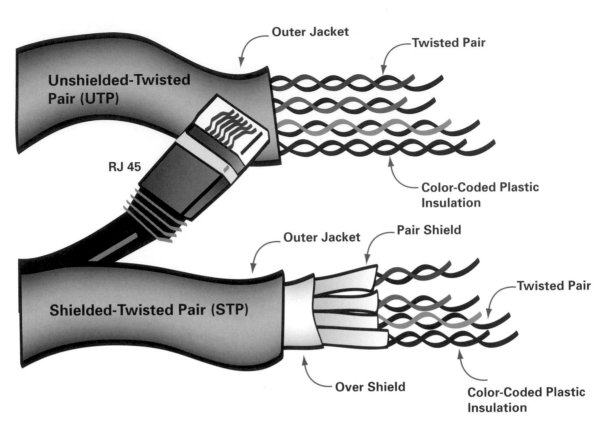

Outer Jacket

Twisted Pair

Unshielded-Twisted Pair (UTP)

RJ 45

Color-Coded Plastic Insulation

Outer Jacket

Pair Shield

Shielded-Twisted Pair (STP)

Twisted Pair

Over Shield

Color-Coded Plastic Insulation

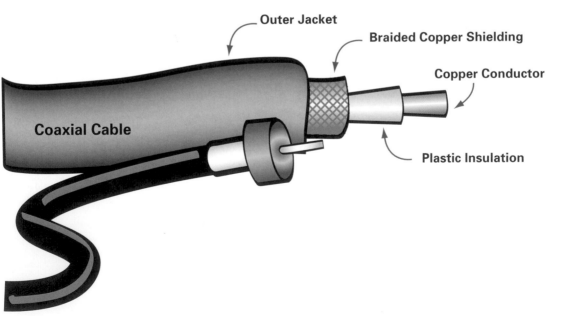

Outer Jacket

Braided Copper Shielding

Copper Conductor

Coaxial Cable

Plastic Insulation

Wireless Networks

Wireless communications use radio frequencies (RF) or infrared (IR) waves to transmit data. Wireless networks (the RF kind, which are by far the most common) are based on the same technology as your FM radio in your car, but with very sophisticated technologies to transmit data at very high speeds. If your PC does not come with a pre-installed wireless NIC, you will have to install one before your computer can communicate with a wireless network. Wireless allows many new options for network designers because no cable is required to connect end stations (which is great for installation in houses or offices where cabling would be difficult or expensive).

Firewire

Firewire is a new cabling standard that is growing in popularity. Developed by Apple, Firewire allows for extremely fast data transfer (up to 400 Mbps), making it ideal for multimedia applications such as streaming video to a monitor or playing high-end digital recordings on a stereo. Firewire only has a range of 4.5 meters (about 15 feet). You can get a Firewire cable longer than that, but the throughput or data speed will be greatly diminished.

Firewire is pretty expensive per foot compared to the other cabling standards discussed here, but if you are serious about audio/video quality or if you share a lot of data between two end devices, Firewire is a good cabling choice.

Comparing Media Types

Table 2-2 compares the various media types.

Table 2-2   Comparison of the Media Types

Media Type	Maximum Length	Speed	Cost	*Notes*
UTP	100 m (328 ft)	10–100 Mbps	Cheap	*Easy to install but prone to interference*
STP	100 m (328 ft)	10–100 Mbps	More than UTP	*Low interference but hard to work with*
Coaxial	185 m (607 ft)	10–100 Mbps	Cheap but more than UTP	*Little or no interference but hard to work with*
Wireless (air)	About 25-50 m (about 80 to 165 ft)	1–108 Mbps (or higher) depending on the wireless standard used (see Chapter 9 for more details)	Cables cost nothing, but there is a cost for the transmitter	*By far the most convenient to work with when setting up a multicomputer network in an area not prewired*

What Is an IP Address?

As mentioned in Chapter 1, "What's a Network?" a network's purpose is to allow computers to share resources and information. This means that computers must be able to send and receive information to each other. To do this, we must have some form of addressing so that each end device on the network knows what information to read and what information to ignore. This ability is important for both the computers that ultimately use the information and for the devices that deliver information to end stations.

Every computer on a network has two addresses:

- **MAC address**—A manufacturer allocated ID number that is permanent and unique to every network device. MAC addresses are analogous to a social security or other national identification number; you only have one, it stays the same wherever you go, and no two people (devices) have the same number.

- **IP address**—This address is what matters most to basic networking. Unlike a MAC address, the IP address of any device is temporary and can be changed. It is often assigned by the network itself and is analogous to your street address. It only needs to be unique within a home network, and someone else's home network might use the same IP address, much like another town might have the same street (for example, Main Street).

Every device on an IP network is given an IP address, which looks like the following:

192.168.1.101

The format of this address is called *dotted decimal* notation and the period separators are pronounced "dot" as in one ninety-two, dot one sixty-right, dot one, dot one o one." Because of some rules with binary, the largest number in each section is 255.

In addition to breaking up the number, the dots that appear in IP addresses allow us to break the address into parts that represent networks and hosts. In this case, the "network" portion refers to a company, university, government agency, or your private network. The hosts would be the addresses of all the computers on the individual network. If you think of the network portion of the address as a street, the hosts would be all the houses on that street. If you were able to see the IP addresses of everyone who subscribes to the same Internet service provider (ISP) as you, you would notice that the network portion of the address is the same for all subscribers, and the host portion would change from subscriber to subscriber.

An example will probably help. Think of an IP address like you would your home address for the post office:

state.city.street.house number

Each number in the IP address provides a more and more specific location, so that the Internet can find your computer among millions of other computers. The Internet is not organized geographically like the postal system though. So the components of the address (intentionally oversimplified) are

major network.minor network.local network.device

So, in the previous example, 192 could represent an ISP, such as Time-Warner Cable, the 168 could represent a section of their network, such as the central North Carolina region, the 1 could represent a particular neighborhood that is served, such as Northwest Raleigh, and finally the 101 could represent the actual cable modem at the house at 303 Peppermint Street.

There is a small problem, though. There are not enough IP addresses to go around!

Dynamically Allocated IP Addresses

Those of you good at math may be asking yourself how in the world we could possibly run out of IP addresses. After all, with the format of the IP addresses, there are roughly 4.3 billion possible addresses (256 to the power of 4). As it turns out, however, the scheme adopted for addressing only leaves about 250 million usable addresses, and although that may seem like it should be enough, consider all the devices such as computers, cell phones, PDAs, game systems, and many others that are connecting to the Internet. Most experts agree that if "conservation measures" had not been taken we would have already run out of addresses.

One method of address conservation that we will deal with is called Dynamic Host Configuration Protocol (DHCP). Don't worry too much about the name; it is what it does that is important.

Using DCHP, an ISP can have more subscribers than it has host addresses to hand out, which means every ISP requires fewer addresses. The reason that the ISP can do this is because not all subscribers use the network at the same time. Knowing this, the ISP can dole out addresses on an "as needed" basis so that the IP address you get from them today will most likely be different than the one you get when you log on tomorrow. This is usually totally transparent to the end user as it does not matter what your IP address is, so long as the ISP correctly associates your Internet traffic with the IP address assigned to you at any given time.

Domain Name Server (DNS)

Every website you visit is identified by the IP address of the server that hosts the site. Imagine if you had to remember the actual IP addresses of all your favorite websites. Even if you could use the dotted-decimal system, it would be difficult to remember more than a handful. (For example, what if you had to remember 64.236.24.20 is the CNN website and 63.111.66.11 is The Weather Channel website?) If knowing every site's IP address were required, it is doubtful that the Internet's popularity would have exploded the way it did

Fortunately, every webmaster can register to have his or her website associated with a name. This way, you only need to remember www.linksys.com or www.beer.com instead of 192.14.244.24 and 178.22.154.1. (These are not the real addresses by the way.) These name-to-address associations are held in DNS servers that are maintained by ISPs. When you open your browser and type in a website name, your machine queries a DNS server to find out the actual address of the website. Your browser is then directed to the correct server that corresponds to the IP address. Your browser keeps track of these associations for the sites you visit most often.

DNS: Matching Domain Names to IP Addresses

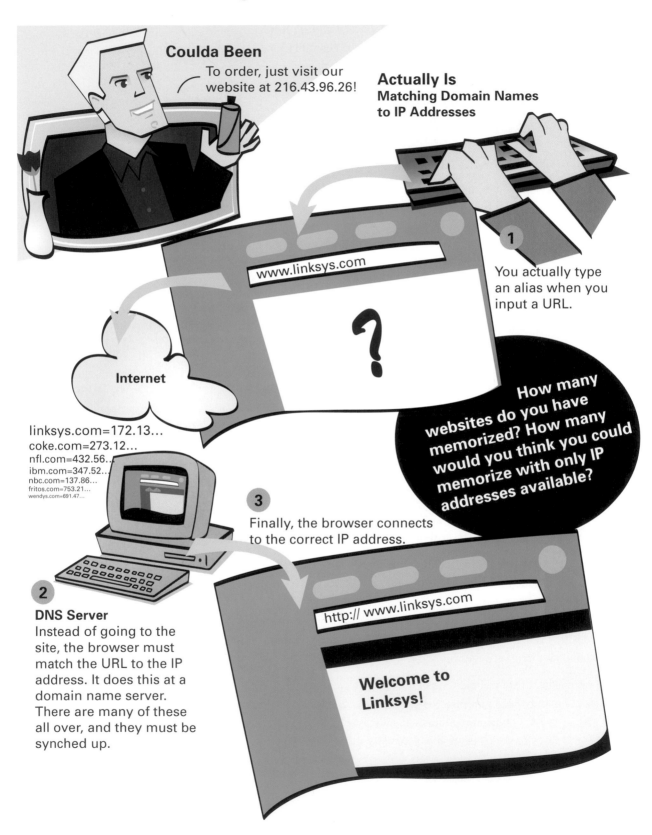

Connecting to the Internet

This chapter begins with a brief description of the Internet—what it is, how it's put together, and how it works. We also cover how e-mail works and what the different options are for creating and using e-mail. This chapter ends with a detailed "How to Build It" section, which shows you how to connect to the Internet (including how to install a modem) and how to configure your e-mail.

The Internet

The Internet is one of the greatest technological wonders of the 20th century. In the 1990s, the availability and usage of the Internet changed the way people communicated, the way they sought entertainment, and the way they did business.

The key to the Internet was the creation of a series of networks that was large enough and easy enough to navigate to allow computers, servers, and other devices to communicate at any time without specific knowledge about the location, owner, or address of the remote systems. Such a feat could only be achieved through the use of an open standard protocol (explained in the next section). In addition, the network allows address aliases (such as Yahoo.com), which make finding a web page much easier to find than it would be if the actual address of the server had to be memorized.

Imagine if you had to access a website using an address like your post office mail:

www.cnn.com@400.Peachtree.Street@atlanta.georgia.usa

This obviously would have killed the usability pretty fast. Fortunately, the Internet provides a completely virtual space where services are separated from their geographic location.

TCP/IP

Computers and devices connected to the Internet communicate using a set of rules called the Transmission Control Protocol (TCP) and the Internet Protocol (IP) or TCP/IP (say just the letters T-C-P-I-P).

TCP was originally invented in the mid 1970s and then modified to TCP/IP a few years later. The protocol was designed to allow for the transfer of files and computer-to-computer communication over a network commissioned by the US Government called ARPANET. ARPANET eventually spawned the Internet, which is not controlled by the CIA or the former KGB despite the convictions of some conspiracy theorists.

TCP/IP is an open standard protocol, which means that its code is open for all to see and use. Open standards encourage broad usage and compatibility across many vendors and products. TCP/IP specifies rules for how computers communicate (how they find each other, communication speeds, error corrections, and so on). After a TCP/IP session is initiated between two computers, other protocols specify rules for applications such as e-mails, web browsers, and file transfers.

A Network of Networks

The Internet is not so much a thing as it is a collection of things. It would be extremely difficult for any single group, business, or government to run and maintain. In fact, if any such group tried to create such a network, it would likely result in several far less capable, noncompatible networks. As it is now, the Internet is made up of several hierarchical layers that all work in concert:

- **Internet service provider (ISP) (bottom layer)**—Typically, an ISP will have a number of connection stations called points of presence (POPs). A *POP* is where all the local subscribers enter the network. POPs are operational only in a small geographic area. An ISP that covers a large area will use several POPs.

- **Regional access provider (not known as a RAP by the way) (middle layer)**—A regional access provider will typically connect several POPs (perhaps from more than a single ISP) to each other and to the larger network. A regional access provider may also provide connection services to businesses or institutions that have large private networks of their own.

- **Backbone (top layer)**—The backbone is made up of multiple, very fast, high-capacity private networks, and are often called "national service providers." These networks overlap and share traffic for increased load balancing, reach, and reliability.

The three layers work in a hierarchy to provide a global network. Think of the hierarchy like a power system, with the backbone being the high-voltage power lines, the regional access provider being the transformer stations, and ISPs being the power poles down your street.

What Are HTTP and HTML and What Do They Do?

You might have noticed that many Internet sites include the letters HTTP in the site address that appears in the address line of your web browser.

HTTP stands for Hypertext Transfer Protocol, which defines the rules for transferring information, files, and multimedia on web pages. Hypertext Markup Language (HTML) is the language used within HTTP. HTML is actually a fairly simple, easy-to-learn computer language that embeds symbols into a text file to specify visual or functional characteristics such as font size, page boundaries, and application usages (such as launching an e-mail tool when a user clicks certain links).

When the developer of an HTTP file (or web page) wants to allow for a jump to a different place on the page, or even a jump to a new page, he simply places the appropriate symbols into the file. People viewing the page just see the link, which is most commonly specified with blue, underlined text.

The ease of jumping from site to site (called "web surfing") is one of the reasons for the proliferation and tremendous growth of websites on the Internet.

Several free and commercial tools allow you to create a web page using HTML without having to know all the rules.

Internet Infrastructure

Access Providers

The web is really made of many networks connected in a hierarchy. Local Internet service providers (ISPs) typically give residential areas and small businesses access to the Internet. Regional providers typically connect several local ISPs to each other and to the back haul providers, which connect with other regional providers.

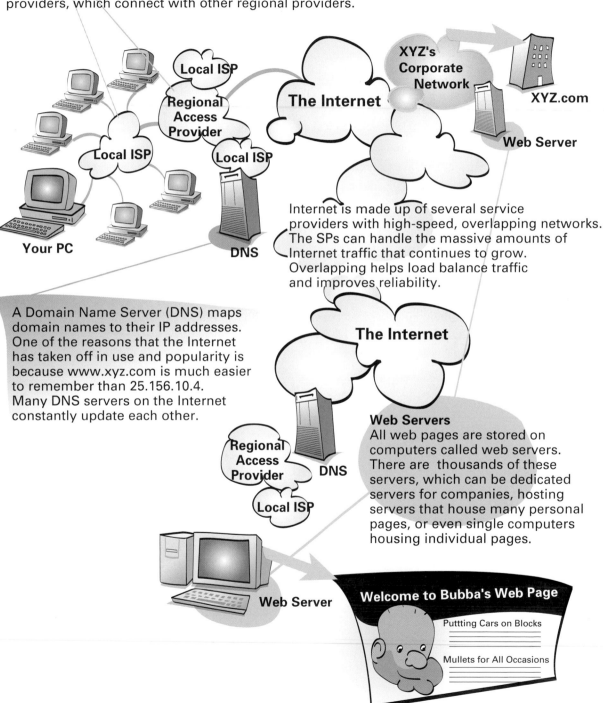

Internet is made up of several service providers with high-speed, overlapping networks. The SPs can handle the massive amounts of Internet traffic that continues to grow. Overlapping helps load balance traffic and improves reliability.

A Domain Name Server (DNS) maps domain names to their IP addresses. One of the reasons that the Internet has taken off in use and popularity is because www.xyz.com is much easier to remember than 25.156.10.4. Many DNS servers on the Internet constantly update each other.

Web Servers

All web pages are stored on computers called web servers. There are thousands of these servers, which can be dedicated servers for companies, hosting servers that house many personal pages, or even single computers housing individual pages.

Your PC

Local ISP

Regional Access Provider

Local ISP

Local ISP

DNS

The Internet

XYZ's Corporate Network

XYZ.com

Web Server

The Internet

Regional Access Provider

Local ISP

DNS

Web Server

Welcome to Bubba's Web Page

Puttting Cars on Blocks

Mullets for All Occasions

One of the issues with HTML is that it is fairly limited to what it can do given that it works only on text and still pictures. In order to achieve some of the really cool moving graphics and web page features, other tools such as Flash, XML, Java, or other scripting languages are needed. These tools are beyond the scope of this book, but if you do a web search on "Flash," you will find some sites with remarkable graphics. (Website creation is beyond the scope of this book.)

Internet Access Options

When the Internet first became popular to a mass audience in the 1990s, accessing the Internet from home was accomplished almost exclusively through a phone line (referred to now as a dialup connection) to an ISP. ISPs began offering multiple phone numbers in any given area with some offering nationwide toll-free numbers. With the growing availability of broadband (high speed) access via cable or digital subscriber line (DSL), traditional phone access is seeing strong competition because broadband is much faster (up to 50 times faster than phone access) and because using the Internet over broadband does not tie up your phone lines, so you can still make and receive calls while on the Internet.

Satellite providers are also offering high-speed Internet services, especially in areas where it is cost prohibitive to run cable TV/Internet lines or start up a DSL service.

With regard to home networking, only having access to dialup presents some issues. The primary issue is that one of the main reasons for home networking is to allow multiple computers to connect to the Internet at the same time. With high-speed, always on, Internet service, this makes perfect sense because even with multiple users downloading large files or generating large amounts of traffic, each user still gets pretty fast response and download times. With dialup, however, it will take anywhere from 5 to 10 minutes for even a single user to download a medium quality picture from an e-mail, for example, with a 1-megabyte attachment. In addition, in a home network using dialup, one computer would need to control the dialing and all traffic would have to run through that single computer. Many popular forms of media-rich web content and Internet entertainment (such as online gaming) are not practical over dialup.

Even with dialup Internet, having a home network can still be very useful as you can do many tasks, such as sharing a printer, setting up a virtual jukebox (although downloading high-quality music over dialup would take forever…give or take a month), and sharing files between computers. Just be aware, though, that you will be very limited with regard to Internet access, so if it is available in your area, and within your budget, broadband is really the way to go.

If broadband is not available in your area, you have other options for receiving high-speed Internet access. Some neighborhoods without access to a standard broadband contract with local ISPs to have a high-speed data line brought right into the neighborhood to be shared by every house in the neighborhood, just as a business would run one to a building. Although this would be expensive for an individual, sharing the cost over a small community would be reasonable and access to the group could be via a wireless system. A security system could be put in place to ensure that only the folks who contribute get access. Some user groups believe that the Internet should be publicly available at no cost and have set up a system like the one just described, but without the security in place so that all within range can have free access.

Modems

If you are going to connect to the Internet from your home, it is almost certain that you will connect to it by using a modem.

We mentioned earlier that no matter how advanced the computer is, it still can only communicate using 1s and 0s. The trick then is to find a way to deliver as many of these 1s and 0s as fast and as accurately as possible over the medium that you have.

The process of converting one information stream into another is called modulation, and the reverse process is called demodulation. The term *modem* is short for "modulator-demodulator," which are the two functions these boxes (or cards) perform.

In the original dialup modems, the 1s and 0s your computer uses were converted to frequency tones (one tone for a zero and different frequency for a one), which allowed them to work over phone lines. Figure 3-1 illustrates these concepts.

Figure 3-1   Basic Concept of Modem Communication

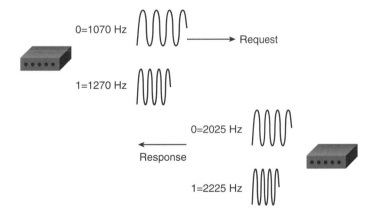

This basic system was in use in nearly all modems up through the initial growth of the Internet. Advances in technology and more complicated modulation schemes allowed the speed of information flow (bit rate) to go from 300 bps, up to the more common 28,800 bps (28.8 kbps) and 56,600 bps (56.6 kbps).

High-speed Internet modems are capable of delivering millions of bits per second by utilizing a broader frequency range than standard modems and by using very advanced modulation schemes that are beyond the scope of this book. However, even the most advanced modulation uses the same principle of representing 1s and 0s in a format that best fits a given medium.

Basic Modem Operation
How to send a l to your friend in Duluth

This figure shows how modems work over phones lines. When people first started using computers, most of the communication was text messages (such as filling out a form on a server.) Instant messaging uses the basic principles shown below.

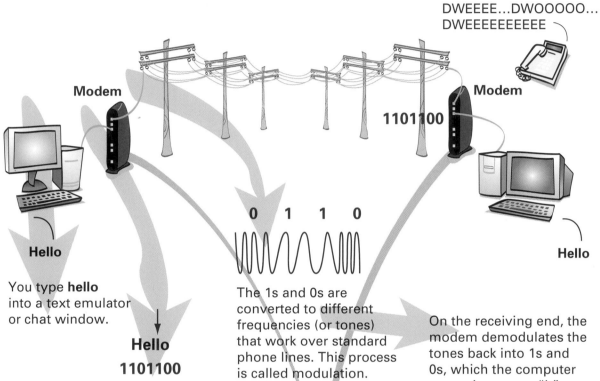

DWEEEE...DWOOOOO... DWEEEEEEEEEE

Modem

Modem

1101100

0 1 1 0

Hello

Hello

You type **hello** into a text emulator or chat window.

Hello

1101100

All the keys on a keyboard have a number associated with them. "l" is 108 in decimal, which is 1101100 in binary.

The 1s and 0s are converted to different frequencies (or tones) that work over standard phone lines. This process is called modulation.

On the receiving end, the modem demodulates the tones back into 1s and 0s, which the computer recognizes as an "l."

If you pick up a phone while someone in the house is using a modem, the squealing sounds you hear are the tones being sent from the remote computer.

Modems connect the same way phones do. After an initial "handshake," data can be passed between the modems.

The Internet and Its Applications

What makes the Internet useful and interesting to the average person is not the network, but rather the applications that operate on the network. The two most common Internet applications in use today are *e-mail* and *web browsers*:

■ E-mail has become a popular tool for communicating with friends and family, for business communication, and for gratuitous commercial solicitations referred to as *spam*. We discuss spam in Chapter 16, "Other Vulnerabilities (Spam, Cookies, Pop-Ups, Spyware, and Scams)."

■ Web browsers allow users to access and view web pages created and maintained by a seemingly endless number of individual, commercial, government, and educational hosts.

This section closely looks at e-mail and the Internet. In the section, we explain how e-mail clients send, receive, and store e-mails. We will also take a look at the Internet explaining how the infrastructure is put together.

We end this chapter with a step-by-step procedure for setting up your e-mail account, and some basics on browser setup and web surfing.

E-Mail

E-mail is one of the most common network applications in use today. Although it might seem relatively new, e-mail was invented in the early 1970s. Back then, of course, there was no Internet as we know it today, so having e-mail was a bit like owning a car before there was a highway system.

Today, e-mail is so widespread that ISPs just assume that you want an e-mail address, and automatically assign you one when you begin your service agreement.

E-Mail Tools

There are two basic ways to create, send, and receive e-mails:

■ E-mail client

■ Web-based e-mail

E-mail clients that are installed on individual machines are in wide use today with the most popular being Microsoft Outlook/Outlook Express. E-mail clients allow for the creation, distribution, retrieval, and storage of e-mails (as well as some other useful features). These types of clients were originally designed so that e-mails to and from an account could be accessed from a single machine.

Some e-mail clients allow for the creation of several aliases, so that different family members can each have their own e-mail space within the same account.

E-mail clients physically move the e-mail from the e-mail server to your PC's hard drive. After the e-mail is downloaded, it no longer exists in the e-mail provider's network. The e-mail exists in your e-mail client program (on the PC's hard drive) until you delete it. Because e-mail clients store the e-mail on your hard drive, it can be accessed even when you are not online.

Web-based e-mail tools, such as Hotmail and Yahoo Mail, allow users to access their e-mail from any machine connected to the Internet. By logging in to the website with their registered name and password, users are given access to a web-based e-mail client that has all the basic abilities of e-mail clients, such as the ability to create, send, and receive e-mails. Many have more advanced features such as the ability to send and receive file attachments and the creation and use of address books.

Almost every ISP offers you the ability to download your e-mail to an e-mail client on your PC or access your e-mail online using their web-based e-mail tool. Web-based e-mail tools differ from e-mail clients in the respect that the e-mail is not downloaded to your PC's hard drive. It exists only on the e-mail provider's network until you delete it. Some people use a combination of web-based e-mail and e-mail client. For example, you may use the web-based e-mail tool to access your e-mail when you are away from home and not using your home PC. When you are at home, you could then use your e-mail client. Because most viruses enter your PC through e-mail, and spam e-mail is increasing at a seemingly endless rate, more and more people are resorting to only web-based e-mail tools to keep the e-mail "at a distance," so to speak, on the provider's network and off your PC's hard disk.

NOTE See Part IV, "Security of Home Networks," for a more in-depth discussion about viruses and spam e-mail.

What Is Up with the @ Sign?

All e-mail addresses are made up of two parts: a recipient part and a domain name. An @ symbol separates the two parts to denote that a recipient is unique within a domain name.

The domain name is usually the name of your ISP (or your company if you have e-mail there), and like a website, an e-mail domain has an associated IP address. This allows (actually requires) the use of a DNS server to translate the domain name portion of an e-mail address to the IP address of the server where the e-mail account resides.

The recipient part is the chosen identifier that you are known by within the e-mail domain. There are a lot of possibilities for choosing the recipient. Here are a few popular styles:

Firstname.Lastname	John.Brown
FirstinitialLastname	JBrown
Nickname	DowntownJohnnyBrown
Personalized License Plate	L8RG8R
Other Obscure Reference	GrassyKnoll63

Choose whatever recipient identifier you want. Because of the large ISP domains these days, Earthlink and AOL for example, it's getting harder to pick a name that someone has not already chosen. So although you want "John.Brown" you might have to settle for "JBrown68." Give it your best shot and just remember that you are going to have to sometimes verbally tell people what your e-mail address is, so "X3UT67B" is not advisable.

Sending E-Mails

E-mails are distributed using a protocol call Simple Mail Transfer Protocol (SMTP). SMTP normally operates on powerful computers dedicated to e-mail distribution, called SMTP servers.

When you create and send an e-mail, your e-mail client sends the file to the SMTP server. The server pulls out the addresses from the message. (You can send e-mails to multiple recipients.) For each domain name, the SMTP server must send a message to a DNS to get the IP address of each recipient's e-mail server. If the recipient is on the same server as you (that is, if you send an e-mail to someone with the same domain name), this step is not necessary.

After your SMTP server knows the IP address of the recipient's server, your SMTP server transfers the e-mail message to their SMTP server. If there are multiple recipients in different e-mail domains, a separate copy of the e-mail is transferred to each recipient's SMTP server. According to the name of the protocol, this is all pretty simple.

Receiving E-Mails

E-mail is often received via a different server than the one that sends e-mail. The type of server depends on which type of e-mail tool you use.

For those using an e-mail client, your e-mail is probably delivered to you via the most common method, POP3 (Post Office Protocol 3) server. (We have no idea what happened to the first two.) The POP3 server receives all its e-mails from SMTP servers and sorts them into file spaces dedicated to each user (much the same way mail would be put into post office boxes at a local post office, thus the name).

When you open your e-mail client, it contacts the POP3 server to request all the new e-mails. The e-mails are then transferred to your PC and in most cases the e-mails are erased from the POP3 server.

Another common method (or protocol) for mail retrieval is an IMAP (Internet Mail Access Protocol) server. The IMAP server receives and sorts e-mail much in the same way as a POP3 server. Unlike POP3, however, IMAP does not transfer the e-mails to the machine of the account holder; instead, it keeps e-mail on the server. This allows users to connect to use their e-mail account from multiple machines. IMAP also allows for *server-side filtering*, a method of pre-sorting e-mail based on rules before it even gets to your PC. Kind of like having a friendly mailman that sorts all your bills to the top, and magazines on the bottom.

Two main issues with IMAP servers are storage space and working offline. Most Internet e-mail services put a limit on the amount of storage each subscriber gets (some charge extra for additional storage space). In addition, these services often limit the file size of attachments (such as photos).

How E-Mail Works

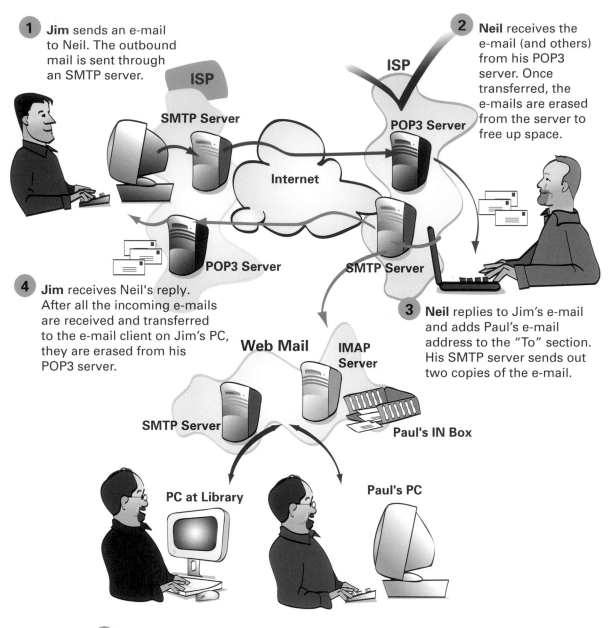

1 **Jim** sends an e-mail to Neil. The outbound mail is sent through an SMTP server.

2 **Neil** receives the e-mail (and others) from his POP3 server. Once transferred, the e-mails are erased from the server to free up space.

ISP

SMTP Server

ISP

POP3 Server

Internet

POP3 Server

SMTP Server

4 **Jim** receives Neil's reply. After all the incoming e-mails are received and transferred to the e-mail client on Jim's PC, they are erased from his POP3 server.

3 **Neil** replies to Jim's e-mail and adds Paul's e-mail address to the "To" section. His SMTP server sends out two copies of the e-mail.

Web Mail

IMAP Server

SMTP Server

Paul's IN Box

PC at Library

Paul's PC

5 **Paul** subscribes to an Internet e-mail service, so he must log onto the service's e-mail site with his name and password. Paul can do this from any PC with an Internet connection. His incoming server is an IMAP server, and the e-mails remain on the system until he erases them.

The other issue is the ability to work *offline* or when not connected to the Internet. One solution is called *caching*, which temporarily places the subscriber's e-mail information on whatever PC they wish to work offline with. When the user reconnects, any e-mails created while offline are sent and any new incoming e-mails can be viewed.

 Geek Squad Get a web-based e-mail account. A web-based e-mail means that your e-mail is entirely accessed over the Internet, not tied to your computer or your ISP. This allows you to change Internet providers, but keep the same e-mail address forever. This is similar to being able to keep your mobile phone number but switch phone companies when better offers come along. We like Yahoo!, Hotmail, and Google the best.

How to Build It: Connecting to the Internet

If you plan to connect to the Internet with high-speed broadband DSL or cable service, you can most likely skip this section because you don't need an analog modem. However, some people may decide they want an analog modem as a backup in case their broadband service is not working.

Most desktop computers and laptops sold today come with a built-in modem by default, so installing one is most likely not a concern. If a modem is already installed in your computer, skip to the section, "Set Up a Dialup Connection to the Internet."

If you are starting from scratch, here's a brief overview of the steps we will go through:

- Decide on the type of modem
- Physically install the modem
- Configure Windows to "talk to" the modem
- Set up a dialup connection to the Internet
- Set up access to e-mail

Decide on the Type of Modem

Decide whether you want to add the modem inside or outside the computer. Adding the modem inside your computer is a bit more work, but it's probably the right way to go because it's typically cheaper, and there's one less box sitting on your desk for your spouse to complain about. The form factors for internal PC and laptop modems are a bit different and are not compatible (see Table 3-1).

On the other hand, external modems can be easily moved between computers, offering good flexibility for less money.

Purchase an internal or external modem that is compatible with at least the V.90 standard, and preferably the V.92 standard. This gives you the best chance of getting the highest speed connection over your phone line to the Internet (which is at best 56.6 kbps, so you need all the help you can get!). Table 3-1 shows an example of each modem type (by Creative Labs). Expect to pay about $20–50 for an internal modem and $50–80 for an external modem.

Table 3-1   Modem Types

Internal Desktop Modem	Internal Laptop Modem	External Modem
Creative Labs Modem Blaster V.92 PCI	Creative Labs Modem Blaster V.90 PCMCIA	Creative Labs Modem Blaster V.92 USB

Physically Install the Modem

For this section, skip to the subsection that matches the type of modem you have.

Internal Modem in a Desktop Computer

To install an internal analog modem in a desktop computer, follow the manufacturer instructions that came with the card you purchased. In general, you will do the following:

1. Shut off and unplug the computer, and then open it up.

2. Plug the new modem card into an available slot.

3. Close up the computer.

4. Plug your phone line into the port on the newly installed card labeled "Line."

5. If you have a fax machine or house phone connected to the same line, plug that into the newly installed card labeled "Phone."

6. Put the CD that came with the modem into your CD drive.

7. Turn on your computer and let your operating system boot.

Internal Modem in a Laptop Computer

To install an internal analog modem in a laptop, the procedure will be very similar to an internal modem for a desktop, but instead of opening up the computer you will plug the modem card into an available PCMCIA slot in your laptop.

One difference with laptops is that after the first installation, you can remove the card and plug it back in when you need it, as often as you like, and even while the laptop is still running. This is advisable if you put your laptop in a carry bag; you don't want your PCMCIA cards hanging out the side where they can likely cause damage to the laptop slots or cards themselves.

External Modem

To install an external analog modem in a desktop or laptop computer, the procedure will be very similar to an internal modem, but instead of opening up the computer, you will use either a serial cable or a USB cable to connect the external modem to a port on the outside of your computer.

In general, fewer and fewer devices, such as modems that are sold today, use a serial cable. USB is faster and allows for multiple devices to share the same physical port. So unless you have an older modem already, or just bought one on eBay, it's probably best to go with a USB modem.

Configure Windows to "Talk To" the Modem

After you physically install the modem, turn the PC on and let Windows boot. While booting, Windows will automatically detect the new modem and help finish installing it. The following procedure shows the steps that take place in Windows 98, Me, and 2000 (as mentioned in the Introduction, the scope covered is only Microsoft Windows as the operating system):

Step 1   Turn on the PC. While Windows is booting, a dialog window will appear that shows that the modem has been detected (see Figure 3-2). The example shown is for a PCI internal desktop modem. Other modem types will appear slightly differently. Insert the CD that came with the modem and click **Next**.

Figure 3-2   Windows Detects a New Device

Step 2   Select **Search for the best driver for your device (Recommended)** and click **Next** (see Figure 3-3).

Step 3   Select **Specify a location** (see Figure 3-4). For some modem products you can click **CD-ROM**; for others, like the example here, you need to click **Browse** to locate the correct driver directory on the modem's CD for your operating system. Reference the installation documentation that comes with the product to see which is required. Click **Next**. (Windows 2000 requires an extra step: Click **OK.**)

Figure 3-3   Search for a Driver

Figure 3-4   Specify Where to Look for the Driver

Step 4   Windows confirms it has located a suitable driver on the CD (see Figure 3-5). Click **Next**.

Figure 3-5   Driver Located

Step 5   You're all done. Click **Finish** (see Figure 3-6).

Figure 3-6   Modem Is Installed

Set Up a Dialup Connection to the Internet

Now that the modem is installed and ready to use, you still need to tell Windows how to use the modem to call the ISP, who provides your dialup service to the Internet.

When you first subscribe to a dialup service, such as Earthlink, AOL, or MSN, you are provided three key pieces of information, which are required to set up your service:

- Local phone number to dial up for connection (or how to find it)

- User ID

- Password (The ISP provides an initial password that you should change!)

Table 3-2 walks you through the necessary steps to set up your dialup Internet connection. The steps are shown side-by-side for Windows 98SE and Windows XP, so the similarities and differences can be seen.

Table 3-2   Setting Up a Dialup Internet Connection

Steps	Windows 98/Me/2000	Windows XP
Step 1: Using the mouse, select **Start > Control Panel > Internet Options**. Click the **Connections** tab, and then click **Setup**.	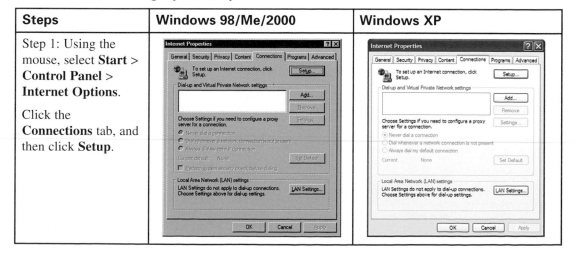	

Table 3-2   Setting Up a Dialup Internet Connection

Steps	Windows 98/Me/2000	Windows XP
Step 2: The Windows Internet Connection Wizard starts. Select **I want to set up my Internet connection manually** and click **Next**. Note the improvement in Windows XP to now display three dialog boxes to ask the same question.		
Step 3: Select **I connect through a phone line and a modem**. Click **Next**.		
Step 4: Windows might need to copy additional files from the Windows CD. Insert it in the CD drive, click **OK**, and follow the instructions. Click **OK** again.		There is no XP-equivalent screen. Proceed to the next step.

Table 3-2   Setting Up a Dialup Internet Connection

Steps	Windows 98/Me/2000	Windows XP
Step 5: Type the local phone number given to you by your ISP. Uncheck **Dial using the area code and country code**. Click **Next**. Type the user name and password given to you by your ISP. Click **Next**. Type in a name for your dialup connection (any name you choose is fine). Click **Next**. Note that for Windows XP, the order is slightly different. XP asks you to name the connection first, and then asks for phone number and user ID/password.		
Step 6: If asked "Do you want to set up an Internet mail account now," select **No**. (You will need to do this at a later time though.) Click **Next**.		There is no XP-equivalent screen. Proceed to the next step.
Step 7: Click **Finish** to complete your dialup connection.		

Table 3-2   Setting Up a Dialup Internet Connection

Steps	Windows 98/Me/2000	Windows XP
Step 8: Windows might need to reboot (thankfully, the latest versions of Windows will probably skip this step). Click **OK**.	*System Settings Change dialog: You must restart your computer before the new settings will take effect. Do you want to restart your computer now? Yes / No*	There is no XP-equivalent screen. Proceed to the next step.
Step 9: Windows will display the Dialup window. If not displayed, double-click it from the desktop. Click **Connect** to test the connection.	*Dial-up Connection dialog: Select the service you want to connect to, and then enter your user name and password. Connect to: Dial-Up Internet Connection; User name: ms650646; Password: ********; Save password; Connect automatically; Connect / Settings... / Cancel*	*Connect Dial-Up Connection dialog: User name: ms650646; Password: [To change the saved password, click here]; Save this user name and password for the following users: Me only / Anyone who uses this computer; Dial: 9260020; Dial / Cancel / Properties / Help*
Step 10: The modem should dial your ISP and connect.	*Connected to Dial-Up Internet Connection: Connected at 36,000 bps; Duration: 000:00:23; Bytes received: 2,900; Bytes sent: 1,916; OK / Disconnect / Details >>*	*Dial-Up Connection Status (General / Details): Connection Status: Connected; Duration: 00:00:36; Speed: 45.2 Kbps; Activity Sent / Received; Bytes: 1,879 / 1,654; Compression: 0% / 0%; Errors: 0 / 0; Properties / Disconnect / Close*

After testing the connection, you should now be able to use Internet Explorer (or Netscape) and browse the Internet. Launch Internet Explorer and type in a web address such as

www.yahoo.com

www.cnn.com

www.weather.com

Congratulations, you are now connected to the Internet!

Troubleshooting Tips: Modem Connection

If the modem does not make a connection, try the following:

- Check the cables to make sure you made the right connections.

- Watch the display during the dialup process to see at what point the connection is failing. Making sure that sound is turned on in the modem can help also, as you can hear the dial-tone, dialing, and so on.

- If the error message indicates there is no dial-tone, it is most likely a cabling problem between your modem and the phone jack on the wall.

- If the modem detects dial tone, dials the ISP number, and goes no further, check that the ISP number being dialed is correct. Also check to see if a ten-digit number (including area code) needs to be dialed in your calling area.

- If the modem connects to the ISP but then you receive an error message such as "Login Invalid" or "Invalid Password," chances are you made a typo entering the user ID/password for the service provided by your ISP.

- On some operating systems (such as Windows XP), the built-in Firewall or a software firewall program you installed (such as ZoneAlarm) might be preventing a connection. In this case, you need to bring up the firewall management program and enable the Internet access. See Chapter 14, "Protecting Your Network from Intruders," for a more detailed discussion on firewall software programs.

- Read the "Troubleshooting" chapter in the installation manual that came with the modem. Often, it is now provided on CD-ROM instead of paper.

Set Up Access to E-Mail

If your Internet is now working, we are ready to set up access to e-mail. Most likely your e-mail account is being provided by the same ISP that provides your dialup (or broadband) service.

When you first subscribe to an Internet service, you will be provided (at least) five key pieces of information that are required to set up and access your e-mail account (see Table 3-3).

 NOTE Whether you intend to use dialup or broadband service to access the Internet, you need to set up your e-mail account this way.

Table 3-3   E-Mail Account Information You Need

Info	Notes	Example
E-Mail Domain	Each ISP has one or more domains.	mindspring.com
E-Mail ID	Can be same or different from your account user ID. Each family member has a unique e-mail ID.	John.Brown
E-Mail Password	Can be the same or different from your account password. Always change the initial password set by the ISP	Ynotl8r
Outgoing Mail Server	Server used to send e-mail (a.k.a. SMTP server).	mail.mindspring.com
Incoming Mail Server	Server used to receive e-mail (a.k.a. POP or POP3 server)	pop.mindspring.com

Often, the ISP provides a number of e-mail accounts included with Internet service as a package, so each member of the family can have his own e-mail. Typically, there is an "anchor" account that the service is tied to, and then other family members can create additional accounts with the ISP. This procedure for setting up access to e-mail will need to be done for each account. Table 3-4 walks you through the necessary steps to set up your e-mail. Once again the steps are shown for both Windows 98SE and Windows XP to show the similarities and differences.

 NOTE We assume for the purposes of this example that Microsoft Outlook Express is being used for e-mail. If another mailer program is going to be used, consult that program's documentation for instructions.

Start by running Outlook Express. To do so, choose **Start > Programs > Outlook Express**. Another way to start this program is to double-click the Outlook Express icon on the desktop.

Table 3-4   Setting Up E-Mail with Outlook Express

Steps	Windows 98/Me	Windows XP
Step 1: Outlook Express may start the e-mail account process automatically. If so, jump to Step 2. If not, select **Tools > Accounts > Add**.	*[screenshot: Internet Accounts dialog box]*	There is no XP-equivalent screen. Proceed to the next step.

Table 3-4   Setting Up E-Mail with Outlook Express

Steps	Windows 98/Me	Windows XP
Step 2: Enter the name you want to be displayed in e-mail that you send. Click **Next**.		
Step 3: Enter the full e-mail address (E-mailID@domain). Click **Next**.		
Step 4: Select **POP3** as the incoming e-mail type (confirm this with your ISP). Enter the incoming and outgoing mail server names. Click **Next**.		
Step 5: Enter the e-mail account ID and e-mail password. Click **Next**.		
Step 6: Click **Finish**.		

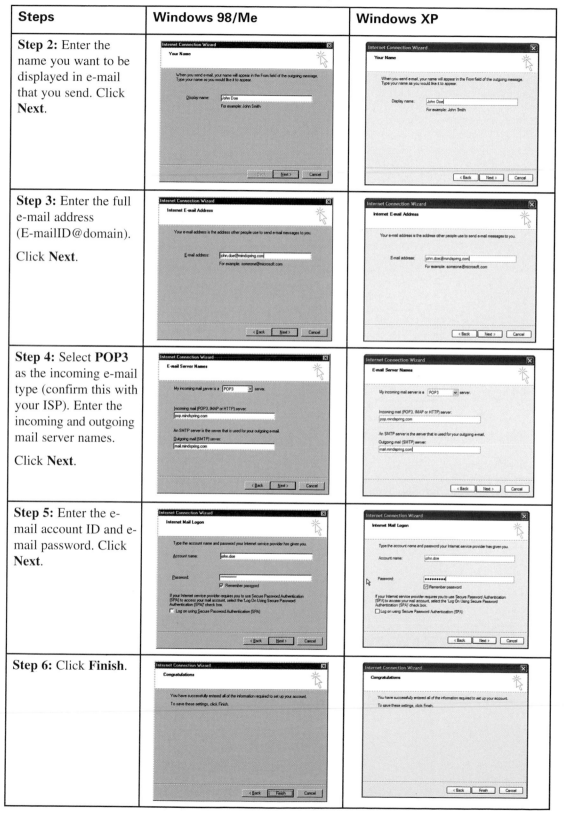

The e-mail account should now be set up. Outlook Express (or whichever mail program you chose to use) should now be able to access the e-mail account and both send and receive e-mail.

Try sending yourself a test e-mail by addressing the e-mail (in the **TO** field) to yourself. Type something clever in the subject and message body, then click **Send**. You should see the e-mail client (Outlook Express in this example) contact the ISP, send the outgoing e-mail, then receive the incoming e-mail. Due to a delay on the e-mail server, you may need to click **Send/Receive** a couple times.

If the message is sent and then you receive your test e-mail back, congratulations, you just set up e-mail!

 Geek Squad Remember to keep your Sent Items folder cleaned out. People often clean up their Deleted Items folder but don't look at Sent Items. So when the Geek Squad shows up on a call about Outlook Express taking forever to open, we find a gigabyte in the Sent Items folder and another gigabyte in the Jokes folder.

Troubleshooting Tips: Setting Up E-Mail

If something goes wrong, try the following:

- Check to see that you have an Internet connection by trying to access a web page with your Internet browser.

- If an error message is displayed during the sending process, verify that you entered the correct SMTP server name, user ID, and password.

- If an error message is displayed during the receiving process, verify that you entered the correct POP3 server name, user ID, and password.

- Double-check with your ISP to make sure your e-mail service has been activated.

- Try the Outlook Express Troubleshooter. Click **Help > Contents and Index > Troubleshooting**.

From the Geek Squad Files

Before you proceed, here are a few tips to make facing any technical problem less painful than it has to be:

- **Keep a log**—What a computer is doing when it misbehaves can tell you a lot about why it is misbehaving. Whether you are just setting up or experiencing problems for the first time, take notes about what you were doing when it happens. Even if the error messages look cryptic, copy them down verbatim. It can save you hours of frustration (and money) by helping the geek on the other end fix it faster. You may notice a pattern yourself eventually and be able to fix it without calling the teenager down the street.

- **Stay calm**—Follow our Ten Minute Miracle: When a problem occurs, after taking notes, turn everything off. Go get a cup of coffee and come back in ten minutes. Power everything back on and you will be surprised how often this helps the situation. If you are already a high-strung person, we suggest decaf.

- **Backup**—If you haven't experienced data loss yet, it's only a matter of time before you do. Hard drives, CDs, and applications can be replaced, but not your photos, financial records, or e-mail. Actually, we don't blame you for not backing up religiously. It has always been a major pain to back up quickly and easily. The advent of CDR (CD-recordable drives) has made it cheap and easy to back up your data. As of the publication of this book, it appears something even easier has emerged: the keychain drive. Fitting on your keychain and the size of a house key, this solid state device comes in capacities from 128 MB up to 4 GB.

- **Antivirus**—Until the last few years, most viruses were more annoying than dangerous. All that has changed. It is a direct effect of the increased number of people online—combined with "always on" Internet connections. These factors make it attractive for virus writers to use unsuspecting (and unprotected) home and office computers to launch their attacks. Bottom line: Get antivirus software, and keep it current by enabling the built-in auto-update feature.

Creating a Basic Home Network

In Chapter 3, "Connecting to the Internet," we got our toes wet by connecting one computer to the Internet. This was pretty much the status quo a few years ago, but today most households have a need for at least a small network of computers.

In this chapter, we will walk you through some basic design principles and best practices, review some of the devices you will likely be using, and provide a step-by-step walk-through on setting up a basic home network.

Planning a Network

When we first networked our homes several years ago, our spouses and kids thought we were pretty geeky. They wondered why we couldn't connect a single computer to the nearest phone line and leave it at that. Today, they call us at work when they can't access the Internet from the back deck. You may think you need just two computers connected with a cable, but chances are, you will outgrow that pretty quickly.

Because of this, it's important to sit down with some blank sheets of paper and think about what you have today, what you are likely to have six months from now, and what you would love to have two years from now, in a home network.

Designing Your Network

Here's an example worksheet we found useful for planning a network. Fill it out twice: once for today, once for what you think your home network may look like one to two years from now. The table can either be written on a piece of paper, or better, in a spreadsheet program. The examples shown in Table 5-1 are based on our houses. Yes, we are both gadget freaks, but we wrote this book because we strongly believe that all of you are going to need to do some extent of this or risk getting left behind. Trust us, the first time your 12-year-old daughter comes to you complaining that she can't connect to her teacher's website to download her homework...all will become apparent.

Table 5-1   Planning Your Network: Example Worksheet

Today					
	Desktop PCs	**Laptops**	**Printers**	**Video Games, Cameras, etc.**	**Other**
How many?	1	1	1		
What rooms are they in?	Master bedroom	Any room	Master bedroom		
How are they connected?	Separate dialup	Separate dialup	Parallel cable		
1–2 Years					
How many?	2	2	2	1 Video camera 1 Xbox	1 TV (networked) 1 Stereo (networked)
What rooms will they likely be in?	Master bedroom Kids' bedroom	Any room	Master bedroom Kids' bedroom	Any room	Family room
How will they be connected?	1 Wired 1 Wireless	Wireless	Parallel cables	Wireless	Wireless

At this point, several other factors need to be considered in our planning:

- What type of Internet access do you have today? Will it have the bandwidth (transfer speed) adequate for your needs?

- Where is the Internet access physically located in your house? Is it convenient?

- Do family members need to share resources like printers?

- Do you have computer-savvy neighbors or family members who can help?

Throughout the following chapters, we take the unconnected "stuff" listed in Table 5-1's "Today" section and progressively work toward the networked home shown in the "1–2 Years" section. The steps we take to get there are

1. Network two computers together, sharing some files and printers.

2. Upgrade to high-speed Internet service.

3. Deploy a wireless network to further extend the home network.

4. Make sure your newly built network is as secure as you can make it.

5. Get into some really cool stuff, like video surveillance and online gaming.

You might need some of these parts to network your computers or all of them—choose the parts you need. By reading this book, you learn about networking options that you might not need now or years from now, but the information is there in case you change your mind (which people have been known to do).

Building Your Network

The network we work toward is wireless. Not going wireless just doesn't make any sense. It's affordable, relatively easy, and saves a ton of time as your network grows. It also allows you to use your PC in places that would not be available if you were "wired." We structured this book with this ultimate goal in mind and have taken care to recommend purchases that will be usable later.

As a final note for planning, everything we build from here on out will be connected to the network. As a result, every device we want to add to the network is going to need a network interface card (NIC). *NICs* are simply cards that enable a PC, laptop, printer, or other device to talk to other PCs, laptops, and so on. There are two distinct types of NICs:

- **Wired**—Uses cables to connect to other computers

- **Wireless**—Uses the air to connect to other computers, much like your cell phone

One thing to keep in mind is that most new PCs and laptops come with built-in NICs, and many new laptops have built-in wireless capabilities.

Don't worry too much yet about understanding all of it, we will explain more as we build out our network. For now, just have a look at the worksheet shown in Table 5-2, which will also be useful for planning your network. This is an example where we have two desktop PCs and two laptop computers each identified by their primary user. We also have a video camera and a video game system that we want to include on the network. Later, we will consider options for each of the items we don't yet have and make the best choice based on our needs. After you inventory your equipment, you may want to create a table similar to what's shown in Table 5-2 for your own needs.

Table 5-2   Network Readiness

	Wired Desktop	Wired Laptop	Wireless Desktop	Wireless Laptop	Wireless Other
Desktop PC 1 (Mom)	Has		May Need		
Desktop PC 2 (Son)			May Need		
Laptop 1 (Dad)		Has		Has	
Laptop 2 (Daughter)		Has		Has	
Video Camera					Has
Video Game					May Need

Examples of Home Networks

Home Network with Broadband Internet

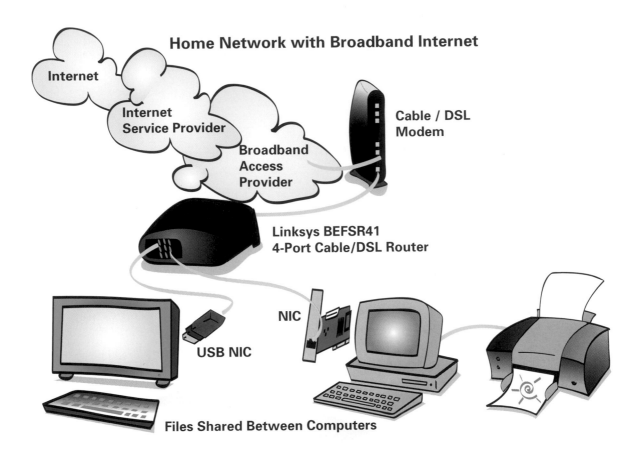

Home Network Without Broadband Internet

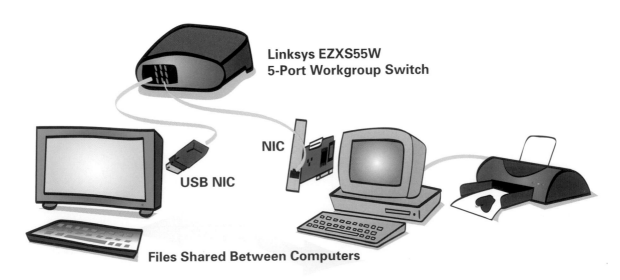

How to Build It: Connecting Two Computers

Now that we have thought about our current and future needs and inventoried our network devices, we will actually build our first network: two computers connected together.

Here's a brief overview of the steps we will go through to connect two computers:

- Decide on the type of NICs.

- Determine if they are already present.

- Physically install the NICs if not already installed.

- Configure Windows to "talk to" the NICs.

- Build a network between the two computers.

- Set up the network in Windows.

NOTE If you plan to build a wireless network, you may choose to skip some parts of this section. However, even in a wireless network, there is most often a need for at least one computer to be cable-connected (wired) in your home network, so this section is still relevant.

Many desktop computers and laptops sold today come with built-in NICs by default, so installing one may or may not be a concern. If NICs are already installed in your computers, skip to the section, "Build a Network Between the Two Computers."

Decide on the Type of NICs

One of the most important decisions to make is whether you will need NICs that are wired or wireless:

- **Wired (cabled) NICs**—Recommended whenever there is a relatively fixed location for the computer, which is in close proximity to the primary location of the Internet service in your house.

- **Wireless (not cabled) NICs**—Recommended whenever a computer is used in different locations (such as a laptop) or is difficult to reach with cabling in your house.

NOTE In subsequent chapters, we will cover how to build a wireless network. The majority of your NICs will likely be wireless, so it's probably not a good idea to run off and purchase a handful of wired NICs. You need at least one for the "primary" computer that is closest to your Internet service in your house.

For demonstration purposes in this section, we are going to select and install two wired NICs and connect two computers. This is useful in situations where you only have two computers you will ever connect, both of them are in close proximity to each other, and their locations in your house are very unlikely to change. Typically, that's pretty restrictive, but we will use it as an example to understand basic networking.

Like modems, NICs come in several connection "styles," including those shown in Table 5-3. For our two-computer wired network, we purchased one Linksys LNE100TX for installing inside a desktop PC and one Linksys USB200M for connecting externally to a laptop. The USB NIC may come in handy for your laptop when you take it on the road and need to connect at a hotel. Expect to pay about $20–30 for either the desktop PC or USB NIC, and $30–40 for the laptop PCMCIA version.

Table 5-3   Different Styles of NICs

Internal Desktop NIC	Internal Laptop NIC	External NIC
Linksys LNE100TX Etherfast 10/100 LAN Card	Linksys PCM100 Etherfast 10/100 Integrated PCMCIA Card	Linksys USB200M Compact USB 2.0 10/100 Network Adapter

Physically Install the NIC

For this section, skip to the section that matches the type of NIC you chose.

Internal NIC in a Desktop Computer

To install an internal NIC in a desktop computer, follow the manufacturer instructions that came with the card you purchased. In general, you will do the following:

Step 1   Shut off and unplug the PC, and then open it up.

 Geek Squad: Because of the potential damage that can be caused by static electric discharge, it's a good idea to take precautions so that you don't zap your computer. As long as you don't shuffle across your shag carpet wearing your socks or play with balloons beforehand, you're probably OK. But you should touch a metal door-frame or doorknob to discharge yourself.

Step 2   Plug the new NIC into an available slot (see Figure 5-1).

Step 3   Close up the computer.

Step 4   Turn on your computer and let your operating system boot.

Step 5   Put the CD that came with your NIC into your CD drive.

Step 6   The install program on the CD should start by itself. If it does not, open a directory window and double-click the install or setup icon in the CD directory.

Figure 5-1   Plug the NIC into a Slot

Internal PCMCIA NIC in a Laptop Computer

To install an internal NIC in a laptop, plug the NIC into an available PCMCIA slot in your laptop (see Figure 5-2).

Figure 5-2   Plug the NIC into a PCMCIA Slot

External NIC for a Desktop or Laptop Computer

To install an external NIC, the procedure is to plug the USB NIC into an available USB port on the outside of your computer (see Figure 5-3).

Figure 5-3   Plug the USB NIC into the USB Port

Configure Windows to "Talk To" the NIC

After you physically install the NIC (either inside the computer, or plugged into the outside of the computer), turn on the PC and let Windows boot. While booting, Windows automatically detects the new NIC and helps you finish the installation. Table 5-4 shows the steps that take place (in Windows 98, Me, and XP). The steps involved are very similar to those we just completed for the modem installation.

 GEEK SQUAD If you are reading this book, chances are, there is obviously a certain amount of geek in you already, and a certain lack of a social life. And that's OK, I mean we take pride in it.

Table 5-4   NIC Installation

Steps	Windows 98/Me	Windows XP
Step 1: Turn on the PC. While Windows boots, a dialog box appears that the NIC has been detected. Insert the CD that came with the NIC and click **Next**.		There is no XP equivalent screen. Proceed to the next step.
Step 2: *For Windows 98:* Select **Search for the best driver for your device**. *For Windows XP:* Select **Install from a list or specific location**. Click **Next**.		

Table 5-4 NIC Installation

Steps	Windows 98/Me	Windows XP
Step 3: Select **CD-ROM drive**. Click **Next**.	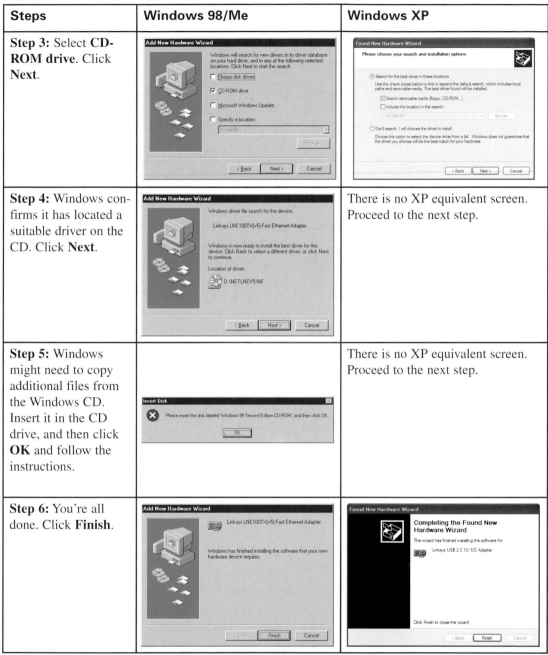	
Step 4: Windows confirms it has located a suitable driver on the CD. Click **Next**.		There is no XP equivalent screen. Proceed to the next step.
Step 5: Windows might need to copy additional files from the Windows CD. Insert it in the CD drive, and then click **OK** and follow the instructions.		There is no XP equivalent screen. Proceed to the next step.
Step 6: You're all done. Click **Finish**.		

Build a Network Between the Two Computers

Now that the NICs are installed and ready to use, we still need to construct a connection between them, and tell Windows what we want the connection to do. There are several different ways we can accomplish the connection. In this section, we focus on two methods:

- Back-to-back

- Using a hub, switch, or router

Back-to-Back

Computers can be connected "back-to-back" directly, with the right connecting cable. There are two types of network cables:

- **Cross-over (a.k.a. PC-to-PC cable)**—A specialized network cable to connect two computers or devices directly, without first going through a network hub or switch.

- **Straight (a.k.a. PC-to-Network cable)**—By far, these are the most widely used cables because they connect just about any computer or device to the network.

VERY IMPORTANT: **By the way, most NICs do not include the cable when you purchase them, so you will need to buy these separately. Expect to pay $5–10 each, with cross-over cables being a bit more expensive.**
Be careful when picking these up on the store shelf not to get a cross-over when you intended to get a straight cable. Rule of thumb: If it does not explicitly say "cross-over" on the package, it's almost certainly a "straight," but keep in mind these cables will look almost identical. Just to be safe, you might want to verify with a store employee.

Back-to-back networking is pretty rare because it has distinct limitations, including that it only works for exactly two computers and is not extendable. The connection procedure for back-to-back network cabling is straightforward: plug one end of the cross-over cable into the NIC in one computer, and the other end into the NIC in the second computer (see Figure 5-4).

Figure 5-4   Back-to-Back Network Cabling

| Computer 1 | Standard PC NIC | Cross-Over Ethernet Cable | USB NIC | Computer 2 |

Using a Hub, Switch, or Router

The most common way for computers to be connected is through a network device, like a hub, switch, or router. Using one of these devices is more common than back-to-back networking because the options are extremely flexible and the network can be easily extended. So what's the difference between each device? Table 5-5 compares the devices.

Table 5-5   Comparison of Hub, Switch, and Router Devices

	Hub	Switch	Router	Wireless Router
Description	"Dumb" device, just connects computers electrically	More intelligent, allows simultaneous transmissions	Most intelligent, includes a switch	It's a router, but also has built-in wireless functions
Cost	$	$$	$$	$$$
Example	Linksys EFAH05W 5-port Workgroup Hub	Linksys EZXS55W 5-port Workgroup Switch	Linksys BEFSR41 4-port Cable/DSL Router	Linksys BEFW11S4 4-port Cable/DSL Router

Which device you choose—hub, switch, router, or wireless router—depends on your requirements:

- Hubs are not very common any more and have largely been replaced with switches.

- Switches will do a fine job for a wired home network or small office, but are not ideal for connecting to most high-speed broadband Internet services.

- Routers are designed to provide network ports just like a switch but are also able to "bridge" to other networks, such as a broadband Internet service. Routers are much more intelligent than switches, and, therefore, take more effort to install in your network.

- Wireless routers are just like routers, only they also provide network access to computers without using cables.

If you plan to connect multiple computers to the Internet using a high-speed broadband service, such as cable or DSL, a router (or wireless router) is the best option.

 NOTE Before buying a switch or wired router, decide if you plan to deploy a wireless network in your house. In Part III, "Look Ma, No Wires!," we will walk through how to do so. Only purchase a wired router at this point if you plan to run cables through your house to connect all the computers and devices you want to put on your network.

For the purposes of learning, we are going to use a switch in this chapter to avoid the need to configure the device. (Switches work out-of-the-box, but routers require some information to be entered.)

The connection procedure using a switch is also very straightforward: For each computer, plug one end of a "straight" Ethernet cable into the NIC and the other end into a port on the switch (see Figure 5-5).

NOTE Avoid the port marked "Uplink," which has a special purpose.

Figure 5-5   Connecting Your Network by Using a Switch

Computer 1   Standard   Straight   Ethernet   Straight   USB   Computer 2
                  PC NIC   Ethernet Cable   Switch   Ethernet Cable   NIC

After properly connected (and don't forget to plug the switch in), both the NICs should display a green light showing connectivity has been established.

Set Up the Network in Windows

Now that our two computers are physically connected in a network, we can start to take advantage of the reasons we wanted to connect computers together in the first place, namely to communicate, share information, and share resources.

To complete our small network, we need to tell each computer about the network it's on and how to talk to other computers over the network. Windows fortunately makes this pretty easy to accomplish.

Let's start by getting our Windows 98 desktop (Computer 1) to communicate with our Windows XP laptop (Computer 2). Here are the steps we need to take for Computer 1:

> **Step 1**   Using the mouse, navigate to **Start > Settings > Control Panel > Network** (see Figure 5-6).

Figure 5-6   Network Dialog Box

> **Step 2**   Click the **Identification** tab (see Figure 5-7).

Figure 5-7   Identification Tab

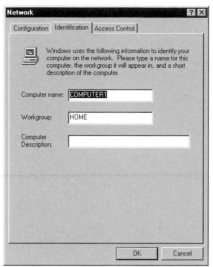

Enter a name for the computer as you want it to appear on the network to other computers (COMPUTER1 in this example). This is *different* for each computer on your network.

Enter a workgroup name that identifies your network (HOME in this example). This is the *same* for each computer on your network. There is a 15-character limit for workgroup names and the name may only include letters, numbers, and hyphens. In addition, the workgroup name must not be the same as any PC names.

Also, remember to write down usernames and passwords you create on the network worksheet you started earlier.

Click **OK**.

Step 3   Windows might need to copy additional files from the Windows CD. Insert it in the CD drive, and then click **OK** and follow the instructions (see Figure 5-8). Click **OK** again.

Figure 5-8   Insert the CD

Step 4   Windows must be rebooted to make the new network settings effective (see Figure 5-9). Click **Yes**.

Figure 5-9   Reboot Your Computer

Step 4   When Windows reboots, a new dialog will now appear each time you boot your PC, asking for your Windows networking username and password (see Figure 5-10).

At this point, no username exists, but entering one creates a new one. It is optional whether you want to create a user ID and password. If both are left blank, none is required. Later in the book, we will provide some tools for parental control so it is best to leave this blank, as it will be one less thing to keep track of.

If you do wish to, enter both a user ID and password. REMEMBER THEM as it is exceptionally difficult to recover a user ID if the password is lost.

Optionally, you can enter just a username and leave the password blank. Leaving the password field blank has the effect of having a user ID that does not require a password.

Click **OK**.

Figure 5-10   Enter New Password Dialog Box

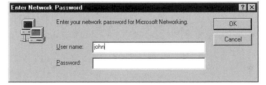

Here are the steps we must take for Computer 2, which uses Windows XP:

Step 1   Using the mouse, navigate to **Start** > **Control Panel** > **Network Connections** (see Figure 5-11). Select the newly installed network adapter, and then click **Set up a home or small office network**. This brings up the Network Setup Wizard (see Figure 5-12). Click **Next**.

Step 2   A Before You Continue dialog box appears (see Figure 5-13). We have already done everything on the list in prior sections. Click **Next**.

Figure 5-11   Network Connections Dialog Box

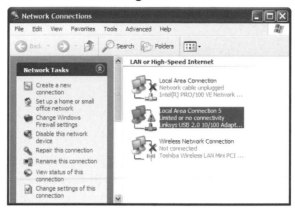

Figure 5-12   Network Setup Wizard

Figure 5-13   Before You Continue Checklist

Step 3   Select **This computer connects to the Internet through another computer on my network or through a residential gateway** (see Figure 5-14). Click **Next**.

Figure 5-14   Connection Method

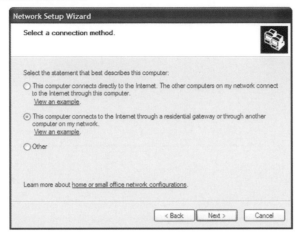

Step 4   Enter the computer name for this computer (see Figure 5-15). This will be *different* for each computer on your network (COMPUTER2 in this example). Click **Next**.

Figure 5-15   Name Your Computer

Step 5   Enter the workgroup name for your network (HOME1 in this example—see Figure 5-16). This will be the *same* for each computer on your network. Click **Next**.

Step 6   A confirmation dialog box appears so you can look over your settings. Check that you typed the computer name and workgroup name correctly (see Figure 5-17). Click **Next**.

Figure 5-16   Choose a Workgroup Name

Figure 5-17   Confirm Your Settings

Step 7   Windows now updates the computer as you have instructed (see Figure 5-18). While doing so, you are entertained with this nice little animation.

Do you ever wonder who gets paid to do these? Wonder if his job title is "Engineer of Entertaining Animations for Users with Short-Attention Spans." Hmmm.

When it's finished, click **Next**.

Step 7   You are asked if you want to create a disk/CD (see Figure 5-19). This is useful mainly for small offices where you want to replicate the network settings across several computers.

Select **Just finish the wizard, I don't need to run the wizard on other computers**. Click **Next**.

Figure 5-18   What Beautiful Animation!

Figure 5-19   Replication Disk Option

Step 8   You're all done. Click **Finish** (see Figure 5-20).

Thankfully, later versions of Windows, including XP, do not need to reboot to make the settings active.

Whew! You made it. So now that we have told our two computers about the network we want them to communicate on, with any luck they will now be happily talking to each other, catching up on old business, planning the next Skynet, and so on.

As a check, let's see if our network is really connected the way we think it is:

■   For Computer 1 (running Windows 98), double-click the **Network Neighborhood** icon on your desktop. Figure 5-21 shows that both Computer 1 and Computer 2 are in your network.

Figure 5-20   Your Computer Is Successfully Set Up

Figure 5-21   Verifying Your Network on Computer 1

■ For Computer 2 (running Windows XP), double-click the **My Network Places** icon on your desktop. Then click **View workgroup connections**. Figure 5-22 shows that both Computer 1 and Computer 2 are in your network.

Figure 5-22   Verifying Your Network on Computer 2

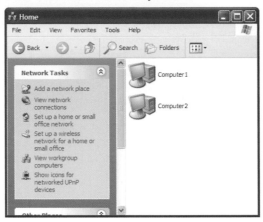

On both computers, you should be able to see the two computers that are now part of our network displayed as icons with the computer names you assigned. Congratulations, you just built a network!

Troubleshooting Tips: Building a Network

If you don't see the computers as part of your newly created network, check these things:

- Is the cabling correct? Do you have the right cables? Are the green lights lit on the NICs?

- If a personal firewall, such as ZoneAlarm, is running on either or both of the computers, that could (for security reasons) block some important network traffic that lets Windows computers see one another. See Part IV, "Security of Home Networks."

- In older versions of Windows such as 98, "sharing" must be enabled before Windows networking can see other computers on the network. See Chapter 6, "Sharing Network Resources," which covers file sharing and print sharing. Windows XP enables sharing by default.

- If an older version of Windows, such as 98, is one of the computers on the network, make sure the network name does not use special characters (such as #, $, &, -, and so on) and is 15 characters or less.

- Double-check in the network properties (by selecting **Control Panel > Network Connections**) that the TCP/IP protocol service is configured for the NIC. If it does not appear in the properties, try uninstalling and then reinstalling the NIC.

Sharing Network Resources

Remember when just a few people had cell phones and those of us who could not afford them would sneer as we stepped up to the pay phone? Today, most people have cell phones and feel naked if they leave them at home. New uses for cell phones have developed that were not foreseen, such as having a built-in digital camera, taking a photo or even video and e-mailing it wirelessly to someone. Many phones are Internet ready now as well.

Home networks are evolving much the same way. First, they were just for nerdy computer types, but they are quickly becoming mainstream, with new uses popping up all the time. Kids take computer networks as a given. They will find uses for them that we never imagined. For example, your daughter could use Instant Messaging (IM) to send short text messages over the Internet to your cell phone to tell you that you are late for dinner (again) and Mom is in "a mood."

In Chapter 5, "Creating a Basic Home Network," we built a small computer network, and "taught" the two computers how to communicate with each other. We tested our network by seeing if each computer could "see" the other over the network. In this chapter, we start taking advantage of all the hard work by making it do something more useful.

There are a lot of reasons we wanted to build a network, including

- Make it easy to share files between computers

- Share printers and other devices

- Provide simultaneous access to the Internet

- Enable some fun stuff, like online gaming and video cameras

This chapter covers file sharing and printer sharing. Later in the book, we explore more advanced uses for our network, including internet connection sharing.

File Sharing

First up, file sharing. What is it, and why would we want to do it? Whether you realize it or not, files surround us in our daily lives. A school report written on a computer, a digital picture in a camera, a news report on cnn.com, a joke a friend sent in an e-mail, a song on an audio CD, and a DVD movie we watch...all of them are files. The problem with all these files is they seem quite often to not be where we need them to be:

"Honey, where's that digital picture you took at the beach? I want to put it on my computer as a background. It's on your computer? Well that doesn't help me."

"Sweetie, can you get off that computer? I need to check something on our taxes and I put them on that computer."

Digital multimedia, such as audio CDs, digital photography, and DVDs have extended the need for file sharing in homes even further. Very soon, families will have a photo library, music library, video library, and game library in a central location (or spread out) in their home. File sharing will allow them to have access to those interesting bits from wherever they are. For example, what if you could have a home movie library that you could view on any TV in your house?

Figure 6-1 shows the basics of file sharing. Someone sits at Computer 2 and realizes the letter he's working on is on Computer 1. Computer 1 is being used by another family member. Without file sharing, we have a family squabble looming.

Figure 6-1   Life Without File Sharing

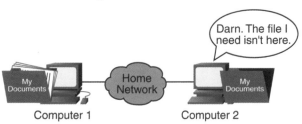

With file sharing, we can easily solve the problem. On Computer 1, we make the folder containing the documents a shared folder on the network. Then when we use Computer 2, we can view and use the folder just as if it was on Computer 2. We can edit it, save it, copy it, print it, and whatever else is important to us.

The files never leave Computer 1. They reside on Computer 1's hard disk, and the Windows networking file sharing service provides the perception that the file is on Computer 2 (see Figure 6-2). Any change that we make to the files are actually made to the files residing on Computer 1.

Figure 6-2   Life with File Sharing

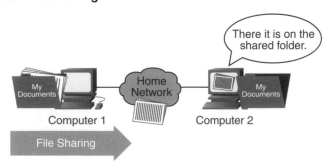

We could choose to copy or save the modified file locally to Computer 2. However, it is important to understand that doing this means that two physical copies of the file now exist: the original on Computer 1 (and the shared network folder) and the modified copy on Computer 2 (see Figure 6-3). People sometimes get confused and believe the changes they made were "lost" by the computer, when in reality, they saved their changes to a different location than the original file.

Figure 6-3   Locally Saving the Modified File

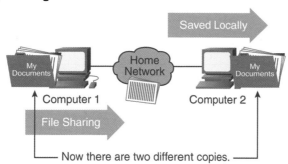

File sharing requires some forethought. If you don't think ahead and put the file in the shared folder on Computer 1, when you need it on Computer 2, you would be out of luck. So it's a good idea to think about what types of information your family might want to share and put the folders in place ahead of time. Get in the practice early of using the folders regularly to store information.

VERY IMPORTANT: **By the way, it is NEVER a good idea to simply share the entire C:/ drive of your computers on the network. It seems like a simple shortcut to always make all of your files available all the time, but it can also expose your computer to viruses and inadvertent corruption of important Windows operating system directories. This will be discussed later in more detail in the section, "Practicing Safe Share."**

Printer Sharing

Printer sharing is similar to file sharing. In most homes, you will have at least one printer, possibly more. Printer sharing is useful for a couple of reasons:

- Allows people to share a printer instead of purchasing one for every computer in your house.

- Some printers are specialized; for example, photo quality for digital camera pictures. Again, you don't want to have to purchase a printer for every computer that may want to print a digital picture.

- Printer sharing provides added convenience over file sharing alone. Users are not required to log in and print all of their files from just one computer.

- Even if you do have multiple printers in your house, invariably one of them will run out of ink, most likely when you need it most.

With printer sharing, it becomes very easy to maximize the investment in printers. Figure 6-4 shows the basics of printer sharing. Someone sits down at Computer 1 on our network and prepares taxes using a tax software program. When completed, the tax documents need to be printed for mailing and record keeping. But Computer 1 has no printer. The only family printer is connected with a parallel cable to Computer 2.

Figure 6-4   Life Without Printer Sharing

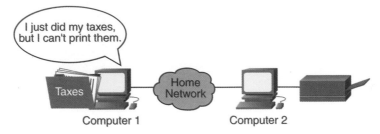

With printer sharing, we can easily solve the problem. On Computer 2, we make the printer a shared printer on the network. Then when we use Computer 1, we can view and use the printer just as if it was connected to Computer 1 (see Figure 6-5).

Figure 6-5   Computer 1's File Prints on Computer 2's Printer

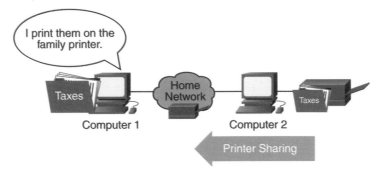

The tax software program we are using to prepare the tax documents has no knowledge of whether the printer is attached to the same computer or another computer on the network. It does not need to know this because Windows networking handles this for us.

We could also have used file sharing by putting the tax documents in a shared network folder on Computer 1, walked over to Computer 2, loaded the tax documents into the program on Computer 2, and then printed it from there. But that's not always possible.

In many situations, a software program that you have purchased might only reside on a single computer. In this example, if we needed the tax software to print documents that only reside on Computer 1, we cannot necessarily use file sharing to print them from Computer 2 because the tax software might not be installed there.

There is also the small matter of the person who may be using Computer 2 at the time, and now you have to "kick him off" for a few minutes while you do your copying and printing. If you don't get it right the first time, family members can become annoyed with you.

With printer sharing, the steps just become so much easier. Computer 1 just "sees" the printer being shared by Computer 2, and your software programs print to it over the network.

Geek Squad: If after reading this book, you decide to install WiFi network at home, consider a WiFi-enabled printer or a WiFi device that turns your current printer into a wireless one. With them, you can place the printer almost anywhere within your home or office, and it doesn't require another computer to "host" the printer.

Caveat: Not all WiFi printers are created equal. We've tried several and most were difficult to install—and we're geeks. Best bet: Consult some online product reviews before you buy.

Practicing Safe Share

Securing your network is covered in more detail in Part IV, "Security of Home Networks," but there are some security concerns specifically related to file and printer sharing that we must cover here. To understand the concerns, it is first helpful to understand the basics of how Windows networking works. Whenever Windows networking is enabled on a home network, each computer on the network sends out information about the resources that are available for other computers to use (see Figure 6-6).

Figure 6-6   Computers Share Their Information to All Other Networked Computers

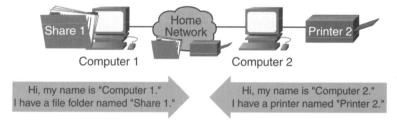

Each computer on the network then collects a list of all the available computers, file folders, and printers that are "advertised." This is what enables us to use Windows functions such as Browse Network Neighborhood (on Windows 98 and 2000) and My Network Places (on Windows XP). The information messages are called "broadcasts." They can be received by anyone on the network who also has Windows networking enabled.

This communication is very desirable. But a complication happens when we add Internet access to the picture. Windows networking was designed to operate in local networks and was not really intended (at least originally) to be used in complex networks where there are local networks (such as home networks) connected to other remote networks (like the Internet). The functions work just dandy, but some undesirable side effects can result.

Figure 6-7 shows one such side effect. In this case, the broadcasts of what computers, file folders, and printers are available on the network can inadvertently be sent to others outside the home network. Windows tries to be helpful by making sure everyone on the network receives the "advertisements." In this case, we do not want anyone but computers on our home network to ever receive information about our network. Doing so can lead to hackers gaining valuable information about our network, leading to attempts to compromise it.

Figure 6-7   Your Network's Broadcasts Can Be Inadvertently Sent Outside Your Network

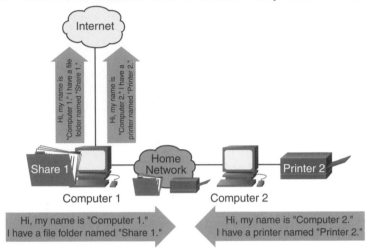

This issue only appears when a single computer on the home network is also providing Internet access for the rest of the network. This is a concern for dialup access, where it is common to have a computer containing a modem providing a shared Internet access.

It is also a concern for high-speed broadband Internet access because these types of connections are "always on." But we will see that the recommended network designs in this book solve this concern quite easily. We discuss this more in Chapter 7, "High-Speed Internet Access."

Another issue that can occur involves other legitimate users on our home network inadvertently updating shared information, such as files, on the network. Suppose on Computer 1, we had a library of digital photos that we upload regularly from a digital camera. Now one of our kids using Computer 2 views the digital photos but, not realizing they have full access, accidentally erases a number of them.

Fortunately, we can take steps to prevent both unintended broadcast of Windows networking information as well as unintentional file modification or deletion. They fall into two categories:

- Sharing guidelines
- Network design guidelines

The "How to Build It" section details the steps you need to take to prevent unintentional broadcasts of your information using both of these categories.

Sharing Guidelines

The following list gives you rules that should keep your private network information from being broadcast on the Internet.

- For each folder you share on the network, decide if other people on the network really need to be able to modify the files, or whether viewing is the only purpose. For folders to be viewed only, we can set the share "access" to be "read-only." You may need to reorganize your folders so that the read-only files are grouped together.

- For each folder and printer we decide to share on the network, we can ask the user for a "password" to verify they are a trusted member of our home network.

- *Never* share the entire C:/ drive of your computer on your home network. This is just asking for trouble. Accidental modification of some of the Windows systems files on a computer can occur, resulting in computer woes.

- Use common sense when deciding what type of information to put in shared folders on your network. *Never* store documents containing invaluable personal information, such as credit card numbers, bank statements, and so on.

- Choose sensible file names when creating files in shared folders. Having to open up files to figure out what is inside is risky. Good filenames make it easier for everyone to find the files they need quickly, reducing the likelihood of accidentally changing or deleting them.

Network Design Guidelines

The section provides some best practices for building a basic home network. You don't have to follow every recommendation, but you should have a good reason for not doing so.

- If using dialup Internet access, *always* disable Windows networking over the dialup connection (we will show how to do this later).

- If you use a computer to connect to both a high-speed broadband Internet service and to the home network (this requires the computer to have two NICs installed), *always* disable Windows networking on the NIC that's connected to the Internet.

- Use a router and firewall to connect to the high-speed broadband Internet service. We will see in later chapters that the router products naturally separate our home network from the Internet, providing a pretty thorough level of security.

- Use a software firewall product, such as ZoneAlarm, on each of the computers in the home network. These products naturally ensure that access to shared files and printers on your network are only from within your home network. This will be covered more extensively in Chapter 14, "Protecting Your Network from Intruders."

 Note: Keep in mind that the security concerns and solutions raised in this chapter err on the side of caution (and near paranoia). A detailed discussion of overall security for your home network will appear in Part IV.

How to Build It: File and Printer Sharing

In this section, we go through the necessary steps to share files, folders, and printers on your home network.

Here's an overview of the steps we will go through to share network resources:

- Enable file and printer sharing

- Share a file over the network

- Map a shared file folder as a disk drive

- Share a printer over the network

- Add security precautions for sharing

Enable File and Printer Sharing

With Windows 2000 and Windows XP, file and printer sharing are enabled by default whenever you install a NIC and enable Windows networking. Further, Windows XP automatically creates a new directory for you titled "Shared Documents" and shares it on the network. You can verify whether this is the case by double-clicking the **My Computer** icon on the desktop or from the Start menu. The human hand underneath the folder icon means that this folder is shared (see Figure 6-8).

Figure 6-8   Locating the Shared Folder with Windows XP

Note: For Windows 98 and Windows Me, you must enable file and printer sharing before they can be used. They are not automatically enabled, like in Windows XP.

Table 6-1 shows the steps to enable file and printer sharing. Both Windows 98 and Windows XP procedures are shown, just in case someone has disabled the feature on XP. You have to enable file and printer sharing on each computer on your network that will share file folders or printers. This is only necessary if you intend to share file or printers on a computer.

VERY IMPORTANT: If you have a laptop from work, there is a good chance that your IT department has assigned it to a workgroup or domain on the corporate network. Take extreme caution in trying to incorporate a work computer into your home network. Changing the workgroup name, for example, can entirely lock you out of your network at work.

Table 6-1   Steps to Enable File and Printer Sharing

Step	Windows 98/Me	Windows XP
Step 1: Windows 98: Select **Start > Control Panel > Network**. Windows XP: Select **Start > Control Panel > Network Connections**. Click the **Local Area Connection** icon, and then click **Change the settings of this connection**.		
Step 2: Windows 98: Click **File and Print Sharing**. Checkmark both **I want to be able to give others access to my files** and **I want to be able to allow others to print to my printer(s)**. Windows XP: Checkmark **File and Printer Sharing for Microsoft Networks.** Click **OK**.	File and Print Sharing ☑ I want to be able to give others access to my files. ☑ I want to be able to allow others to print to my printer(s).	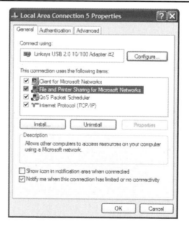
Step 3: Windows XP: You are done. Windows 98: You have a few more steps. An entry for "File and printer sharing" should now appear in the Network list. Click **OK**.		There is no XP equivalent screen. Please proceed to the next step.

Table 6-1   Steps to Enable File and Printer Sharing

Step	Windows 98/Me	Windows XP
Step 4: Windows 98 might need to copy additional files from the Windows CD. Insert it in the CD drive, click **OK**, and follow the instructions.		There is no XP equivalent screen. Please proceed to the next step.
Step 5: Windows 98 needs to be rebooted to make the new network settings effective. Click **Yes**.		There is no XP equivalent screen.

Share a File Over the Network

Now that file and printer sharing are enabled on your network's computers, we can begin sharing files. As mentioned earlier, Windows XP automatically creates a folder called "Shared Documents" and shares it on the network. This is a start, but it may or may not meet our needs. For Windows 98/Me, no such default directory gets created and shared.

Table 6-2 walks you through an example of file sharing on the home network we built earlier with our two computers. On each computer, we are going to create a file folder. This can be named anything you want, but we are going to go with the boring "Shared Documents." Then we are going to share these folders on the network. When we do so, we are going to have to pick a name for the file folder to be known by on the network. This can be the same as the actual name on the computer, or different. It's usually a good idea to give the folder a meaningful name so that it's easy to figure out where it actually resides. For this example, we share our Shared Documents folder from Computer 1 on the network with the name C1 Shared, and share our Shared Documents folder from Computer 2 on the network with the name C2 Shared (see Figure 6-9).

 Note: If an older version of Windows, such as 98, is one of the computers on the network, make sure the network name does not use special characters (like #, $, &, -, and so on) and is 15 characters or less.

 Note: In this case, Computer 1 is running Windows 98 and Computer 2 is running Windows XP, so that we can see the similarities and differences.

Figure 6-9   Planning Shared Folders on the Network

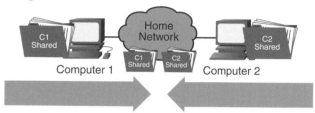

Table 6-2   Sharing Files on Your Home Network

Steps	Computer 1 (Windows 98)	Computer 2 (Windows XP)
Step 1: Create a new file folder named Shared Documents. With the mouse on the folder icon, click the right mouse button. Select **Sharing** from the pull-down menu. If you do not see the Sharing option, file sharing is not enabled.		
Step 2: Windows 98: Click **Shared As** and type the name you want the folder to have on the network. Windows XP: Click **Share this folder on the network** and enter its name. Click **OK**.	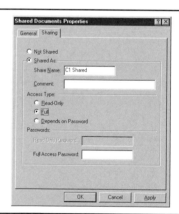	
Step 3: The file folder now appears with a human hand underneath it, meaning it is being shared with the network.		

Now that the folders are being shared, let's check to see if each computer can see the other's folder:

- For Computer 1 (Windows 98), double-click the **Windows Explorer** icon on your desktop. Click the **+** to the left of the Network Neighborhood icon. Then click the **+** to the left of both the Computer 1 and Computer 2 icons (see Figure 6-10).

Figure 6-10 Exploring the Shared Folders on Windows 98

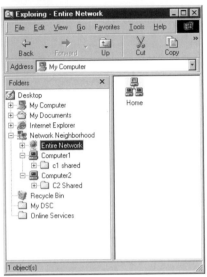

- For Computer 2 (Windows XP), double-click the **My Network Places** icon on your desktop. You may need to click on "View Workgroup Computers," and then double-click on the Computer 1 icon (see Figure 6-11).

Figure 6-11 Exploring the Shared Folders on Windows XP

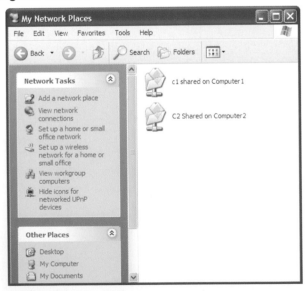

Note: Creating subdirectories in a shared folder makes the subdirectories shared as well.

Map a Shared File Folder as a Disk Drive

Now that we have successfully shared folders across the network, we want to make it really easy to use those shared folders each time we want to access files. *Mapping* a shared folder as a disk drive on our computer is a handy way to use shared folders.

Here's what *mapping* means: When we purchase our computer, it comes from the factory with a pre-installed disk drive for us to store documents and other files, usually called the C:/ drive. The C:/ drive is the "hard disk" inside our computer that, by default, holds information we put into the computer, including programs, files, and so on. We are also able to copy and exchange files with other types of disk drives, such as a floppy disk drive (usually A:/) and often a CD-ROM drive (usually D:/ or E:/ or sometimes Z:/).

To make copying files really simple from and to our newly shared folder, we can make it appear to the computer that there is another "disk drive," even though it happens to physically reside on a different computer across your home network.

Table 6-3's step-by-step guide shows how to "map" shared network folders as a disk drive. In this example, we map the shared folder called "C2 Shared" residing on Computer 2 to a drive on Computer 1 named "S:/" (for Shared, to make it easy to remember). And then we will do the same on Computer 2, mapping the folder named "C1 Shared" residing on Computer 1 to a drive named "S:/" on Computer 2.

 Note: Once again, Computer 1 is running Windows 98 and Computer 2 is running Windows XP so we can see the similarities and differences.

Table 6-3   Steps to Map Shared Network Folders as a Disk Drive

Steps	Computer 1 (Windows 98)	Computer 2 (Windows XP)
Step 1: Windows 98: Start by double-clicking the **Network Neighborhood** icon on the desktop. Windows XP: Double-click the **My Network Places** icon on the desktop.		

Table 6-3   **Steps to Map Shared Network Folders as a Disk Drive**

Steps	Computer 1 (Windows 98)	Computer 2(Windows XP)
Step 2: Double-click the icon for the other computer on the network. This displays the resources that the other computer is currently sharing. Click the mouse on the shared folder you want to map, and then click the right mouse button. Select **Map Network Drive** on the pull-down menu.		
Step 3: Select a disk drive number you want the shared folder to be known as. (We chose S:/ for this example.) Make sure to check-mark the **Reconnect at Logon** option. Click **OK**.		

Now that the folders are mapped, let's check to see if each computer can see the other's folder as a "drive":

- For Computer 1 (Windows 98), double-click the **My Computer** icon on your desktop. You can see that Computer 1 now has an S:/ drive mapped to Computer 2's shared folder (see Figure 6-12).

- For Computer 2 (Windows XP), double-click the **My Computer** icon on your desktop. You can see that Computer 2 now also has an S:/ drive mapped to Computer 1's shared folder (see Figure 6-13).

Now whenever we are using any program, we can open, copy, or save files to the shared folder on the other computer by selecting the S:/ drive in the program. Figure 6-14 shows an example of using the Save As option in Microsoft Word.

Figure 6-12   S:\ Drive on Somputer 1

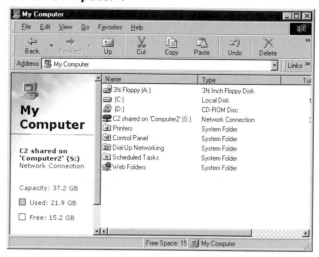

Figure 6-13   S:\ Drive on Computer 2

It's not necessary to map shared folders in this manner, but it really makes things a lot easier when you want to use files. Windows makes it so that the programs you use don't care or need to even know if the location of the file is on your same computer or on another computer in your home network.

Figure 6-14 Saving to the Shared Drive

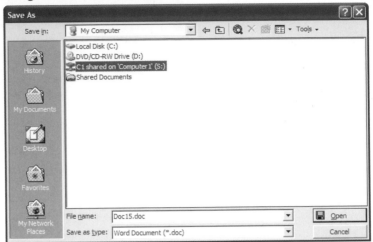

 Note: One thing to note is that if the other computer is not powered on and booted up, you will not be able to connect to it's shared folders (or printers). So it's very important to plan accordingly, perhaps by placing a shared folder on a PC in the house that is nearly always turned on.

Share a Printer Over the Network

Printer sharing is similar to file sharing. The process that follows walks through an example of printer sharing on the same home network example we built earlier. In this example, we have a printer attached with a parallel cable to each computer. When we share these printers on the network, we are going to have to pick a name for each printer to be known by on the network. This can be the same as the actual name on the computer, or different. It's usually a good idea to give the printer a meaningful name so that it's easy to figure out which printer it is. For our example, we are going to share the Printer/Fax/Scanner product attached to Computer 1 on the network with a name of "C1 Officejet," and share the printer attached to Computer 2 with a name of "C2 Printer." Figure 6-15 shows this.

 Note: If an older version of Windows, such as 98, is one of the computers on the network, make sure the network printer name does not use special characters (like #, $, &, -, and so on) and is 15 characters or less.

Figure 6-15   Sharing Printer Devices

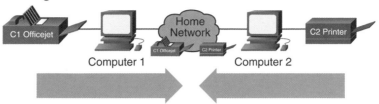

Table 6-4 shows what we need to do to share the two printers.

Table 6-4   Steps to Share a Printer

Steps	Computer 1 (Windows 98)	Computer 2 (Windows XP)
Step 1: Select **Start**, **Control Panel**, **Printers**. With the mouse on the printer icon, click the right mouse button. Select **Sharing** from the pull-down menu. In Windows XP, you could alternatively click on **Share this printer** in the left section of the dialog.		
Step 2: Windows 98: Checkmark **Shared As** and enter the name you want the printer to be known by on the network. Windows XP: Checkmark **Share the printer** and enter the network name.		
Step 3: The printer now appears with a human hand underneath, meaning it is being shared with the network.		

Now that the printers are being shared, let's check to see if each computer can see the other's printer:

- For Computer 1 (Windows 98), double-click the **Windows Explorer** icon on your desktop or in the Start menu. Click the **+** to the left of the "Network Neighborhood" icon. Then click the **+** to the left of the Computer 2 icon. You can see that Computer 1 recognizes the printer on Computer 2 (see Figure 6-16).

Figure 6-16 Explore the Shared Printer Using Windows 98

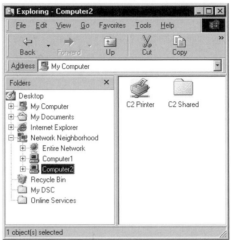

- For Computer 2 (Windows XP), double-click the **My Network Places** icon on your desktop or in the Start menu. Double-click the **Computer 1** icon. You can see that Computer 2 recognizes the printer on Computer 1 (see Figure 6-17).

Figure 6-17 Explore the Shared Printer Using Windows XP

Congratulations, you just shared printers!

Map a Shared Printer

Now that the printers are shared and visible on the network, the next step is to map the shared printers to each computer, so that the computer considers the printer part of it's "pool" of potential printers it can use. Table 6-5 shows what we need to do to map the two printers.

Table 6-5   Steps to Map a Shared Printer

Steps	Computer 1 (Windows 98)	Computer 2 (Windows XP)
Step 1: Select **Start > Control Panel > Printers**. Windows 98: Double-click the **Add Printer** icon. Windows XP: Click **Add a Printer** in the left section of the dialog.		
Step 2: The Add Printer Wizard starts. Click **Next**.	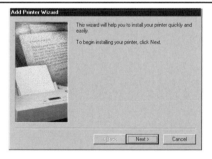	
Step 3: Checkmark **Network Printer**. Click **Next**.		

Table 6-5   Steps to Map a Shared Printer

Steps	Computer 1 (Windows 98)	Computer 2 (Windows XP)
Step 4: Windows 98: Click **Browse**. Windows XP: Checkmark **Browse for a printer**, and click **Next**.	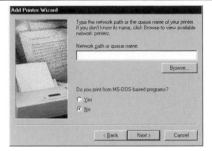	
Step 5: Click + to the left of the Network Neighborhood icon. Then click the + to the left of the other computer icon. Select the printer you want to map, and then click **OK** (or **Next**).		
Step 6: The driver for the exact printer model needs to be installed. Select the manufacturer and printer that matches your printer, and then click **OK** (or **Next**). If it is not listed, you may need to insert the CD that came with your printer and click **Have Disk**, and follow the instructions.	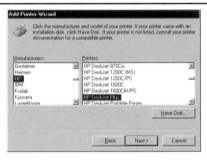	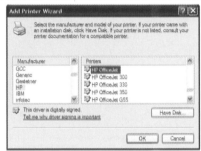

Table 6-5   Steps to Map a Shared Printer

Steps	Computer 1 (Windows 98)	Computer 2 (Windows XP)
Step 7: Windows 98 allows you to name the printer, while Windows XP does not. If the computer has its own local printer, choose **No** to make this printer the default. If the network printer is the only printer available, choose **Yes**. Click **Next**.		
Step 8: Windows 98 asks to print a test page, which is a good idea. Windows XP does not. Click **Finish**.		
Step 9: We can now see the new shared printer mapped to our computer.		

As a further check, go into any program on Computer 2 that normally uses a printer, such as Microsoft Word, open a file previously edited, and then click **File** > **Print**. The Printing dialog box should appear. Click the arrow next to the printer selection list. We should see the C1 Officejet printer as an option (see Figure 6-18).

Figure 6-18   Try Printing to the Shared Printer

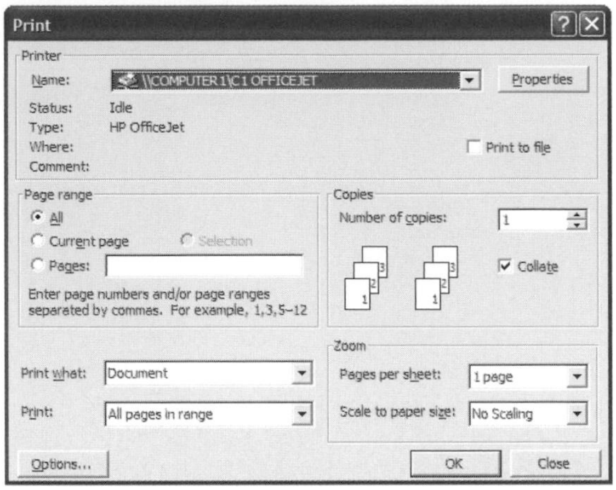

Add Security Precautions to File and Printer Sharing

As discussed earlier in the section, "Practicing Safe Share," you need to take some security precautions to make sure that your file and printer sharing does not compromise your home network.

First, if we want the files in a shared folder to be visible by other computers on the network, but not modifiable, we can set the folder to be read-only. To do this, you just need to take one additional step:

- For Computer 1 (Windows 98), during Step 2 of the file sharing steps, select the **Read-Only** radio button (see Figure 6-19). Click **OK**.

Figure 6-19   Making a Shared Folder Read-Only with Windows 98

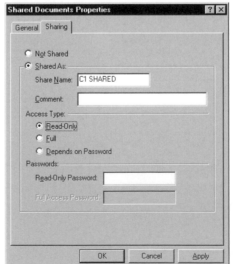

- For Computer 2 (Windows XP), during Step 2 of the file sharing steps, Uncheck the **Allow network users to change my files** checkbox (see Figure 6-20). Click **OK**.

Figure 6-20   Making a Shared Folder Read-Only with Windows XP

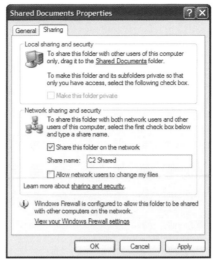

Finally, there is a specific network design that is vulnerable to security issues. If we have a situation where we have a single computer providing shared Internet access for a network, such as shown in Figure 6-21, we need to take additional steps to secure the network.

Figure 6-21   Security Concern with Internet Connection Sharing

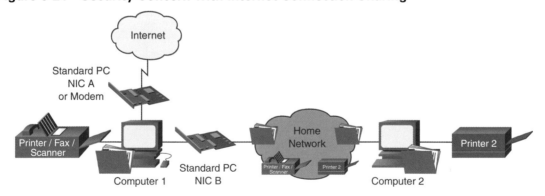

In this example, Computer 1 has either a modem providing dialup Internet or a NIC (shown as NIC A) providing high-speed broadband Internet access for the network. A second NIC (shown as NIC B) connects Computer 1 to the home network.

For file and printer sharing to work properly, we need NIC B to send and receive the appropriate broadcasts regarding available shared folders and printers on the home network. However, we do *not* want NIC A/modem to make those "broadcasts" available outside of the home network, such as to the Internet. By default, Windows networking enables dialup connections and network connections to be able to support sending and receiving this traffic. So we need to disable this feature on the dialup/NIC A.

Two examples are shown here:

To disable Windows file and printer sharing on a dialup interface under Windows 98 (Computer 1):

Step 1   Select **Start** > **Control Panel** > **Network**.

Step 2   Select the dialup NIC and click **Properties** (see Figure 6-22).

Figure 6-22   Select the Dialup NIC

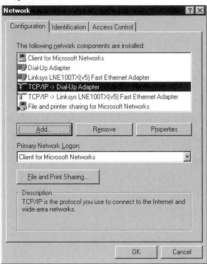

Step 3   Click the **Bindings** tab.

Step 4   Uncheck the **Client for Microsoft Networks** and **File and printer sharing for Microsoft Networks** checkboxes (see Figure 6-23). Click **OK**.

Figure 6-23   Disable File and Printer Sharing on the Internet Dialup or NIC

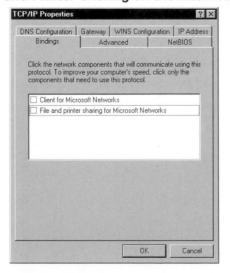

Step 5 A warning is displayed (see Figure 6-24). Click **No**.

Figure 6-24   Ignore the Warning Dialog Box

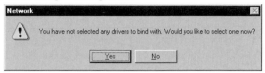

Step 6 Windows 98 needs to reboot to make the new network settings take effect. Click **Yes**.

Figure 6-25   Windows 98 Needs to Reboot

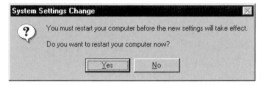

To disable Windows file and printer sharing on a dialup (or Internet connection sharing) NIC under Windows XP (Computer 2):

Step 1 Select **Start > Control Panel > Network Connections**.

Step 2 Select the NIC connected to the Internet and click **Change settings of this connection** (see Figure 6-26).

Figure 6-26   Change the NIC Settings

Step 3   Uncheck the **Client for Microsoft Networks** and **File and Printer Sharing for Microsoft Networks** checkboxes (see Figure 6-27). Click **OK**.

Figure 6-27   Disable Windows File and Printer Sharing

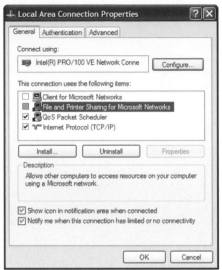

After Windows networking and file and printer Sharing have been disabled on the dialup/Internet NIC, the security exposure is now mitigated.

There are two additional precautions that can be taken, both of which will be discussed in subsequent chapters:

- Install a router between the home network and the Internet. See Chapter 7, "High-Speed Internet Access."

- Install personal firewall software, such as ZoneAlarm, on each of the computers on the home network. See Part IV for more information.

High-Speed Internet Access

If you don't have high-speed (broadband) Internet, you have a problem. Actually, you have two problems:

- If you are on dialup, it's not so easy to share an Internet connection, and then even if you do find a way to share a connection, you will either tie up your phone line for hours at a time or have to get a second phone line, which adds to your monthly expenses.

- The world is leaving you behind. Even before the wide availability of residential high-speed Internet access, many people thought dialup seemed pretty slow. Web pages took way too long to load, e-mails that included photos took forever to download, and forget trying to download your favorite song (legally, of course) or software updates.

Today, high-speed Internet is widely available and affordable. When high-speed access (also referred to as broadband) first came out, it was not a big deal for the folks still on dialup. Most websites still catered to the slow modem crowd, and if one of your friends with broadband started showing off by sending e-mails with 20 photos attached every night they would usually get flame (angry) e-mails sent by all the recipients still on dialup. Unfortunately for those of you still using dialup, a lot of people now have broadband. So many, in fact, that most website developers really only cater to folks who can download at a blazing 1–3 Mbps (20–100 times faster than dialup). Because there are also enough people with high-speed access, sending large e-mail attachments, or several large attachments, is no longer a breach of e-mail etiquette. The good news is that if you are still on dialup and want to get broadband service, you have many options for upgrading.

Broadband Revolution

The availability of broadband access for the home has dramatically changed the way people work, seek entertainment, and connect to the rest of the world. More and more small businesses are also using broadband connections for their Internet access. Whether working from home using high-speed voice over IP (VoIP), downloading movies online, or sending pictures to friends and family, broadband has made the promise of true multimedia capable home connections a reality.

The key to broadband access to the home was finding a way to offer the service at a price that would be acceptable to the majority of users while still being profitable for the service providers. With the decreasing cost of high-speed routers and switches, the major cost component of the service was connecting local high-speed aggregation points with the homes in the area. This part of the network is referred to as "the last mile."

So, the entire business case boiled down to this: The only way to make broadband access profitable was to already have the last-mile infrastructure in place, and the only businesses who had that were

- Local phone companies

- Local cable TV providers

Both industries then figured out innovative ways to solve the technical issues of making broadband work.

A new player comes along, and so does an old one

One of the issues with broadband Internet access is accessibility. If you live in an area not serviced by cable or if you live too far away from a phone company switching point, you can't get broadband Internet. If this is the case, there are still two alternatives to regular dialup:

- If you live in North America and have a clear view to the southern sky from either your yard or your house, you can now get Internet over satellite. Satellite service is a bit slower than the cable and DSL high-speed services, but it is still much faster than dialup. Expect the startup and monthly costs for satellite broadband service to be significantly higher than cable and DSL.

- If satellite is not an option, you can subscribe to an accelerated dialup service that speeds up Internet browsing and some other Internet functions. This is often referred to as high-speed dialup, but that's more about marketing than data speeds.

Different Types of Broadband

Four different types of broadband connections exist:

- **DSL**—Access comes from existing phone wires

- **Cable**—Access comes from existing cable television cables

- **Satellite**—Access comes from satellites in orbit

- **Wireless**—Access comes from your existing cellular phone services

- **Accelerated Dialup**—Access comes from your existing phone wires (not really broadband, best a next best option)

The section explains how each type of broadband works.

DSL

Digital subscriber line (DSL) uses existing phone wires connected to virtually every home in most countries. The twisted-pair wires that provide phone service are ideal because the available frequency ranges on the wires far exceed those required to carry a voice conversation, which occupies frequencies of roughly 4000 hertz (4 kHz) or less. The copper wires that provide phone service can carry in the range of 1–2 million hertz (MHz), which provides lots of bandwidth for you. To protect your phone (and your ears), DSL requires that you put a filter on all the phone jacks in your house to prevent you from hearing high-pitch tones.

Residential DSL is typically set up to provide more downstream data (from the Internet to you) than upstream data (from you to the Internet) based on how most people use the Internet. This ratio of download to upload speed can be changed for businesses or those running web servers, but you have to ask for it. Figure 7-1 shows the typical frequency allocation.

Figure 7-1   Typical Frequency Allocation of DSL

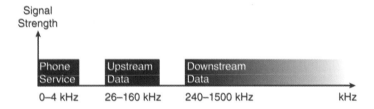

DSL is typically offered with 1.5–6 Mbps download speeds. To get DSL, you must be in a market where the service is offered (which is fairly widespread) and must be within three miles of the local phone company distribution center due to distance limitations with the technology. Access fees typically run from $25–40 per month. Keep in mind that you may not be able to achieve the maximum advertised bandwidth because of factors such as distance from the telephone company, quality of telephone wiring in your house, and so on.

DSL

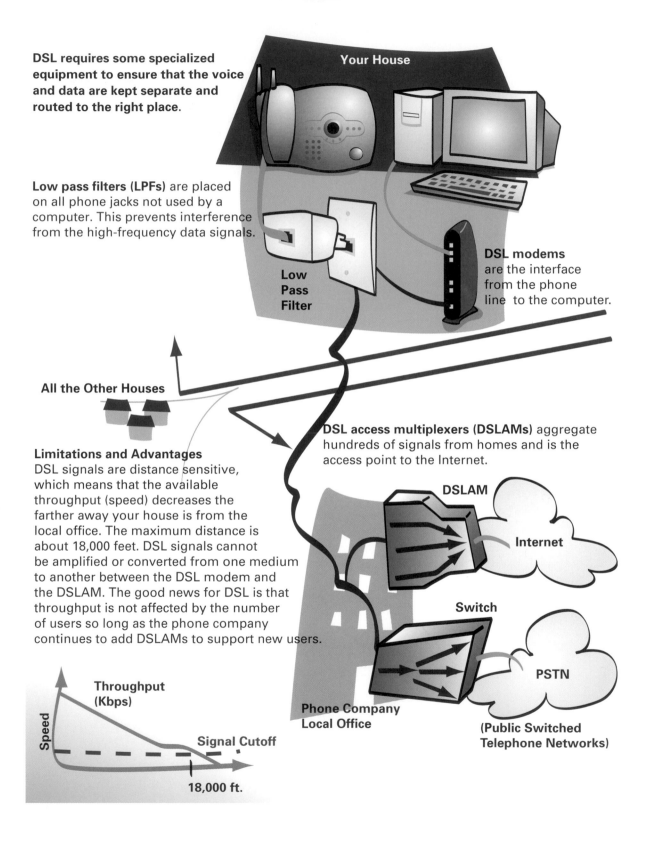

DSL requires some specialized equipment to ensure that the voice and data are kept separate and routed to the right place.

Your House

Low pass filters (LPFs) are placed on all phone jacks not used by a computer. This prevents interference from the high-frequency data signals.

Low Pass Filter

DSL modems are the interface from the phone line to the computer.

All the Other Houses

DSL access multiplexers (DSLAMs) aggregate hundreds of signals from homes and is the access point to the Internet.

DSLAM

Internet

Limitations and Advantages
DSL signals are distance sensitive, which means that the available throughput (speed) decreases the farther away your house is from the local office. The maximum distance is about 18,000 feet. DSL signals cannot be amplified or converted from one medium to another between the DSL modem and the DSLAM. The good news for DSL is that throughput is not affected by the number of users so long as the phone company continues to add DSLAMs to support new users.

Switch

PSTN

Phone Company Local Office

(Public Switched Telephone Networks)

Throughput (Kbps)

Speed

Signal Cutoff

18,000 ft.

Cable

Like DSL, broadband cable uses only a small amount of its available bandwidth to provide an Internet connection (but unlike DSL, it uses a coax cable like your TV cable, instead of a telephone wire, obviously). Cable is slightly different, though, in the way it divvies up its available frequencies.

The cable spectrum was already divided into several hundred 6 MHz blocks to account for the various cable channels. Your cable-ready TV simply tunes its receiver to the frequency that corresponds to the channel you choose. To add Internet capabilities, each user is assigned one or more blocks for downstream data. (Each channel is good for about 30 Mbps of data.) For the upstream piece, the lower end of the spectrum (below 65 MHz) was divided into 2 MHz blocks as most people pull more information down than they upload. Each subscriber is assigned one or more 2 MHz blocks. Figure 7-2 illustrates the frequency usage for high-speed cable.

Figure 7-2   Cable Spectrum

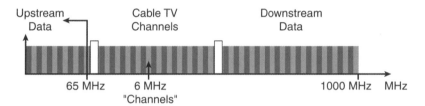

With broadband cable, you do not need additional filters for your television sets because a *cable-ready TV* means that the television is already capable of picking a single channel and blocking out the rest of the signals.

High-speed Internet over cable typically offers the fastest residential access with blazing download speeds of up to 6 Mbps (many customers actually get between 1–2 Mbps). Most areas serviced by cable television now offer broadband Internet access over cable as well. Prices typically run around $40–50 per month for service.

Cable

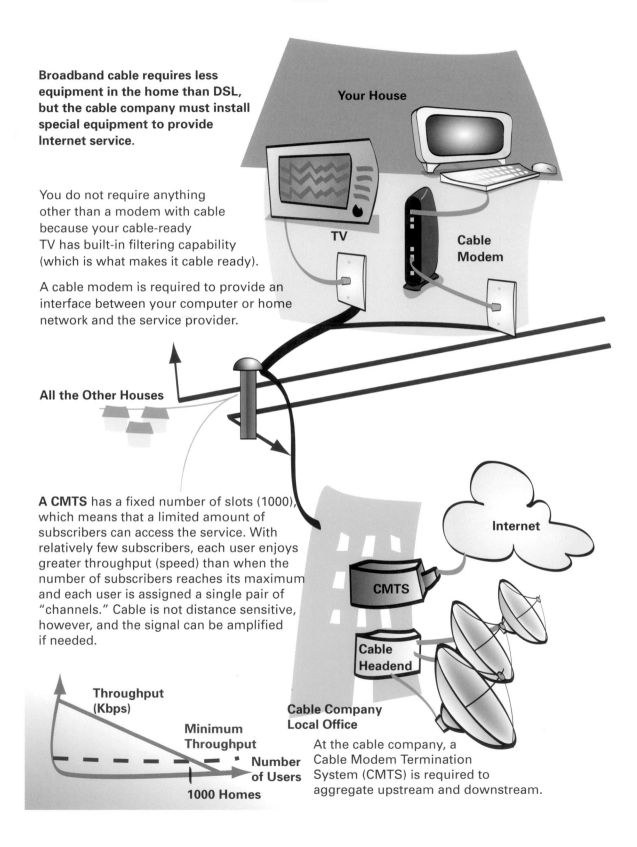

Broadband cable requires less equipment in the home than DSL, but the cable company must install special equipment to provide Internet service.

You do not require anything other than a modem with cable because your cable-ready TV has built-in filtering capability (which is what makes it cable ready).

A cable modem is required to provide an interface between your computer or home network and the service provider.

Your House

TV

Cable Modem

All the Other Houses

A CMTS has a fixed number of slots (1000), which means that a limited amount of subscribers can access the service. With relatively few subscribers, each user enjoys greater throughput (speed) than when the number of subscribers reaches its maximum and each user is assigned a single pair of "channels." Cable is not distance sensitive, however, and the signal can be amplified if needed.

Internet

CMTS

Cable Headend

Cable Company Local Office

At the cable company, a Cable Modem Termination System (CMTS) is required to aggregate upstream and downstream.

Throughput (Kbps)

Minimum Throughput

Number of Users

1000 Homes

Satellite

When standard broadband is not available, broadband Internet via satellite can be a viable option. Satellite Internet works on the same principle as cable and DSL in that the system uses unused frequencies reserved for Internet access.

With satellite Internet, a transmit function must be added to the system you already have (assuming you currently subscribe to satellite TV). If you live in North America, you need a clear view of the southern sky as the satellites are in orbit around the earth's equator. Typically, you must replace your small round satellite dish with a larger oval dish.

Download speeds over satellite are around 500 kbps to 1 Mbps but are affected by heavy rains or snow. Startup fees for satellite Internet (including the special dish) can run $500 or more, with fees between $60–100 per month. One of the cool things about satellite Internet is that you can attach a dish to a recreational vehicle (RV) and have broadband Internet access everywhere you go.

Satellite

Broadband over satellite uses different satellites than the ones used for TV. Therefore, you will contract both an access provider (who routes your traffic through its satellite) and an ISP (who provides access to the Internet and gives you an e-mail address).

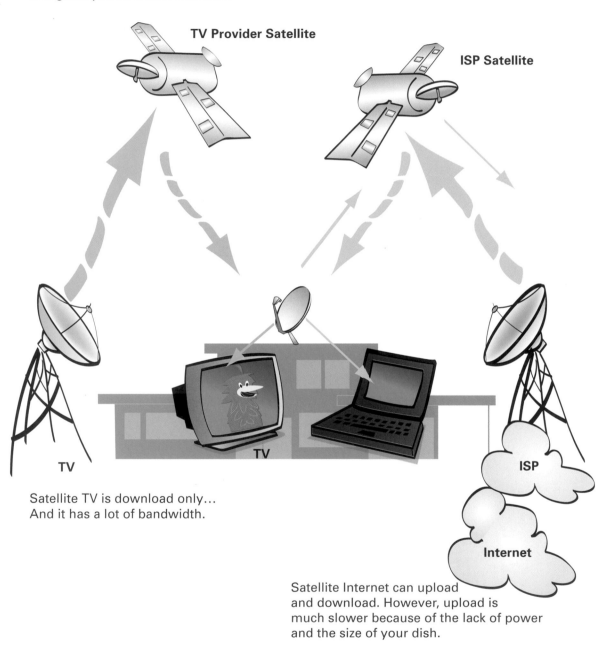

TV Provider Satellite

ISP Satellite

TV

TV

ISP

Internet

Satellite TV is download only... And it has a lot of bandwidth.

Satellite Internet can upload and download. However, upload is much slower because of the lack of power and the size of your dish.

Wireless (Cellular)

A new service just being offered is Internet access over the cellular phone network. This service uses the same network as your cell phone and can offer download speeds comparable with DSL. The service runs in limited markets at this time but is growing rapidly.

Others services being piloted are WiMax (wide-area wireless) and, believe it or not, Broadband over Power Line (BPL). If the standard broadband options do not work for you or are not available, one of these connection methods might work for you.

Accelerated Dialup

If you find yourself in the unfortunate position of living in an area not serviced by cable, too far away from the phone company to get DSL, and just to the north of a very large mountain or redwood forest, you can still do something to speed up your Internet connection.

A new service called accelerated dialup can speed up many parts of your Internet experiences with a combination of filtering, compressing, and caching (pronounced like *cashing*) the information you download and view. Some services claim that on average you will see a fivefold increase in download speed for certain web pages and e-mails. Prices are comparable to regular dialup service.

Accelerated Dialup

A new service called "accelerated dialup" can speed up many parts of your Internet experiences with a combination of **filtering**, **compression,** and **caching** the information you download and view over a standard phone line. Some services claim that, on average, you will see a 5x increase in download speed.

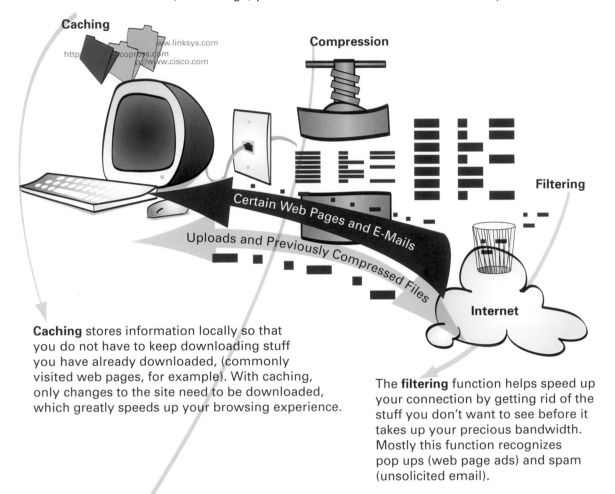

Caching stores information locally so that you do not have to keep downloading stuff you have already downloaded, (commonly visited web pages, for example). With caching, only changes to the site need to be downloaded, which greatly speeds up your browsing experience.

The **filtering** function helps speed up your connection by getting rid of the stuff you don't want to see before it takes up your precious bandwidth. Mostly this function recognizes pop ups (web page ads) and spam (unsolicited email).

The **compression** function "squeezes" or removes information on web pages, e-mail (text), and pictures viewed with a browser that you can't see or don't notice, which greatly speeds up browsing and some downloads. The bad news is that it can't help you with streaming media (online movies), e-mail attachments, or software downloads, which are usually already compressed as much as they can be. The service also does nothing for uploads, so if you e-mail someone pictures of your cute kids, it will still take approximately forever to send the e-mail.

Providers

At this point, it's necessary to talk about the different types of providers as this can be a bit confusing. The two types of providers you run into are

- **Access Service Providers (ASPs)**—Simply provides access to a high-speed medium, such as cable

- **Internet Service Providers (ISPs)**—Connects you to the Internet

In some cases, your ASP will also be your ISP and, in some cases, they will be different.

Let's look at an example of each case. We mentioned high-speed Internet over cable. In most cases, a community with cable TV service has a single cable company that serves that area. For the purposes of cable TV, the U.S. government allows a local, regulated monopoly to the cable company. For Internet access, however, the cable company must offer other service providers the use of their circuits so that consumers can have a choice of providers. In most cases, your cable company will offer high-speed Internet and if you obtain service from it, that company will be both your ASP and your ISP. One example of this is having Time Warner Cable service and Road Runner Internet service, both of which are owned by AOL Time Warner. You have the option, however, to use the physical cable owned by your cable company to reach a different ISP. In this case, your local cable company is the ASP, and your ISP is whomever you go with. For example, you could also have Time Warner Cable for your TV, but subscribe to EarthLink high-speed Internet. Which you choose depends on your own selection criteria. In these cases, you only pay the ISP, who includes that cable usage fee as part of the monthly subscription cost.

Now, in some cases, you will have to have a separate ASP and ISP. One example of this is satellite Internet access. The company that owns the satellite does not offer Internet service, only access to the medium. You will need to find a service provider after you are connected through the satellite company (in other words, EarthLink does not own a satellite so you need to "rent access" to the satellite to reach EarthLink).

It would seem that having a single provider be both your ASP and ISP would be the least expensive option, but this is not always the case. Sometimes, you can receive package discounts (for example, having a combined cable TV/cable Internet service or combined telephone/long distance/DSL service.

 GEEK SQUAD As with your cell phone company, there are more and more options for Internet access. It's a good idea to review your choices once or twice a year. Not only will there be new choices for you to access the Internet, but as new choices emerge, the cost of other forms of access will likely come down. For example, as broadband Internet has grown, it has driven down the cost of slower forms of Internet access, and made it more competitive.

Need for Speed

The availability of high-speed Internet connections begs the question, "why does anyone need high-speed connections in the first place?" With the availability of all forms of multimedia in demand on the Internet, Figure 7-3 offers some perspective. This figure compares each media's elapsed time to download a high-quality digital recording of a song, which is typically about 10 MB.

Figure 7-3   Download Times for a 10 MB File

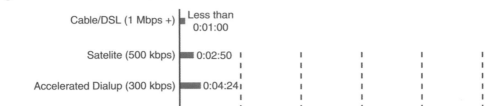

Hours: Minutes: Seconds

Table 7-1 summarizes the different types of Internet access and their attributes and costs. There may be some local variances (particularly in price) so do your own research to make sure you have up-to-date information to base your purchase decision on.

Table 7-1   Comparison of the Different Types of Internet Access

	Dialup	Accelerated Dialup	DSL	Cable	Satellite
Maximum Download Speed	Up to 56 kbps	Up to 500 kbps (for certain media types)	Up to 3 Mbps	Up to 6 Mbps	Up to 1 Mbps
Maximum Upload Speed			Up to 768 kbps	Up to 2 Mbps	Up to 100 kbps
Always On?	No	No	Yes	Yes	Yes
Availability	Anywhere you can find a phone	Anywhere you can find a phone	Most major markets, but must be close to local phone office	Most major markets	Anywhere you have line of sight to the southern sky (from US and Canada)
Access	Dial in to your ISP	Dial in to the ISP accelerator	DSL access provider, possibly a separate ISP	Cable access provider, possibly a separate ISP	Satellite access provider, plus an ISP
Installation	$0	$0	$0–25	$0–50	$100–700
Cost per Month	$15–25	$25–35	$25–55	$35–60	$50–100

Selecting a Broadband Service

When choosing a broadband service, you must consider numerous factors, including

- **Availability**—What is offered in your neighborhood.

- **Speed**—How fast the connection is; it's important to consider both uplink (house-to-Internet) and downlink (Internet-to-house).

- **Cost**—Competition has made pricing reasonable; consider both monthly and installation costs as well as bundled savings (for example, having both cable TV and Internet services).

- **Contract**—Services are starting to bundle in free equipment and options for one or two year agreements, very similar to cell phone services.

- **Equipment**—A broadband modem might be included or it might be an extra one-time or monthly cost.

- **Multiple Computer Restrictions**—A small number of providers want to start charging you extra for implementing a home network where more than one computer shares the broadband Internet connection. Our advice is to avoid such providers as there are usually alternative providers that will not.

- **IP Address(es)**—Decide how many you need; if it's "static" or "dynamic," most people only need a single "dynamic" address. Usually, additional addresses and "static" addresses cost extra. Unless you are hosting a website or some other service, you most likely don't need a "static" address.

- **E-Mail Accounts**—If the broadband access provider will also be your e-mail provider, how many e-mail accounts are included in the monthly service fee.

- **Security Add-Ons**—Additional features available such as parental controls, spam blocking, personal firewall, and so on.

- **Other Add-Ons**—Competition is creating some interesting deals, such as tossing in discounted or free home networking equipment, such as routers.

- **Support**—Most are very similar; ask friends and neighbors about their experiences and see if the provider offers a free support "Chat" service

Online Resources to Help You Choose a Broadband Provider

Several good websites can help you:

- Find out what the options are for your neighborhood

- Compare the services to help you select the best deal

One good website is http://www.broadband.com. Simply enter your home phone number and it will search dozens of broadband service providers and give you a nice list of options (other sites are available for those outside the United States). Table 7-2 shows a sample list, similar to what you can see on http://www.broadband.com. You can checkmark the options you want to explore further and click a Compare button, which displays a comprehensive report comparing all the listed factors and more. Finally, if you so choose, you can even click a **Select Plan** button, which starts the ordering process for you.

Table 7-2   **Sample List of Local Broadband Options**

Carrier	Plan	Access Method	Download Speed	Setup Fee	Monthly Fee
EarthLink	EarthLink high-speed Internet	Cable	Up to 3 MB	$0	$41.95
Sprint	DSL 1.5 m Annual contract	ADSL	Up to 1.5 MB	$9.95	$49.99
DiRECWAY	"Home" plan with easy monthly payments	Satellite	Up to 500 K	$99.99	$99.99

Another easy way to learn about and pursue your broadband options is to check out EarthLink service at http://www.earthlink.net/home/highspeed/. By entering your home phone number and complete address, you can perform a similar search of broadband options. EarthLink "resells" DSL, cable, and satellite broadband services of many of the major providers, sometimes at a better deal than getting the same subscription from the provider directly. This search service only works if you have a wired home phone (not cellular). However, having a phone is not a requirement for Internet service.

The key is to shop around. Monthly fees are pretty comparable, but sometimes speeds can vary widely. One major point to find out is who pays for the broadband modem. Many providers kick one in for free if you sign up for a year. Some, however, want to stick you with the cost. If it's $2–3 per month, it's probably still worth going with the provider's modem. However, for example, if your broadband cable service is the only service you can receive in your neighborhood, and they want to charge you $15/month to rent the cable modem, you should consider purchasing your own, such as the Linksys BEFCMU10 cable modem.

Just make sure your broadband provider supports the particular modem you purchase, if you must purchase one. Again, the first option should be to seek a service that provides the broadband modem for free or for a nominal monthly fee. EarthLink once again seems to excel in this area, offering ongoing promotions that include free cable and DSL modems for subscribing through their services.

A final factor to consider is reliability. This is difficult to evaluate as a consumer. One possible resource is the website http://www.broadbandreports.com/gbu, which consolidates thousands of feedback reports from consumers and provides report card–like data for different providers. We tend to be a little skeptical about feedback at such sites as it might be skewed toward the negative. (People are typically more motivated to report bad experiences than good ones.) But you can at least read some feedback and perhaps draw some general conclusions about providers in your area.

Cable/DSL Broadband

Cable Broadband

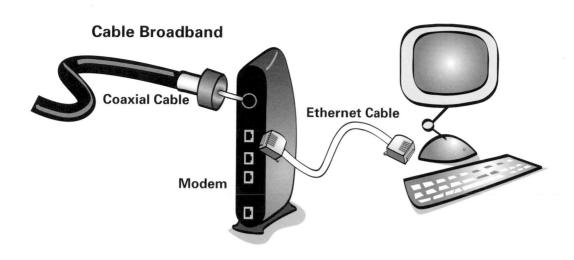

Coaxial Cable

Ethernet Cable

Modem

DSL Broadband with Modem

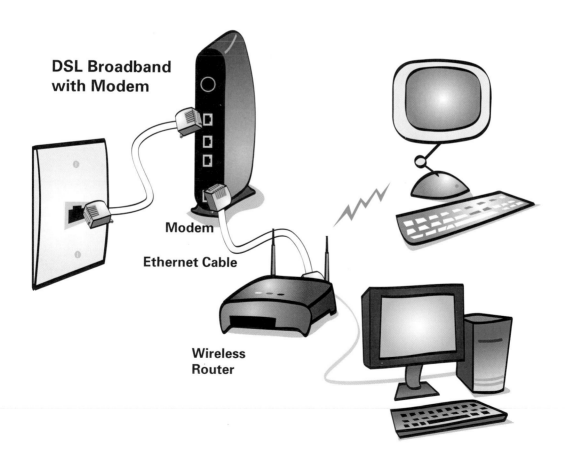

Modem

Ethernet Cable

Wireless Router

Keep This Important Information

When you do finally sign up, the broadband provider is going to give you some critical pieces of information, summarized in Table 7-3.

Table 7-3   **Broadband Provider Account Information**

	Cable	DSL	Example
IP address	"Dynamic"—no further info needed "Static"—the actual address	"Dynamic"—no further info needed "Static"—the actual address	DHCP (dynamic) 192.168.3.102 (static)
Hostname	Some providers require you to have a hostname.	N/A	jdoe1
Domain	Some providers require you to have a domain.	N/A	rr.com
Username	N/A	Always required	johndoe1
Password	N/A	Always required	Xy8fr9Z

If the broadband provider also provides you with e-mail, the information shown in Table 7-4 will also be provided to you.

Table 7-4   **Broadband Provider E-Mail Information**

	Example
Account	John.Doe@earthlink.com
Password	YRUlaughing2
Outgoing server	mail.mindspring.com
Incoming server	pop.mindspring.com

Hang on to all this info; you will need it later to install!

How to Build It: Broadband Internet Access

A primary reason for building a computer network is to improve access to the Internet for your family members. As more family members become computer savvy, the two main issues that quickly develop are more than one person wanting to access the Internet at the same time and needing more connection speed. Dialup just doesn't cut it anymore, so we need to install a broadband service.

In this section, we will go through the steps to select, install, configure, and use a broadband cable/DSL service.

NOTE There are other service types available, such as satellite and fixed wireless; however, we will only cover cable and DSL as together they comprise more than 90 percent of the broadband subscriptions in the United States.

Here's a brief overview of the steps we will go through to set up your broadband Internet:

- Decide on a home network design
- Set up the broadband equipment
- Configure the router for broadband service
- Configure the router for the home network
- Check the access to the Internet

NOTE It is important to understand that this section covers how to install a wired home network using a router. In Part III, "Look Ma, No Wires!" we will also cover a wireless network, which has obvious advantages to simplify installing a home network. However, for both the wired and wireless deployments, it is necessary to perform the steps in this chapter, as they deal with setting up the home network with a broadband service. So, even if you plan to go directly to a wireless home network, read on, as you will need to perform these steps regardless.

Decide on a Home Network Design

So far, we focused on connecting the computers on your home network. This may be all that some people need, but increasingly many households want to allow more than one computer on the home network to share access to the Internet over a broadband connection. Before we actually start connecting the cables to receive broadband, we need to take another look at the devices that will be on our home network, and that's going to determine some basic things about how we will connect to the broadband service.

One-Computer Network

Even if you only have one computer today, you will still greatly benefit from broadband Internet service. The home network design in this case will look like Figure 7-4.

Figure 7-4   Broadband Connection for a Home with One Computer

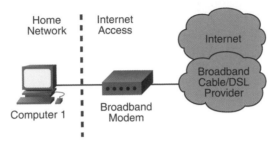

Two-Computer Network

If we have exactly two computers, we could connect to the Internet with "back-to-back" networking as described in Chapter 5, "Creating a Basic Home Network." Figure 7-5 shows a network with two computers using back-to-back networking.

Figure 7-5   Possible Broadband Connection for a Home with Two Computers

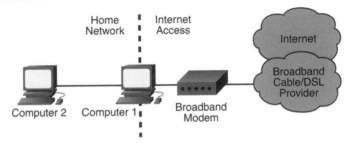

In this case, Computer 1 serves a dual role on the network:

- It is a computer that can be used to access the Internet.

- It is also acting as a "gateway" for Computer 2 to reach the Internet.

This is called *Internet Connection Sharing* in Windows. Computer 1 and Computer 2 are connected on the home network with network interface cards (NICs). Computer 1 has a second NIC that's connected to the broadband modem.

Multiple-Computer Network

Although the back-to-back configuration can be useful, it only works for exactly two computers. As soon as you need a third computer (and you will), you have to look at using a hub or a switch to add more devices to the network. Figure 7-6 shows this.

Figure 7-6   Possible Broadband Connection for a Home with Three or More Computers

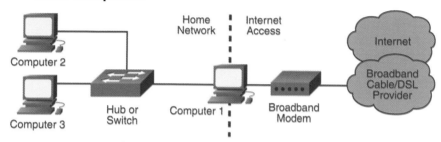

This lets more devices access the network for sure, but this home network has some disadvantages:

- Computer 1 must handle all the Internet accesses from Computer 2 and Computer 3, which means Computer 1 will need to be powered on. Depending on where Computer 1 is located, this could be a hassle.

- There is more security exposure if we have a computer directly connected to the broadband service.

- If you are going to invest in a hub or switch, you might as well add a few dollars more and buy a router product instead. Actually, we have to purchase one less NIC, so the cost is nearly equal.

With a router, the network design looks like what's shown in Figure 7-7.

Figure 7-7   Broadband Connection for Multiple Computers Using a Router

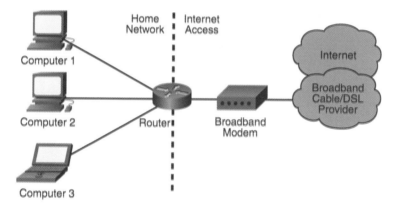

The design shown in Figure 7-7 eliminates many of the disadvantages of the prior designs. The router performs quite a few functions for us:

- Providing four or more "ports" to connect computers and devices (more with a wireless router)

- Serving as the Internet "gateway" for simultaneous sharing of the broadband service, keeping you from having to have the gateway computer powered on all the time.

- Inserting a level of security between the Internet and our home network to minimize security exposure to hackers

- Managing the addresses of computers on the network automatically for us, instead of doing this ourselves

Wireless Network

Finally, as we mentioned earlier, a wireless network has obvious benefits in terms of not having to physically run cables through the attic and walls and crawl spaces. For just about the same price or a few dollars more than a router, we can purchase a combination router/wireless product. This greatly simplifies our network implementation. This is the ultimate objective in this book, and we will cover wireless networks in depth in Part III. Adding wireless to our home network will result in the network shown in Figure 7-8.

Figure 7-8   Broadband Connection Using a Wireless Router

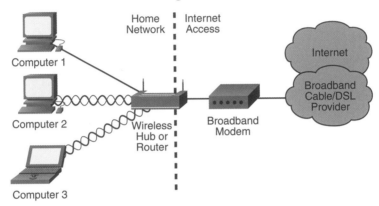

Functionally, this network and the previous wired network are nearly identical. The main difference is in how Computer 2 and Computer 3 are connected. For example, we can have Computer 1 in a central location in the house next to a cable/DSL outlet and modem. But we can essentially place Computer 2 and Computer 3 anywhere else we want in the house without having to worry about how to get an Ethernet cable into that room. Very handy indeed.

We mention this now so that you think about what you ultimately want your network to look like before you run out and buy a wired router product. If you think you will go wireless, hold off on a purchase until you read Part III. If it's easy to run cables and you are happy with a wired router implementation, that's a good approach also.

Router Comparison

Table 7-5 compares a couple different router products from Linksys.

In the rest of this chapter, we are going to use the Linksys WRT54GS wireless broadband router to demonstrate how to configure and set up your home network.

NOTE Note the wider price range for wireless routers. In Part III, we explore the many different wireless features and options, and help you choose which wireless product is right for your home network, as well as show how to configure the wireless network itself.

Table 7-5   Comparison of Linksys Routers

Model	Linksys BEFSR41 Broadband Router	Linksys BEFSR81 Broadband Router	Linksys BEFSX41 Broadband Router/Firewall	Linksys BEFW11S4 Broadband Wireless Router
Description	Wired router	Wired router	Wired router with firewall	Router with wireless access
Ports	4	8	4	4+ (many wireless)
Use It When	Wired access only	Wired access only, need more than 4 ports	Wired access only, need a strong firewall	Wireless access desired
Cost	$	$$$	$$	$$–$$$$
Looks Like				

Whether or not you choose a wired or wireless router product, you will need to go through similar steps to set up the router to connect to your broadband service; so follow the rest of this section, even if you plan to build a wireless home network.

Set Up the Broadband Equipment

After you find a broadband service and order a subscription, the next step is to install the service. Some providers will offer professional installation for a nominal fee. More and more providers are encouraging self-installation (big surprise). If a professional installation will be performed, usually they require a single computer in the household to be designated as a primary computer, and the installer will install a configuration that looks something like what was previously shown in Figure 7-5.

A single computer is connected to the broadband modem, and, of course, the broadband modem is connected to either the cable or DSL line. Traditionally, the connection to the broadband modem will be with an Ethernet cable connected to a NIC installed in the computer. Some installation kits include a free NIC. The newest broadband modems are supplying a USB connector as an alternative connection method for a single PC.

Broadband Cable Connection

For broadband cable service, Figure 7-9 shows a typical connection. The cable provider will install service in the cable system, and then any cable wall jack in your house can be used for a connection. The steps are

Step 1   Plug a coax cable (just like the one that connects your TV) to the wall jack, and the other end to the cable jack on the cable modem.

Step 2   Connect an Ethernet cable to the Ethernet port on the cable modem, and the other end to the Ethernet port on the NIC in the computer.

Step 3   Make sure to plug in the power cable for the cable modem.

Figure 7-9   Typical Broadband Cable Connection

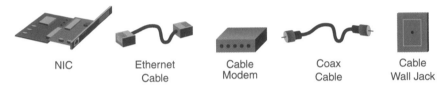

| NIC | Ethernet Cable | Cable Modem | Coax Cable | Cable Wall Jack |

Broadband DSL Connection

For broadband DSL service, Figure 7-10 shows a typical connection. The DSL provider will install service in the telephone system, and then any phone wall jack in your house can be used for a connection. The steps are

Step 1   Plug a phone cable (RJ11)—just like the one that connects your phone—to the wall jack, and the other end to the DSL port on the DSL modem.

Step 2   Connect an Ethernet cable to the Ethernet port on the DSL modem, and the other end to the Ethernet port on the NIC in the computer.

Step 3   Make sure to plug in the power cable for the DSL modem.

Figure 7-10   Typical Broadband DSL Connection

| NIC | Ethernet Cable | DSL Modem | Phone Cable | Phone Wall Jack |

In addition to installing the actual DSL modem and connecting it to your computer, in most cases, you also need to install *filters* on all the phones in your house *except* for the DSL modem. This prevents noise from developing during phone calls because of the DSL service. The filters are normally provided as part of an installation kit. Check with the DSL service provider to see if filters are required and how they should be installed to be compatible with their DSL service. Figure 7-11 shows what typical filters look like.

Figure 7-11   DSL Filters

Filters are easy to install. Essentially wherever you have a phone in your house, you unplug the phone, plug the phone into the filter, and then plug the filter back into where the phone was originally plugged into.

VERY IMPORTANT: **Do not put a filter on the phone wire that connects your DSL modem to the wall jack. This renders your DSL service inoperable!**

There will be variations from provider to provider, so the best advice is to follow the broadband service provider's installation instructions. Normally, the provider includes a CD-ROM in the installation kit, which installs software on your primary computer (which is the computer you or the installer will use to configure the modem) and then guides you through the install.

Configure the Router for Broadband Service

Connecting the router to the broadband service takes an extra step added to what we did before to connect a single computer to the Internet via dialup. The steps to follow are (as shown in Figure 7-12)

Step 1   Connect the cable modem to the wall outlet just like we did before.

Step 2   Connect an Ethernet cable between the cable modem and to the port on the back of the router labeled WAN (for wide-area network).

Step 3   Connect another Ethernet cable between the NIC in the computer and of the ports in the router labeled 1, 2, 3, or 4.

Figure 7-12   Adding a Router to Your Broadband Connection

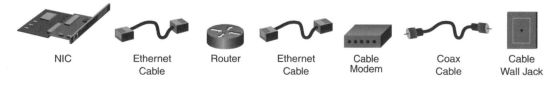

| NIC | Ethernet Cable | Router | Ethernet Cable | Cable Modem | Coax Cable | Cable Wall Jack |

Now we can plug up to three computers in the other ports (labeled 1, 2, 3, or 4). Even if this is a wireless router, we are going to need to plug in at least one computer with a wired Ethernet cable to configure the router (this is only necessary when installing, making changes to, or troubleshooting the router).

So if you did have a professional installation done for your broadband service, and it's now connected to a primary computer in your house, what you need to do is insert the router between that computer and the cable/DSL modem. The Ethernet cable from the cable/DSL modem is plugged into the WAN port on the router. Then the Ethernet cable from your computer is plugged into any of the available switch ports on the router (labeled 1, 2, 3, and 4). To make it easy to remember, you might want to plug the primary computer into port 1.

NOTE If the cable/DSL modem is powered on at this point while you are cabling, unplug it and plug it back in. This resets the modem so that it will properly communicate with the router instead of the primary computer that was originally plugged in.

Linksys router products come out of the box preconfigured with some default options to make it pretty easy to set up your home network. We may need to tweak a few things, but in general, it's almost (sometimes completely) functional just taking it out of the box and plugging it in. As mentioned earlier, we show you how to configure the Linksys WRT54GS, but just about every Linksys router product (whether wired or wireless) will be similar.

Configuration of the Linksys router products is done using any Internet browser on any computer, such as Internet Explorer in Windows. The "look and feel" is a little different on Windows 98 or Windows XP, but the options configured are the same, so we only show one operating system (OS) in the step-by-step guide to configuring your products.

Here are the configuration steps that we need to configure your router for broadband service:

Step 1   Find the Internet Explorer (or whatever browser you use) icon on your computer desktop and double-click to launch it. Because there is probably no connection to the Internet yet, it will most likely say "The page cannot be displayed." That's normal.

Step 2   Type **192.168.1.1** in the Address field in your browser and hit **Enter** (see Figure 7-13). This is the address of the Linksys router on the network.

Step 3   The Linksys router prompts for a username and password. Leave the User name field blank, and type **admin** in the Password field (see Figure 7-14). Click **OK**.

NOTE Address 192.168.1.1 and the "admin" password are the default settings for almost every Linksys wired and wireless router product.

Figure 7-13   Using Internet Explorer to Access the Router

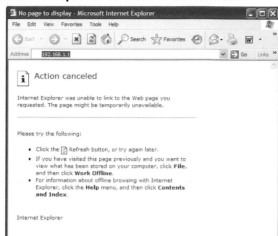

Figure 7-14   Enter the Default Password

Step 4   The main Linksys router configuration dialog now appears in the browser
(see Figure 7-15).

The first setting is the Internet Connection Type (or, on some Linksys routers, WAN
Connection Type). This is going to be based on what your service provider specified
when you signed up for service. The most common are

- **Cable**—DHCP or dynamic

- **DSL**—PPPoE

- **Static**

Find out which your service is, and then go to the appropriate part of Step 5.

Figure 7-15   Main Router Configuration Screen

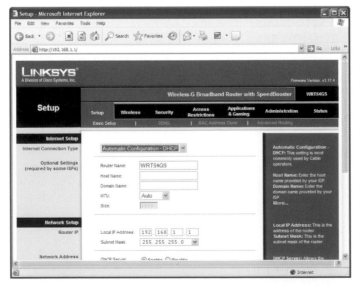

Step 5   Go to the appropriate step based on your service.

For cable broadband service:

Generally, you will select **Obtain an IP Automatically** or, in some Linksys routers, the menu choice is simply **DHCP**.

If the ISP gave you a host name and domain name to use, enter it in those fields (see Figure 7-16). Click **Save Settings**.

Figure 7-16   Select Automatic/DHCP for Cable

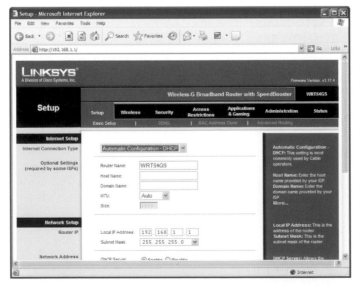

For DSL broadband service:

Generally, you will select **PPPoE**.

This will change the fields that are displayed. This is normal.

Enter the username and password that the ISP gave you for accessing the DSL service (see Figure 7-17). Click **Save Settings**.

Figure 7-17   Select PPPoE and Enter User/Password for DSL

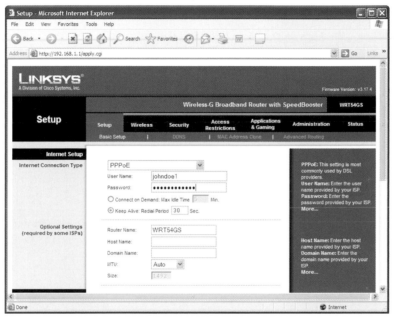

For a broadband service with a static IP address:

In some cases, the broadband provider may assign you a static IP address, which means that you are being assigned a permanent address on the Internet. Generally, this also means you will be paying more for your broadband service. Most of the general public will use a dynamically assigned address. There are some situations where you want a static address, for example, if you are running a web server out of your house.

 NOTE These are fairly advanced topics, so we will not cover them in-depth in this book. If you are running a web server, chances are you probably know how to do most everything in this book.

In the event your broadband provider assigns you a static IP address, here are the steps:

Select **Static IP**. This changes the fields that are displayed. This is normal.

Your ISP will also give you a whole list of items that need to be entered, including

- Static IP Address

- Subnet Mask

- Default Gateway

- Primary DNS

- Secondary DNS

Enter all this information in the appropriate fields (now you see why "dynamic" is so handy). (See Figure 7-18.) Click **Save Settings**.

Figure 7-18   Select Static IP and Enter Parameters

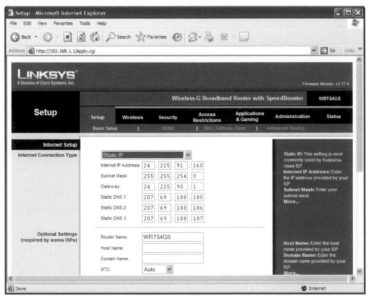

Step 6 We want to immediately change the password for the Linksys router so that it is not the default of "admin" any longer. We do not want anyone hacking into our home network. To do this, follow these steps:

Click the **Password** tab on the Linksys menu. (On some Linksys routers, this is under the Administration tab.)

Enter a new Password that you have chosen in both the **Password** field and the **Re-enter to Confirm** field (see Figure 7-19). Write down your password somewhere! Click **Save Settings**.

NOTE Choose a strong password consisting of a combination of uppercase letters, lowercase letters, and numbers. Do not use words, names, and so on. Passwords and security are covered in more depth in Part IV, "Security of Home Networks."

Figure 7-19   Change the Router Password

Step 7   At this point, the router should be communicating with the cable/DSL broadband modem. Here's how we can check to see if everything is set up correctly at this point:

Step 8   Click the Status tab on the Linksys menu.

You should see a confirmation of the connection type (in other words, DHCP, PPPoE, or Static IP). (See Figure 7-20.) Click **Refresh**.

Figure 7-20   Check the Router Status

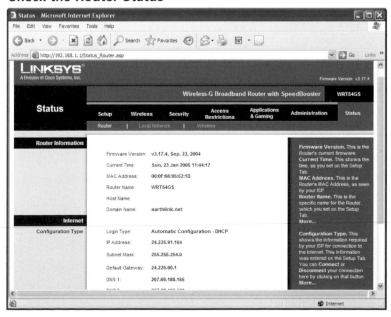

Under the Internet section (listed as WAN on some routers), you should also see the actual IP addresses now assigned for

- IP Address

- Subnet Mask

- Default Gateway

- Primary DNS

- Secondary DNS

Congratulations! You have now configured your router!

Troubleshooting Tips: Configure the Router for Broadband Service

If you see 0.0.0.0 assigned for any field, something is wrong. Here are some things to check and try. Between each step, go back and click the **Refresh** button to see if the problem is corrected:

- Check the cables to make sure you made the right connections.

- Check that the Ethernet ports on the cable/DSL modem, router, and primary computer are all lit as green. If not, remove power from the router, check all the cables for good connections, and return power to the router.

- Check that the broadband service subscription information from your ISP was entered correctly, and that you chose the correct Internet connection type (for example, DHCP, PPPoE, or Static IP).

- Try powering off the cable/DSL modem and the Linksys router, and shut down the primary computer. Power up the cable/DSL modem, then the Linksys router, and then reboot the primary computer.

- Check with your ISP to see if it has locked your service to the MAC address of your primary computer. Occasionally, the broadband system remembers the physical NIC of the computer that was used to install the broadband service. Power cycling the cable/DSL modem will often correct this. If it does not, call your ISP to see if the service is locked to your MAC address. If so, try the following:

    Step 1 Obtain the MAC address from the primary computer. Typically, there is a sticker on the NIC or on the bottom of the laptop computer. It will be a series of six number/letter pairs separated by colons.

    Step 2 Click the **MAC Address Clone** or simply **MAC Clone** tab on the Linksys router menu.

    Step 3 Type in the MAC address and select **Enable** (if this option is present). (See Figure 7-21.)

    Step 4 Click **Save Settings**.

Figure 7-21   Locking the Router to a MAC Address

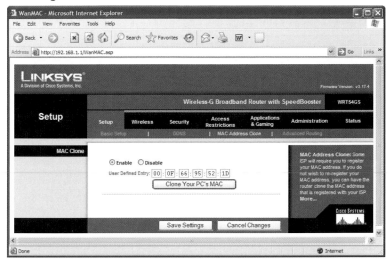

 GEEK SQUAD Many problems are solved using the "10-minute miracle." Unplug everything and walk away for 10 minutes. Come back and plug everything back in. It's magic!

- Check to make sure the broadband DSL or cable connection in your house is not experiencing interference from other devices (phones and televisions) that may be connected to the same wall outlet. It is best to "split" the connection as early as possible after entering your house and keep the Internet access line separate from the other service line (phone or cable TV). Talk to your broadband provider about the best way to properly separate the two types of services inside your house wiring.

- Read the "Troubleshooting" chapter in the installation manual that came with the Linksys router. Often, it is now provided on CD-ROM instead of paper.

Configure the Router for the Home Network

Now that we have taken care of the broadband service part of configuring your router and verified that it is communicating properly with the broadband service network, we need to tell the router how it should provide and manage the home network.

First, it's useful to have a basic understanding of how IP addresses are assigned by the router to the home network. It is important to understand that there are actually two networks connected by the router (see Figure 7-22):

- Home network (Inside)
- Internet (Outside)

Figure 7-22   Inside and Outside IP Addresses

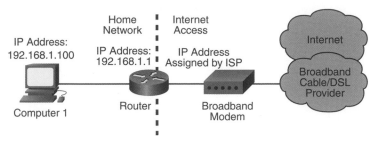

In the section, "Configure the Router for Broadband Service," you took care of the Internet addressing, or outside. The outside addressing is typically provided and managed by the broadband modem. We need not know or care what it's doing and what addresses are being used.

For the home network addressing (inside), the router is going to provide and manage the addresses that our computers use to communicate on the home network. It also has to assign itself an address, so that computers know how to reach the router itself.

The default address assigned to the router itself is 192.168.1.1. Then each computer (or device) that gets connected to the home network is going to ask the router for an address to use, and will be assigned an available address from 192.168.1.100, 192.168.1.101, 192.168.1.102, 192.168.1.103, up to 192.168.1.149.

In Figure 7-22, Computer 1 was the first computer attached to the router. When it was booted, its NIC requested an address to use, and the router said, "Here, use 192.168.1.100." This is the essence of dynamic address assignment. After we initially set this up on the Linksys router, we do not need to care about it again; we just let the router manage it for us.

Just in case these are not set properly, or you purchased a used router from eBay, let's verify the settings:

Step 1   Return to the main Linksys router configuration menu and click the **Setup** tab.

Verify that the Local IP Address (on some Linksys routers, it is called the LAN IP Address) is set to 192.168.1.1 (see Figure 7-23). Click **Save Settings**.

Step 2   On some Linksys routers, the information for this step is on the same Setup tab, on others it might appear under a tab named DHCP. Click the appropriate tab.

Verify the following settings, which are the defaults (see Figure 7-24):

- DHCP Server: **Enable**

- Starting IP Address: **192.168.1.100**

- Maximum Numbers of DHCP Users: **50**

Click **Save Settings** (or **Apply** on some Linksys routers).

Figure 7-23   Verify the Local IP Address

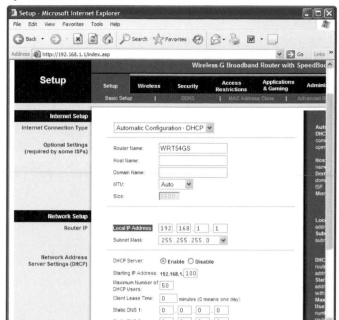

Figure 7-24   Verify the DHCP Server Settings

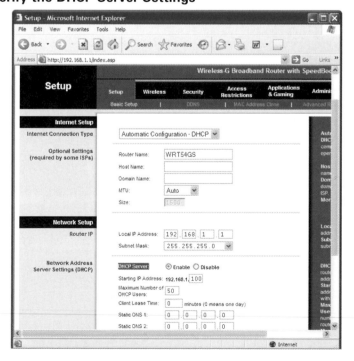

After the home network addressing (inside) of the router is configured, we can check that it is operating as expected. First, check if the NIC on Computer 1 has in fact been assigned the address we expected it to be (192.168.1.100). Here's how to do it in Windows 98 and Me:

Step 1   On the primary computer, select **Start > Run**, type the program name **winipcfg** in the dialog box, and press **Enter**. An information screen will appear (see Figure 7-25). If you have more than one NIC, you may have to select the one connected to the Linksys router.

Figure 7-25   Verify That the Router Assigns an IP Address to Computer

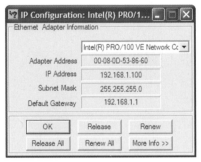

Step 2   Check that the IP address assigned is 192.168.1.100.

Step 3   Check that the Default Gateway assigned is 192.168.1.1.

Doing the same thing in Windows 2000 and XP requires, unfortunately, a little more work. For some unexplained reason, Microsoft stopped shipping this invaluable utility with the introduction of XP.

NOTE   There must have been a public outcry about the removal of this invaluable utility program, as Microsoft provides a way to download it for 2000 and XP as well. Here's the URL where you can go to do so:
http://www.microsoft.com/windows2000/techinfo/reskit/tools/existing/wntipcfg-o.asp.

Here's an alternative method for verifying on Windows 2000 and XP:

Step 1   On the computer, select **Start > Run**, type the program name **command.com** in the dialog box, and press **Enter**.

Step 2   In the window that appears, type the program name **ipconfig,** and press Enter. (See Figure 7-26.)

Step 3   Check that the IP address assigned is 192.168.1.100.

Step 4   Check that the Default Gateway assigned is 192.168.1.1

If the IP address assigned is 192.168.1.100 and the Default Gateway assigned is 192.168.1.1, the home network (inside addressing) of the router is functioning properly.

Congratulations, you just configured a home network on the router!

NOTE Commit the steps above to memory! The use of this utility will be absolutely invaluable for troubleshooting your home network.

Figure 7-26   Alternative for Verifying IP Address Assignment

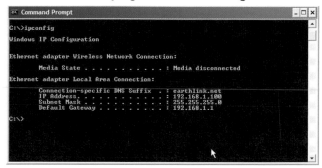

Troubleshooting Tips: Configure the Router for Your Network

If you see 0.0.0.0 assigned for either of these addresses, something is wrong. Here are some things to check and try.

- Repeat the steps listed in the section, "Configure the Router for Broadband Service."

- Double-check that the NIC configuration is set to Obtain an IP Address Automatically, and not set to Use the Following Address (in general, go to **Start** > **Control Panel** > **Network Settings** > **TCP/IP** > **Properties**).

- Shut down and reboot the primary computer to reset the NIC, so that it will request a new address from the Linksys router when it restarts.

- Make sure that if the primary computer was installed directly connected to a DSL broadband service, it may still be configured to run PPPoE on the NIC. Remove the PPPoE settings (you may need some help to do this).

- Read the "Troubleshooting" chapter in the installation manual that came with the Linksys router. Often, it is now provided on CD-ROM instead of paper.

Check the Access to the Internet

After you correctly complete all the previous steps, you should be ready to put the broadband service to work. Start by trying to browse a website on a computer to see if it can reach the Internet:

Step 1   Find the Internet Explorer (or whatever browser you use) icon on your computer desktop and double-click to launch it.

If you had a home page configured, you should see it now.

Step 2   Type your favorite website name in the address field and press **Enter**. See if it is displayed.

So that we don't have people yelling at us about why we didn't pick their site, the example shown is http://www.broadband.com (see Figure 7-27), whom we have already given a "plug" to. (They owe us two beers now.)

Figure 7-27   Success

Congratulations! You just installed a home network sharing a broadband connection! You should now able to access the Internet now from any and all of the computers connected to your home network.

Troubleshooting Tips: Internet Access

If you cannot access the Internet, something is wrong. Start by going back through the verification and troubleshooting sections of this chapter.

Here are a couple of resources on the web where you can get some help:

- **Linksys Tech Support**—http://www.linksys.com/support/TechSupport.asp

- **Linksys Tech Support**—(800) 326-7114

- **Microsoft Online Support**—http://support.microsoft.com/

Of course, if the problem persists, it may be time to bring in the Geek Squad (http://www.geeksquad.com).

From the Geek Squad Files

One thing to keep in mind about the Geek Squad (and, really, about all computer geeks) is that the ability to cite useless trivia is held in very high esteem. So, if one of us mentions that BlueTooth technology (the wireless protocol that allows devices like cell phones and PDAs to communicate with a wireless headset or to exchange business e-cards) is named after a Danish king who united the Viking clans of Denmark and Norway in the 900s, he's just strutting his stuff so to speak. Sure, it's annoying, but it's better than crushing empty beer cans on our foreheads. Anyway, here are a few observations we have made over the years:

- **KISS**—Use the KISS (keep it simple, stupid) principle when trying to solve a problem. Here are some seemingly silly things we have found:

  - Is it (computer, modem, router) plugged in and turned on? If you unplug your wireless router and put it in the closet, you are not going to have Internet access.

  - Your home wireless network will not be available to you if you are in another state.

  - If your house is without power due to a hurricane, it is unlikely you are going to be able to access the Internet.

  - The Internet is not on the AOL disk you get in the mail; you must use the software on the disk to connect to the Internet.

- **Dialup will not die**—For every Coke, there will always be a Pepsi. As cool as broadband is, there will always be a segment of the population that insists on using dialup. Its use as a backup for critical access will keep dialup around forever, so do keep those old modems.

- **AOL CDs**—If you are sick of getting a CD from AOL every other day, here are some suggestions on what you can do with them:

  - They make great drink coasters.

  - Throw them down on the floor, jump on them, and pretend you are surfing the Internet.

  - Hang them in the garden to scare birds away.

  - Use them to make a disco ball.

    – Mirror your dorm or living room.

■ **File sharing**—You have to be really careful putting software firewalls on computers behind a hardware firewall because they can affect file sharing. If you want to simplify the network, you could rely on a hardware firewall and skip the software firewall on each computer.

■ **Back up**—We mentioned backing up your critical data in Part I, "Networking Basics." Here it is again…back up your data. Trust us on this one.

ABGs of Wireless

The remainder of this book focuses on building out the network using wireless technology. Before jumping in, however, it's worth spending a moment discussing why we choose to go this route, and it really boils down to a single word: flexibility.

Wireless technology provides us with a great deal of flexibility when it comes to what devices we put on the network, how many devices, and where we put those devices. Let's look at an example. Start with a person who wants to connect to the Internet using broadband cable (this example works with any type of broadband). This person has three computers in the home, one for herself, her spouse, and her teenager, and they all want to connect to the Internet.

First they must determine where the cable jacks are in the home and decide which one they want to connect to the cable modem. Is one close to where one of the computers will be used? If not, that's a problem. They either have to put a computer where they don't want it or string a long cable across a room. After they decide which cable jack to use, they have to figure out how to get multiple computers to have access to it (because there is only a single cable modem per home). This means they will either need to have a single device connected to the Internet at a time, or they will need to buy a device (router, switch, or hub) that will allow multiple computers to connect to the Internet. They also have to decide how to connect all the computers in the house to the router or hub.

At this point, they have some options:

- Run cables through the walls. If the family was building a new house, they could have it wired throughout for Internet access but this is expensive. If they live in an existing home, they could hire an electrician to run cables, but that is really expensive and messy. If they rent, neither of these are an option.

- String cables all through the house. This is cheap, but it's messy and they will be tripping over cables all the time.

- Move all the computers to where the router or hub is.

- Go wireless.

Now some folks may be a little dubious of using a "new" technology, but the ability to provide wireless networking has been around for a long time, and the only reason you only heard about recently is that it was never really necessary. The need to provide high-speed network access to multiple, somewhat mobile computers really only emerged with the widespread availability of broadband Internet and inexpensive computers. The ability to do this has existed for years, suggesting that for a long time, wireless networking was a solution looking for a problem.

The bottom line is that wireless networking is reasonably easy and affordable. Assuming you start from scratch and have to buy wired network cards for all your computers, and a hub or router to connect them all, by the time you end up adding all the cables you need to connect to a wired system, the price is comparable to what a wireless system would cost. Adding in whatever cost you associate with convenience and absence of clutter, the wireless system becomes a near even trade off.

Wireless LANs

Today's wireless LANs (WLANs) give you much of the speed of a standard wired LAN (and in some cases, more) plus much flexibility.

WLANs can provide up to 54 Mbps (more for some standards) of speed for multiple computers with up to a 200–300 foot range, which is more than enough for most homes. In addition, you don't have to worry about running cables through walls or stringing them across rooms or down hallways.

Unlike wired LANs, the throughput (speed) of WLANs is greatly affected by distance and power. As you move further away from the wireless router or access point (AP), the strength of the signal decreases greatly which, in turn, requires slower transmissions (to reduce data errors), which, of course, lowers the number of bits you can send per second (see Figure 9-1).

Figure 9-1   A WLAN's Signal Decreases as Distance Increases

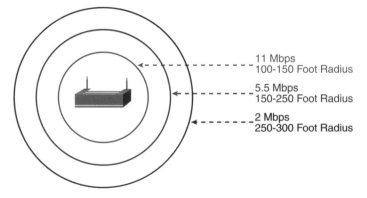

11 Mbps
100-150 Foot Radius

5.5 Mbps
150-250 Foot Radius

2 Mbps
250-300 Foot Radius

In addition, as you move your PC further away from an AP, your wireless NIC must increase its transmit power to maintain high data rates. If you are using a fixed PC that is plugged in to a wall outlet, this is not an issue. If, however, you are using a laptop, you can quickly drain your battery.

GEEK SQUAD The ranges shown in Figure 9-1 are off the box. Don't expect to actually get ranges this good because walls and other obstacles will dampen the signal. A concrete basement is a bad place for a wireless router. This doesn't mean you should yell at the kids that get between you and the wireless router.... It doesn't work that way.

Standards Soup

Hopefully by this point, we have convinced you that wireless is the way to go for home networking. Unfortunately, you may have gone to the store to look at wireless equipment and some boxes said they were G wireless, some said A, and some said B. If you were lucky, the person at the store gave you a good explanation of what this means, but more likely, you got someone who either confused you with too much information or who was not quite sure either. So here is what we hope is a good and simple explanation.

Currently, three wireless LAN standards exist:

- IEEE 802.11a

- IEEE 802.11b

- IEEE 802.11g

IEEE stands for the Institute of Electrical and Electronic Engineers. More than just a bunch of the fellas getting together for beers on the weekend, the IEEE is the worldwide standards body for all sorts of technologies.

The IEEE standards ensure that nearly all devices, technologies, and parts (within the realm of electronics anyway) are standardized and agreed upon. Without such a standards body, it would be extremely difficult for all vendors to make gear that works together. Just think about how much of pain it would be, for instance, if every stereo speaker manufacturer used different types of cables and connectors. The IEEE helps standardize just that sort of thing and many others that may not be so obvious. This type of standardization also allows for very rapid innovations and price reductions. So in cave-man speak: IEEE and standardization good, no IEEE bad.

Okay, back to the point...the IEEE standard that covers WLANs is 802.11.

802.11b

802.11b was the first of the three standards to become widely available. This standard operates at 2.4 Gigahertz (GHz) and offers up to 11 Mbps. It is the slowest of the three standards but is also the least expensive and most widely deployed. 802.11b has a range of about 150 feet in open air before signal degradation (and, therefore, speed) becomes noticeable. If you are using a wireless NIC that supports the B standard, chances are that any hotspot you visit will be compatible with your card.

802.11a

802.11a was the next standard to hit the market. This standard operates at 5 GHz and can achieve speeds up to 54 Mbps. This standard has a limited range of about 75 feet. The 802.11a standard is both expensive and not widely deployed, so unless you have a specific reason to use this standard we recommend using one of the other two.

802.11g

802.11g is the newest of the three standards. Because it features the best of the other two standards, it is seeing rapid deployment. The G standard operates at 2.4 GHz, has a range of about 150 feet, and can achieve speeds of up to 54 Mbps (with proprietary non-standard extensions, speeds can go as high as 108 Mbps). The equipment cost for this standard is a bit more than the B standard but less than the A standard. The G standard is growing in popularity with many hotspots.

Comparing the IEEE WLAN Standards

Table 9-1 shows an easy-to-read, side-by-side comparison of the three standards (courtesy of Linksys). Table 9-1 helps you figure out which standard is right for you, which at this point should be a choice between standards B and G. Before you go out and buy equipment however, there are a few important things to keep in mind, which are covered in the next section.

Table 9-1   A Versus B Versus G

Wireless Standard	802.11b	802.11a	802.11g
Popularity	Widely adopted. Readily available everywhere.	New technology.	New technology with rapid growth expected.
Speed	Up to 11 Mbps.	Up to 54 Mbps (5 times greater than 802.11b).	Up to 54 Mbps (5 times greater than 802.11b.)
Relative Cost	Inexpensive.	More expensive.	Inexpensive.
Frequency	More crowded. 2.4 GHz band. Some conflict may occur with other 2.4 GHz devices, such as cordless phones, microwaves, and so on.	Uncrowded 5 GHz band can coexist with 2.4 GHz networks without interference.	More crowded 2.4 GHz band. Some conflict may occur with other 2.4 GHz devices, such as cordless phones, microwaves, and so on.
Range	Good. Typically, up to 100–150 feet indoors, depending on construction, building material, and room layout.	Shorter range than 802.11b and 802.11g. Typically, 25 to 75 feet indoors.	Good. Typically up to 100–150 feet indoors, depending on construction, building material, and room layout.

Table 9-1   A Versus B Versus G

Wireless Standard	802.11b	802.11a	802.11g
Public Access	The number of public hotspots is growing rapidly, allowing wireless connectivity in many airports, hotels, public areas, and restaurants.	None at this time.	Compatible with current 802.11b hotspots (at 11 Mbps). Also, it is expected that most 802.11b hotspots will quickly convert to 802.11g.
Compatibility	Widest adoption.	Incompatible with 802.11b or 802.11g.	Interoperates with 802.11b networks (at 11 Mbps). Incompatible with 802.11a.

Selecting the Right Wireless Standard for Your Network

So how do you sort through the many wireless options that are available to you and decide on what's best for your home network? Keep in mind that there are two "sides" to this decision process:

■ What to choose for the wireless access point/router, which will "host" your wireless network

■ What to choose for wireless NICs that will allow the computers on your home network to "join" the network wirelessly

The previous sections covered the various wireless standards that exist, and the advantages and disadvantages of each. But what does it all mean? There are four primary factors that you need to weigh:

■ **Compatibility**—How well will it work together?

■ **Speed**—How fast is fast enough?

■ **Cost**—How much?

■ **Other Considerations**—What else should you care about?

As it turns out, compatibility and speed are intimately related. These factors are explored in the following sections, followed by our bottom-line recommendations.

Compatibility

The first really important point to understand is the relationship of the wireless A, G, and B standards to each other. NICs need to be compatible with the access point you purchase. It's fairly straightforward:

- B NICs are compatible with B and G Routers

- G NICs are compatible with B and G Routers

- A NICs are compatible only with A Routers

Now, just so that you understand, let's take it one step further by providing "dual-standard" (also known as dual-band) wireless NICs and routers. So you will see A+B and A+G products. What this means is the product supports both standards. It seems really confusing, but again it boils down to some pretty simple rules.

The next complication is that some vendors provide proprietary extensions to their products to make them run even faster. For example, Linksys provides a "SpeedBooster" version of their wireless G products that improves the transmission speed beyond the standard 54 Mbps. Linksys also provides a "SRX" series of wireless G products that doubles the speed to 108 Mbps. Other vendors have similar product extensions.

There are two things to understand about such extensions:

- They are backward compatible with the base standard.

- The extended speeds typically only work when you are using both that vendor's NICs and routers.

So be a bit cautious when you are thinking of buying products with such extensions. Make sure they are compatible with the base standard, at a minimum.

Is your head spinning yet? Yeah, thought so. Table 9-2 helps sort this out. Along the top are an assortment of wireless NICs with an indication of which wireless standards they support (a couple shown are Linksys proprietary extensions). Along the left side are accompanying wireless routers, again with the wireless standards they support. At the intersection point is an indication of whether the NIC is compatible with the wireless router.

Table 9-2   Wireless NIC and Router Compatibility Chart

Routers \ NICs	Wired	Wireless-B	Wireless-G	Wireless-G with Speedbooster	Wireless-G with SRX	Wireless-A	Wireless A+B	Wireless A+G
Wired	100 Mbps	Not Compatible	Not Compatible	Not Compatible	Not Compatible	Not Compatible	Not Compatible	Not Compatible
Wireless-B	100 Mbps	11 Mbps	11 Mbps**	11 Mbps**	11 Mbps**	Not Compatible	11 Mbps	11 Mbps**
Wireless-G	100 Mbps	11 Mbps*	54 Mbps	54 Mbps**	54 Mbps**	Not Compatible	11 Mbps*	54 Mbps
Wireless-G with Speedbooster	100 Mbps	11 Mbps*	54 Mbps*	72 Mbps	54 Mbps**	Not Compatible	11 Mbps*	54 Mbps*
Wireless-G with SRX	100 Mbps	11 Mbps*	54 Mbps*	54 Mbps**	108 Mbps	Not Compatible	11 Mbps*	54 Mbps*
Wireless-A	100 Mbps	Not Compatible	Not Compatible	Not Compatible	Not Compatible	54 Mbps	54 Mbps	54 Mbps
Wireless A+B	100 Mbps	11 Mbps*	11 Mbps**	11 Mbps**	11 Mbps**	54 Mbps	54 Mbps	54 Mbps
Wireless A+G	100 Mbps	11 Mbps*	54 Mbps	54 Mbps**	54 Mbps**	54 Mbps	54 Mbps	54 Mbps

* Operates at a lower speed than the router supports
** Operates at a lower speed than the NIC supports

Speed

Compatibility is only half the story though; resulting speed is the other. Table 9-2 also gives an indication of the performance you will receive when you use a type of wireless NIC with a type of wireless access point/router.

In general, the different wireless standards offer maximum performance of

- **802.11b**—11 Mbps

- **802.11g**—54 Mbps (up to 108 Mbps with extensions)

- **802.11a**—54 Mbps (up to 108 Mbps with extensions)

 GEEK SQUAD Never trust "marketing numbers" (the ones printed on the box). They test these things over and over in a lab with no walls and no furniture or phones during a full moon. There may be a chicken or two getting sacrificed as well. When they get a number they like, they write it on the box.

However, whether you achieve these speeds depends on distance from the router/access point, interference in your house, and a couple other factors. The combination of NICs and routers you use also matters. For example, a NIC for the 802.11b standard will certainly function with a wireless router for the 802.11g standard, but of course it will only operate at the 11 Mbps rate, not the higher 54 Mbps rate of the G standard. Similarly, a NIC for the 802.11g standard will work just fine with a wireless router for the 802.11b standard. It will just operate at the slower 11 Mbps rate of the B standard.

It's important to understand that the speed of your wireless network has almost nothing to do with the speed you can access the Internet using computers on your network. Even the "slower" B standard (between 2 million and 11 million bits per second) is normally faster than the speed of your Internet connection (typically between 500 thousand and 3 million bits per second). So having a faster A or G wireless network (between 20 and 108 million bits per second) does not mean you have faster Internet access. The wireless network needs to be fast enough, which any of the standards really is.

Cost

Costs have come way down for wireless networking, to the point that it is almost the same cost to put up a wireless network as a wired one. Wireless NICs can be more expensive than wired NICs, but costs are falling rapidly. One thing to note is wireless A tends to be the most expensive option, with wireless G the next most expensive, followed by wireless B, which is the cheapest.

Additional Considerations

There are a couple other things to consider when making your decision, including:

- What types of wireless NICs do you already own versus what you must go out and purchase? Many new laptops (and even some desktops) are sold with "built-in" wireless NICs.

- Do you want to be able to use wireless network access outside your home in a publicly provided wireless network (hotspot)?

The last thing you want to do is purchase a wireless router only to find out that you need to replace a wireless NIC that came with your laptop because it is not compatible. Similarly, you will be quite frustrated if you buy a wireless NIC for your laptop, intending to use it at hotspots, only to find out you bought the wrong standard.

NOTE Like wired NICs, wireless NICs come in various form factors, including PCI for installing in desktop computers, PCMCIA for installing in laptop computers, and USB for connecting to any computer or device with a USB port. Choose whichever makes sense for your network and computers.

Recommendations

Here are our bottom-line recommendations:

- If you just want Internet access, are on a tight budget, or do not anticipate a large amount of internal traffic (from a wireless juke box, for example), either the B or G standards are good choices.

- If you anticipate a large amount of internal traffic, plan on setting up a wireless gaming system, or want a little bit of "future proofing," G is the best choice. G also supports connecting to B networks, so if you plan on using hotspots, or getting on other people's networks, G offers a "best bet" for compatibility.

- A mixture of B and G NICs (for example, if you already own one or two B NICs) is just fine for connecting with G routers. We do recommend a wireless G router.

NOTE If a wireless G network contains a mix of computers with wireless B and Wireless G NICs, it is possible that network performance could be degraded slightly by the slower wireless B devices. Some early wireless G products even reverted the whole network to wireless B (fixed in latest products).

We do *not* recommend the A standard unless you have a specific reason to avoid using B or G. For example, if you are getting known interference from 2.4 GHz cordless phones, the A standard might be an option. Keep in mind, though, that cordless phones are now also being offered in the 5 GHz range, which can potentially interfere with wireless A networks. In any case, we recommend trying G first and swapping out to A only if G is not working out for you.

 GEEK SQUAD We once had a lady who would yell at her kids to stop getting in between her and her wireless router. We assure you, your kids make no difference in your wireless signal, so stop yelling at them. Well, at least about that, anyway.

Going Wireless at Home

This chapter walks you through the setup of your wireless network. We start off with some notes on planning and equipment selection to make sure you get the most out of your home network. After that, we jump right in to building a network and checking it for correct operation. After you have completed this chapter you will be up and running, but don't stop here as the chapters that follow will help prevent you from having security or privacy issues down the road.

Planning Your Wireless Network

The first step in building the wireless network is to sit down and do some planning. A little time spent up front will save you a lot of frustration and rework time later.

One item to note: The chapter assumes you are deploying a wireless router to connect behind a new or existing broadband connection, and that you don't already have a wired router. If you do already have a wired network including a router, you might want to consider deploying a wireless access point behind the router, or replace the wired router with a wireless router.

Wireless Network Topologies

Before we begin laying out the wireless network, we need to understand a very basic concept of wireless network topologies. There are essentially two types of wireless networks:

- Peer-to-peer (also called "ad-hoc")
- Peer-to-access point (also called "infrastructure")

In a peer-to-peer (or ad-hoc) wireless network, there is no central point of access or control. Every computer on an ad-hoc network is considered an equal "peer," having the same rights and access as any other computer on the wireless network. Any computer with a wireless network adapter may connect to any other wireless NIC. Figure 10-1 shows an example of this.

In a peer-to-access point (or infrastructure) wireless network, a central wireless "base station" provides the rendezvous point for all the wireless NICs on the network. In this case, each computer on the network always communicates only with the base station, or wireless access point, never directly to other computers on the network. Figure 10-2 shows an example of this.

Figure 10-1   Peer-to-Peer Wireless Network

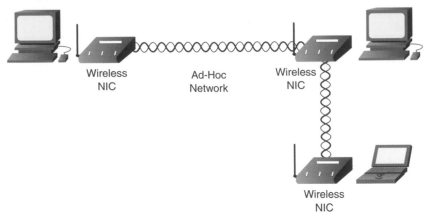

Figure 10-2   Peer-to-Access Point Wireless Network

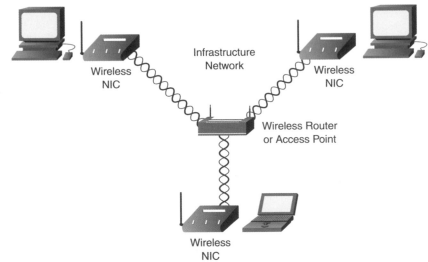

Although it's just as feasible to set up a peer-to-peer wireless network, we are not big fans of that "style" of wireless network for a couple of reasons:

- Because there is no central "authority" as to who can "join" the wireless network and who cannot, security becomes a real concern. (Wireless network security is covered in much greater depth in Chapter 11, "Securing Your Wireless Network.")

- One of the computers must be designated as the "owner" of the high-speed broadband Internet service and provide "gateway" access for all the other computers on the home network.

- Because of the reason just mentioned, if the Internet "gateway" computer is not turned on, all other computers on the home network will not be able to access the Internet.

There is a small cost advantage to a peer-to-peer network because it is not necessary to purchase a wireless router or access point. But this approach has many downsides of its own, which are described in Chapter 7, "High-Speed Internet Access."

It's our opinion that while peer-to-peer wireless networks have their place, the disadvantages far outweigh the benefits. Therefore, we recommend deploying an "infrastructure" style wireless network, and this will be the focus of the rest of this chapter.

Sketching a Network Layout

The next thing to do for planning is figure out where we are going to place our wireless router and where our computers will be placed. It's useful to make a sketch of your house. Nothing fancy is required, just make a sketch of the major rooms.

Now, put a red mark in the rooms where you have the appropriate port for Internet access (cable, DSL, or other). Next, put a blue mark in the rooms where you are likely today or in the future to have a desktop computer (or other device). Finally, put a green mark in the rooms where you can conceive of using a laptop computer. By the way, for health and safety reasons, we don't really recommend using computers in the bathroom. Aside from the obvious electrical shock hazard, well, it's just a little too weird.

In addition, if you have a cordless phone system that operates in the 2.4 GHz band (it should be written on the phone somewhere), you may want to mark the location of the phone's base station on the sketch. These phones can cause interference with your network if the wireless router is too close. Figure 10-3 shows a sample sketch.

Figure 10-3   Sample Sketch of a House

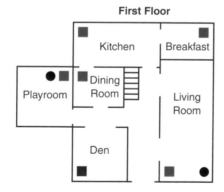
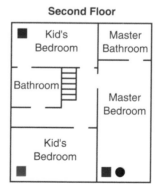

From the sketch, we can make some decisions about where you will put your wireless router, which computers will have wired connections, and which will have wireless connections. Suppose today, we have two desktop computers (a spouse's and a son's), one personal laptop (a daughter's), and one work laptop (mine). Suppose we also happen to have cable outlets in three areas of the house (master bedroom, living room, play room).

We need to have at least one computer with a wired connection (at least during initial setup and sometimes when changes are required). In this example, the family decides to have the high-speed broadband service installed to the outlet in the master bedroom. The wireless router can be placed next to the cable modem, and the "Spouse" desktop computer right next to that as well. All three of these will be cabled together with Ethernet cables.

Because the daughter's laptop and son's desktop computer are in other bedrooms of the house, and not easy to run Ethernet cables to, these computers will have wireless connections. The last computer is the "work" laptop, which is used primarily in the den, but could also be used in the living room, breakfast nook, and on the back deck (once you try this, you will never want to work in your office again). Wireless is definitely the way to go for this laptop as well. By jotting these requirements into the sketch, we have what's shown in Figure 10-4.

Figure 10-4 Adding Wired and Wireless Computers to the Sketch

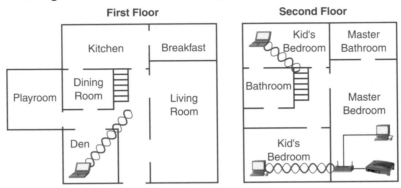

Making a Shopping List

Now we need to figure out what we need to buy to build our wireless home network. It might help to create a table like Table 10-1. Start by making a list of computers (and other devices) that will be on your home network. Decide how they will be connected (wired or wireless) and write that in the "Need" column. See what NICs may already exist in each computer and write that in the "Have" column.

Table 10-1   Example Inventory for Wireless and Wired NICs

	Need	**Have**	**Type to Buy**	**Model**
Desktop PC (Spouse)	Wired NIC	**Wired NIC**		
Desktop PC (Son)	Wireless NIC	**Wired NIC**		
Laptop 1 (Daughter)	**Wireless NIC**			
Laptop 2 (Work)	Wireless NIC	Wired NIC Wireless B NIC		

In this example, we checked the "Spouse" desktop computer and found out there is already a wired NIC installed inside the computer (a PCI card). Then, we checked the "Son" computer and found out it also had a wired NIC (not what we need) but no wireless NIC.

Continuing this process throughout all the computers we plan to connect, we end up with what's shown in Table 10-1, which shows us that we need to purchase two wireless NICs to build our home network.

Looking at the "Work" laptop, we see that it has a built-in wireless NIC that supports the B standard.

Now we need to add to the table information on the products we need to buy. We need to consider what we learned in Chapter 9, "ABGs of Wireless," on wireless standards and NIC to router compatibility.

For the "Son" desktop, we decide that we will use a USB-connected Wireless G NIC to make installation easy. For the "Daughter" laptop, we decide to go with a PCMCIA Wireless G NIC that we can easily insert in the laptop, and is also very portable, so we can take it traveling (it will become apparent later on why this is handy).

We note these in Table 10-2. We also make an entry for the wireless router (lest we forget the most important piece of the network). We decided (in this example) on a Wireless G Router, which will be compatible with the existing Wireless B NIC we already have, as well as provide high-speed wireless for the two Wireless G NICs we intend to buy. Finally, we have a pretty good start to our shopping list.

Table 10-2   Example Shopping List

	Need	**Have**	**Type to Buy**	**Model**
Desktop PC (Spouse)	Wired NIC	Wired NIC		
Desktop PC (Son)	Wireless NIC	Wired NIC	USB Wireless G NIC	
Laptop 1 (Daughter)	Wireless NIC		PCMCIA Wireless G NIC	
Laptop 2 (Work)	Wireless NIC	Wireless NIC Wireless B NIC		
Wireless Router	N/A	N/A	Wireless G Broadband Router	

Next we need to decide on the actual products we want to buy. As we said in the introduction, we chose to use Linksys products because they are the top-selling brand and they work very well. Originally we wanted to provide a product list here in this book, however, consumer electronics products change so rapidly in the marketplace that the list would be outdated as soon as the book published.

Check with the knowledgeable folks at the computer electronics store for the latest products. It may be helpful to take along your sketch and shopping list table, so that you can explain to the person at the store what it is you are trying to do and the thought process you used to come up with your list.

We have also provided a current list of Linksys products online (which we will try to keep updated). See Appendix C, "Linksys Products List," at http://www.ciscopress.com/1587201364.

NOTE Some older computers may lack the horsepower to be able to operate a wireless NIC. For example, Linksys wireless NICs are only supported in computers with 200 MHz Pentium processors and higher. Sometimes, though, we have an older computer such as a Pentium 133 MHz that we still want to use.

The solution to this problem is to go ahead and install a wired NIC in the computer, and then add a wireless Ethernet bridge (such as the Linksys WET11) to provide the wireless connection. The wireless bridge is "self-contained" and does not need the PC to connect itself to the wireless router.

Wireless Ethernet bridges are a little hard to find but can be worth their weight in gold if you absolutely must put an older computer on the wireless network.

Turning Up the Network

Before we actually set up the wireless portion of the network, there are a couple decisions to be made regarding the design.

Select an SSID

The first order of business is to select a service set identifier (SSID). This is the network name that devices will be able to identify that it's your wireless network they are connecting to, not your neighbor's.

An SSID should be selected so that it's very difficult for someone to guess it. Do not use pet names, children's names, or nicknames. Preferably, pick a series of random letters and numbers, making sure some are capital and some lowercase. Write it down! We are going to have to share it with all the devices on the network so we are all singing the same song.

Figure 10-5 shows how an SSID works.

Figure 10-5   An SSID Identifies Your Home Wireless Network

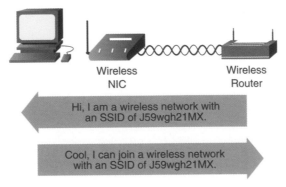

Wireless NIC

Wireless Router

Hi, I am a wireless network with an SSID of J59wgh21MX.

Cool, I can join a wireless network with an SSID of J59wgh21MX.

Select a Wireless Channel

The next thing we need to think about (maybe) is which "channel" the wireless network will use. Each of the wireless standards defines a number of channels that can be used to send and receive signals on. Much like the channels on your television, the wireless channel gets "tuned to" by the wireless router and wireless NICs in order to communicate.

In most cases, the default channel setup in the wireless router will work just fine out-of-the-box. In some cases, if a very close neighbor also has a wireless network using the same channel, or if there is another type of wireless device in your house (such as a 2.4 GHz cordless phone or a wireless room-to-room video signal extender.), you may experience interference with your wireless network and need to use a different channel.

So here's a little information on wireless channels. The 802.11b and 802.11g standards share the same defined channels (1 through 11 in the United States). Only three of them are unique (channels 1, 6, and 11), while the other eight are overlapping. Figure 10-6 shows this (keep in mind 802.11a is different, but we are focusing on 802.11b and 802.11g).

Figure 10-6   11 Channels of 802.11b and 802.11g Standards

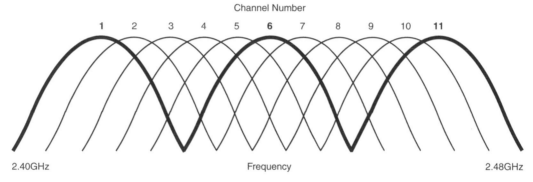

In most cases, let the wireless router use the default channel (Linksys routers use a default of channel 6) to start with (see Figure 10-7). If there are problems with reception (we will talk about how to recognize this later), try channel 1, then try channel 11, and if all three of those are poor, try the others.

Figure 10-7   Wireless NICs Try Channel 6 by Default

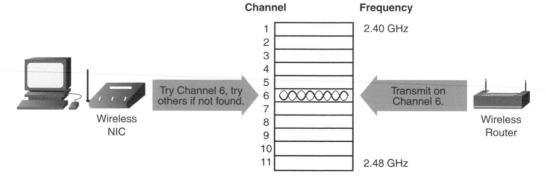

Wireless NICs do not necessarily have to be told in advance which channel the wireless router is going to use. They have the ability to "scan" for the correct channel to use. Essentially, they start at channel 6 looking for a "base station." If found, it locks on; if not, it continues to search for another channel that has a base station that is broadcasting its network.

In the next section, "How to Build It: Going Wireless," we set up the wireless router and wireless NICs and get our basic wireless network up and running.

VERY IMPORTANT: Chapter 11 focuses on how to make the wireless network secure. It is essential that you read and follow the chapter on wireless security!

For now, we are going to set up the network in a very basic way, without the recommended security measures. For those of you reading ahead to Chapter 11, it is *strongly* recommended that you get the network working first, and then go back and secure it. If we do the two steps at once, and it does not work, we will not know whether we made an error in the basic setup or in the security measures.

How to Build It: Going Wireless

Now that we have selected the wireless equipment for our network, and have chosen some basic parameters, we can start building it. We have to set up the wireless router/access point, which will act as the base station for our wireless communications, and we also have to set up wireless NICs in each of the computers (or devices) we want to connect to the home network without using cables.

A little housekeeping first: If you already have a broadband wired router and are adding a wireless network to it, your steps will be somewhat different. The essential wireless configuration is relatively the same for a wireless access point and wireless router. The difference is really that a wireless access point will not have the broadband configuration that we performed in Chapter 7.

By the way, you cannot terminate your broadband service with a wireless access point, as it has no capability to function as a router. In general, it is probably as easy and cost-effective to simply replace your wired router with a wireless router, rather than to try and configure two separate boxes to do the same job.

In any case, if you are installing a wireless router, it is still necessary to perform the steps described in the "How to Build It" section in Chapter 7. This section builds on Chapter 7 by walking you through how to set up the wireless network.

The steps we will go through are as follows:

- Install and set up a wireless router

- Install and set up wireless NICs

- Check wireless network operation

VERY IMPORTANT: **We cannot stress enough: After you complete the steps in this chapter, it is essential that you proceed immediately to the next chapter to secure your wireless network.**

Install and Set Up a Wireless Router

To connect a wireless router to the high-speed broadband service, follow the same instructions in Chapter 7. Even though we are going wireless, at least one of our computers needs to be wired, at least during the installation and configuration. Just like we did when we set up the broadband service, start by connecting a computer to the router with an Ethernet cable to any open port numbered "1," "2," "3," or "4." Now we need to set up the wireless service on the router by following these steps:

NOTE This process is shown with a Linksys WRT54GS Wireless-G SpeedBooster Router (for the 802.11g and 802.11b standards), but the process is similar on all the Linksys wireless routers.

Step 1 Find the Internet Explorer (or whatever browser you use) icon on your computer desktop and launch it.

Type **192.168.1.1** in the address field in your browser and hit **Enter** (see Figure 10-8). This is the address of the Linksys router on the network.

Figure 10-8   Enter the Router's IP Address into Internet Explorer

Step 2 The Linksys Router prompts you for a username and password (see Figure 10-9).

Leave the user name blank, and type the password you created when you set up the router initially in Chapter 7.

If this is the first time accessing the router, type in the default password **admin**.

Click **OK**.

The main Linksys router configuration dialog now appears in the browser.

Figure 10-9   Enter the Password for the Router

Step 3   Click the **Wireless** tab (see Figure 10-10).

By default, the wireless function should be enabled; make sure **Enabled** is selected.

By default, the SSID is set to linksys. Change this to the SSID you have decided for your network. For this example, we chose J59wgh21MX.

Click **Save Settings**.

Figure 10-10 Setting the SSID

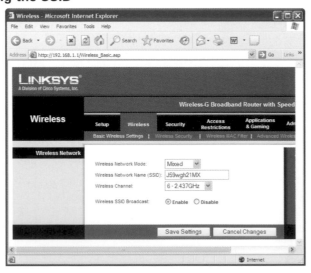

Step 4   Check the channel setting.

By default, the Wireless Channel is set to 6. This setting should be okay. If you experience interference or poor reception, you may want to try a different channel.

For now, leave the setting on 6, and put a bookmark here to come back to if you need to change the channel (see Figure 10-11).

Click **Save Settings**.

Figure 10-11 Setting the Channel Number

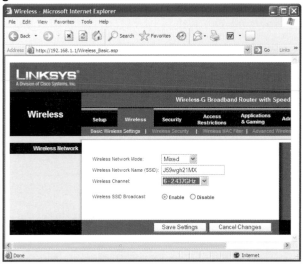

At this point, the wireless router should be up and running, and putting out a signal for computers with wireless NICs to "see." There is not much we can check at this point to ensure it's operating as we think it is. We need to move on and set up a wireless NIC in one of the computers to see if we can establish a connection.

Install and Set Up Wireless NICs

Just like wired NICs, we have a number of options for selecting which wireless NICs we are going to use to set up our network. Continuing the example we started in the section, "Planning Your Wireless Network," suppose we now want to connect our "Son" desktop computer and "Daughter" laptop to the wireless network.

Because the desktop is fairly stationary, portability is not a concern. For a wireless NIC, we could purchase a PCI card and install it inside the computer, or a USB-connected adapter that will plug into the computer externally to any USB port.

For the laptop computer, a USB-connected adapter would also work just fine, but it's not as portable, so we chose a PCMCIA adapter. The PCMCIA adapter is about the size of a thick credit card, so it will be much easier to take with you when you travel, say to a wireless hotspot. The USB adapter is bulkier and requires a USB cable as well, so it's not as well suited to travel.

So that we can get a feel for different install procedures, let's also assume the desktop computer is running Windows 98 and the laptop Windows XP.

VERY IMPORTANT: For Windows 98, Me, and 2000 computers, you will typically need to install the software on the Linksys CD that comes with the adapter before plugging in the NIC. For Windows XP (and presumably later), you will typically plug the network adapter in first and go from there. However, check the instruction sheet of the specific NIC as this is not always true!

Let's install the USB-connected adapter (for this example, we use the Linksys WUSB11 Wireless-B NIC) in the "Son" desktop running Windows 98, and the PCMCIA adapter (for this example, we used the Linksys WPC54GS Wireless-G NIC with SpeedBooster) in the "Daughter" laptop running Windows XP.

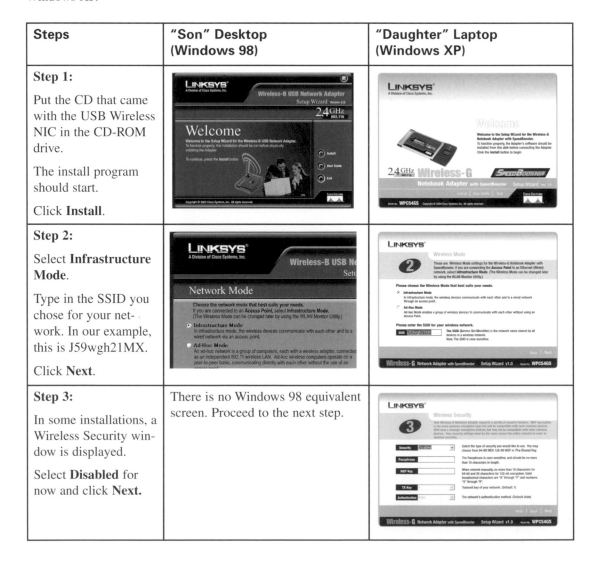

Steps	"Son" Desktop (Windows 98)	"Daughter" Laptop (Windows XP)
Step 1: Put the CD that came with the USB Wireless NIC in the CD-ROM drive. The install program should start. Click **Install**.		
Step 2: Select **Infrastructure Mode**. Type in the SSID you chose for your network. In our example, this is J59wgh21MX. Click **Next**.		
Step 3: In some installations, a Wireless Security window is displayed. Select **Disabled** for now and click **Next.**	There is no Windows 98 equivalent screen. Proceed to the next step.	

Steps	"Son" Desktop (Windows 98)	"Daughter" Laptop (Windows XP)
Step 4: A confirmation window appears. Double-check that the SSID was entered exactly. Click **Next**.		
Step 5: We're done with the install. Click **Exit,** and remove the Linksys CD.		There is no XP equivalent screen. Proceed to the next step.
Step 6: Windows may need to copy some files. Insert the Windows CD that came with your computer. Click **OK**.		There is no XP equivalent screen. Proceed to the next step.
Step 7: Some versions of Windows will require rebooting the computer at this point. Click **OK** or **Yes** to reboot.		

After the desktop computer reboots, we need to connect the USB NIC to the computer:

Step 1 Plug one end of the USB cable that comes with the NIC into the back of the desktop into an available USB port.

Step 2 Plug the other end into the adapter itself.

There is no power cord required for USB devices; they get their power through the computer they are connected to. Figure 10-12 shows an example.

Figure 10-12 Connecting the USB NIC to the Computer

Desktop Computer   USB Port   USB Cable   Wireless Adapter

Installing the PCMCIA card in the "Daughter" laptop computer is easy. Just plug the card into an open PCMCIA slot, like Figure 10-13 shows.

Figure 10-13 Installing the PCMCIA Card into the Laptop

On top of both of these NICs, you should see a green light labeled Power light up. The NICs immediately begin looking for the wireless router and try to establish a connection.

This covers installing new adapters. We will verify they are operating correctly in the later "Check Wireless Network Operation" section.

Configuring an Existing Built-In Wireless NIC

Let's take a look at enabling a pre-existing wireless NIC to be able to communicate with our network. The "Dad" laptop we referred to earlier in the chapter has a built-in Wireless-B NIC. This is becoming common for laptops you buy today. In fact, if you are considering a new laptop purchase and it does not have a built-in Wireless-B or Wireless-G NIC, we advise shopping around for one that does.

Follow these steps to tell your existing built-in NIC how to "see" your wireless network (by the way, the "Dad" laptop is running Windows XP):

Step 1   Select **Start > Control Panel > Network Connections**.

The red X on the Wireless Network Connection icon means there is no communication to a Wireless base station (such as a wireless router).

Step 2   Click the **Wireless Network Connection** icon in the right section of the window, and then click **Change settings of the connection** on the left (see Figure 10-14).

Figure 10-14 Access the Wireless Settings for the NIC

Step 3   Click the **Wireless Networks** tab. Make sure to checkmark the **Use Windows to configure my wireless network settings** box. In the Preferred networks section, click the **Add** button (see Figure 10-15).

Figure 10-15 Add a New Wireless Network

Step 4   Type in the SSID you chose for your network (see Figure 10-16). (In our example, this is J59wgh21MX.)

VERY IMPORTANT: **The SSID should be the same on your wireless router and network adapters.**

If they're checked, uncheck all other boxes on the screen. Click **OK**.

Figure 10-16 Enter the SSID for the Wireless Network

Step 5   You should now see an entry in the Preferred networks section (see Figure 10-17).

Click **OK**.

Figure 10-17 New Wireless Network Entry Is Added

Step 6   Back to the Network Connections window, the red X should now disappear from the Wireless Network Connection icon (see Figure 10-18).

Figure 10-18 Wireless NIC Should Show Connected

Check Wireless Network Operation

Now that we have configured both the wireless router and all our wireless NICs, they are hopefully happily communicating. In this section, we check to make sure that's the case.

First, let's check if the wireless router can see the computers on the network over the wireless connection. Access the wireless router using your web browser (use the same procedure we have shown a couple times now):

Step 1 Click **Status > Local Network**.

Step 2 Click the **DHCP Client Table** button. You should see something like what's shown in Figure 10-19.

Figure 10-19 Verifying the Wireless NICs Are Seen by the Wireless Router

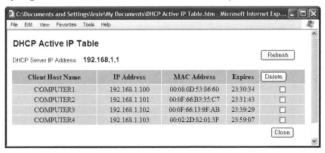

For our example, we can see that we now have all four computers (three wireless and one wired) with assigned IP addresses by the wireless router. You should see one entry per computer on your network. If you do, then congratulations, looking good from the wireless router's perspective!

Let's check the computers with the wireless NICs. We can usually do this a couple of different ways. In Windows XP, we can go back to the Network Connections window, right-click the **Wireless Connection** icon, and select **View Status of this Connection**. This brings up a dialog box that shows the connection status, as shown in Figure 10-20.

Figure 10-20 Checking the Wireless Connection Status

The green bars on the signal strength line tells us that we are connected (these are similar to a cell phone display). We also see a couple other good indications, such as speed being 11 Mbps (top speed for a Wireless-B NIC) and packets being sent and received.

Another way to view operation (if your NIC is a later Linksys model) is using the Linksys WLAN Monitor. If you have this handy utility, you should see an icon like this ![icon] on the far right of your Windows taskbar.

Double-clicking it launches the program. If you don't see such an icon, try going through **Start > Programs > Instant Wireless > Instant Wireless LAN Monitor**.

If the wireless NIC is communicating properly with the wireless router, a window like what's shown in Figure 10-21 appears.

Figure 10-21 Wireless Network Is Connected

If there's an error, a window like what's shown in Figure 10-22 appears.

Figure 10-22 Wireless Network Is Not Connected

The green bars next to Signal Strength and Link Quality tell us that we have a good communication link. If all your computers show a good connection, congratulations, you made it!

Troubleshooting Tips: Going Wireless

If there are no bars or the message "No association with Access Point" is displayed, something is wrong. Here are some things to check and try:

- Check that the wireless router is plugged in and powered on. Make sure the green light labeled "Wireless" on the front of the Linksys wireless router is lit.

- Access the wireless router with your Internet browser and double-check the setup. Make sure the wireless network is "Enabled," the correct SSID is entered, and the security settings (encryption, WEP) are "Disabled" (for now).

- Use the Linksys WLAN Monitor program (or whichever program is used to manage your wireless network adapter[s]) to verify the settings:

Step 1 Double-click the WLAN Monitor icon to launch the program.

Click the **Profiles** tab (see Figure 10-23). Select the home network entry and click **Edit**.

Figure 10-23 Re-Checking the Wireless Network Profile

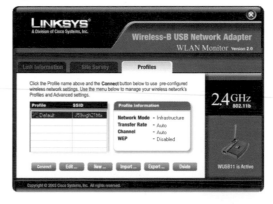

Step 2   Walk through the settings, making sure they match the wireless router (see Figure 10-24):

- Infrastructure mode

- SSID

- WEP: Disabled

Figure 10-24 Review Your Settings

- Shut down and reboot the computer(s) to reset their NICs.

- Try powering off and on the Linksys wireless router.

- Using the Linksys WLAN Monitor utility, watch the Signal Strength and Signal Quality bars for a minute or so. If you see periodic connections, where you briefly see the green bars, then they disappear, you could be experiencing low signal strength. Much like a cell phone, signal strength tells you if you are getting a good signal or not. Poor signal strength could be a number of things:

  — The computer and wireless router could be too far apart—try moving the computer closer to the router to confirm if this is the problem.

  — Try adjusting the external antenna(s) to a new position.

  — There could be interference inside your house from a cordless phone, baby monitor, intercom, or other wireless device—try unplugging such devices and see if this is the problem. If there is an interfering device, such as a 2.4 GHz phone base, try moving the device farther away from the wireless router.

  — A nearby neighbor may already have a wireless home network installed and the two networks are interfering.

    In this case (and you could try it for other steps above as well), try changing the wireless channel on the wireless router to a channel other than the default channel (6). Try channel 1 or 11, as shown in Figure 10-25.

Figure 10-25 Try Changing the Wireless Channel

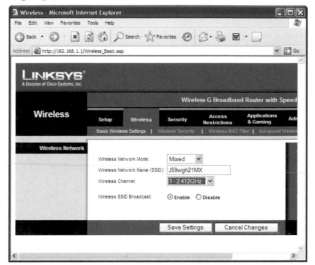

- Check the SSID a third time on the wireless router and wireless NICs. The SSID is case-sensitive. This means that if you enter "A123" as the SSID on the router and "a123" as the SSID on the NIC, the two will never "find" each other. Make sure you entered the exact letters and numbers.

- If a personal firewall software program, such as ZoneAlarm, is running on the computer, try disabling it temporarily to see if it alleviates the problem. Sometimes firewall programs can prevent good stuff from happening.

- Read the "Troubleshooting" chapter in the installation manuals that came with the Linksys wireless router and Linksys wireless NICs.

- If all else fails, contact Technical Support and get some help, or give a call to the Geek Squad!

Securing Your Wireless Network

We already mentioned that a key feature of a wireless network is flexibility. Although this additional flexibility makes wireless networking attractive, it does come at the potential cost of security. This doesn't mean that a wireless network will always be insecure; it just means that you must take additional precautions to ensure that your wireless network is not an easy target for those who know how—and are willing—to take advantage of folks who don't practice safe networking.

Why Should I Worry About Wireless Network Security?

Access to a wired network is easy to control, because people have to be physically inside your house to plug a computer into the router. With a wireless network, people just have to be in the proximity of your house. Physical barriers such as windows and doors do not control access in this case, so we have to take other steps to block intruders.

The security issue with a wireless network stems from the fact that the signal is omnidirectional. Unlike a wired network where signals are fairly well contained, the wireless signal goes everywhere in all directions for 300 feet or more. Anyone that wants to gain access to your signal need only put a receiver (a computer with a wireless NIC) inside the signal range.

 NOTE Why would someone want to access your wireless network? Well, there are lots of reasons. One of your neighbors could "leech" onto your network just to receive free Internet access. Although irritating, this is not all that harmful in itself, if all they are doing is browsing the Internet on your dollar. However, "war-drivers" or professional hackers could use the access to obtain your personal information. For example, eavesdropping while you are conducting an online purchase could expose your credit card information.

One of the most unusual illicit uses of insecured home wireless networks also offers perhaps the strongest reason yet to secure your wireless network. Recently, several instances have surfaced where people conducting illegal activities used wireless networks with inadequate security for the anonymity that they can provide. One fellow parked in a neighborhood, easily gained access to an unprotected home wireless network, and downloaded huge amounts of illegal child pornography. He was fortunately arrested, but due to a traffic violation, not the downloading. If someone commits an illegal activity in this manner, it can easily be traced to your broadband subscription, and now you could end up having to explain to the authorities that it was not you or other family members conducting the illegal activity.

We are always amazed when we drive through a neighborhood and check how people have deployed their wireless networks. Using a free software program, anyone can download from the Internet; we easily found 114 wireless routers, only 45 (roughly 40 percent) of which were protected in any fashion. From such a scan, potential intruders can easily obtain a survey of the available wireless networks, their SSID, channel number, and most importantly which networks have been secured and which have been left wide open (roughly 60 percent). In Figure 11-1, the networks with a circle and a padlock inside indicate that they are at least using WEP encryption. The circles without a padlock are wide open. Anyone can sit on the street near these houses (or businesses), associate to the access point, and access the Internet or try and break into the rest of the home network.

Figure 11-1   Example of Scanning for Available Wireless Networks in a Neighborhood

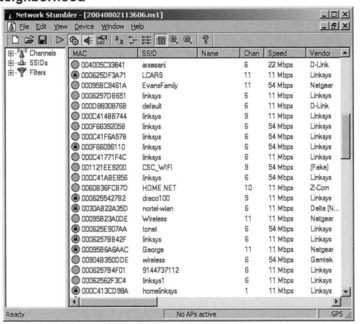

This is unfortunate and easily rectified. We can only assume that the reason so many people leave their networks "open" is because that is the way the various wireless router manufacturers deliver their products. Most products are delivered without security measures enabled, and people do not seem to take the time (or maybe don't understand the need) to lock the door.

What Do I Do About It?

You can take some simple steps to dramatically increase the security of your wireless network. It is not foolproof, but it will keep most of the riff raff out, which is good enough in most cases. People often ask us how to make their networks totally secure, completely secure, or some such variation. The answer is easy; don't turn it on. In other words, if someone who knows what they are doing has enough time, enough money, and the willingness to spend both, that person will crack any security scheme you can come up with. So lesson number one: Never dare or really tick off a hacker. If you do, you're toast. Lesson number two: If you see a white van bristling with antennas parked in front of your house for several hours, turn off your network.

The real lesson, though, is best explained with the help of a funny story that goes something like this: Two friends are walking through the woods when they come across an angry grizzly bear that starts rushing toward them. The first friend quickly starts to lace up his running shoes prompting the second friend to remark "Why are you doing that? You can't outrun a grizzly bear." At this, the first friend replies, "I don't need to outrun the bear, I need to outrun you!"

This is actually a very good model for wireless security and really for all network security. The fact is that although you cannot make your network 100 percent secure, you can take simple steps to make sure that you are not the easiest target in your neighborhood, and in most cases that is enough to keep your network safe. This is really the same strategy as home security in that a dead bolt and an alarm system can be bypassed by expert thieves, but you should still have both. Thieves are usually not looking to hone their lock-picking skills, they are looking to steal without attracting attention and, therefore, usually will pick an easy-to-get-into home over a well secured one. Figure 11-2 shows varying degrees of wireless home network security and the vulnerabilities related with the networks.

Figure 11-2   Security Examples

Wireless Settings
Enabled SSID Broadcast
Default SSID (e.g., linksys)
No Encryption
No MAC Filtering

Wireless Settings
Disable SSID Broadcast
Changed SSID (e.g., fluffycat)
No Encryption
No MAC Filtering

Wireless Settings
Disable SSID Broadcast
Random SSID (e.g., kr90oLMZ)
128-Bit WEP Encryption
No MAC Filtering

Wireless Settings
Disable SSID Broadcast
Random SSID (e.g., Fh560S0eeXt)
WPA2 Encryption
MAC Filtering

Security Issues
Wireless routers come from the store this way. Anyone with a laptop can get on this network, and most hotspot programs will make it easy. Don't do this.

Security Issues
This network will keep most non-hackers off the network, but all your information (including e-mail online shopping data) is sent in cleartext for anyone to see.

Security Issues
This network is secure enough for most people, including encrypting all data sent and received. There are more secure options, but this is the minimum you should do.

Security Issues
This network has the most security possible today and is equivalent to business-class security. However, it's more complex to implement. If you need more than this, hire a professional.

This person is asking for trouble!

This person is still vulnerable.

Secure enough for most people, but a dedicated hacker could take you down.

Very secure.

Knowing this, it makes good sense to secure your network, and given that basic network security is not too difficult to achieve, there is really no reason not to secure your wireless network. How easy, you ask? It takes just two steps:

- Don't advertise your network (turn off SSID broadcast)

- Scramble (encrypt) your wireless signal (use WEP or WPA)

Now for the really good news. All of these steps can be done while in the setup screen for your router and it takes all of about five minutes. Before we get into the "How to Build It" section, though, lets take a closer look at the "what" and "why" of wireless network security.

Don't worry if this seems a bit complicated; it's really not. The "How to Build It" section walks you through the setup so that these basic security features can be turned on in a fairly painless way. Trust us here, though; it's a far worse pain to have people get on and take advantage of your network if you do not implement these steps.

Don't Advertise Your Wireless Network

In the previous chapter, you set up your wireless network and, as part of this, you chose a service set identifier (SSID), which is the name of your network. The first thing you can do to greatly improve the security of your wireless network is to not broadcast the SSID!

Most wireless hubs/routers have the broadcast SSID setting turned on when you take them out of the box. This feature announces the name of your network to every wireless capable computer within range. Although this makes it easy for you to connect to your network, it makes it easy for the rest of the neighborhood, too. Turn this feature off (we show you how in the later section "Stop Advertising Your Wireless Network"). In addition, remember that knowing the name of a network (even if the broadcast function is turned off) gives you the power to get on that network, so you should choose a random SSID name.

Any SSID that is easy for you to remember is probably easy to figure out, so avoid SSIDs that include your name, the word "home," the word "network," or anything related to *your name-home-wireless-network*. We suggest that you rename the SSID to something personal (but not easily guessed, or use a random combination of numbers and upper and lowercase letters. Don't worry about having to memorize this as you can just write it down and keep in a drawer or a folder where you can access it later if you need it.

Remember, however, that these steps will only keep out the nosy neighbors or low-skilled hacker. A real hacker has the means to bypass these attempts so if you are really in need of a highly secured network, call a professional.

Scramble Your Signal

Another thing you can do to improve the security of your network is to turn on encryption.

Introduction to Wireless Encryption

If you are unfamiliar with encryption, the concept is pretty simple. Remember being a kid and making up a list like this:

A	B	C	D	E	F	G	H	I	J	K	L	M	N	O	P	Q	R	S	T	U	V	W	X	Y	Z
1	2	3	4	5	6	7	8	9	10	11	12	13	14	15	16	17	18	19	20	21	22	23	24	25	26

Then your friend writes you a note like

9

12 15 22 5

12 9 19 1

You pull out your handy-dandy decoder table and translate it to "I love Lisa." Congratulations, you were doing encryption.

We are obviously oversimplifying, but encrypting your wireless network is actually a similar concept. You are going to choose a "key" for your wireless network. That key is known to both the sender and receiver, for example, your computer and the wireless router. Every time you send information between each other, you use the key to encode it, transmit it, and then use the key again to decode the message back to its real information.

In the case of wireless encryption, instead of a single letter to number translation, a mathematical formula is calculated using the original information and the key. The result is a highly encoded piece of information that is very difficult to decode without knowing the key. In general, the longer the key, the harder it is to break. Think of an encryption key like a PIN code that has 64 or 128 digits instead of 4. (How the mathematical formulas work are beyond the scope of this book. If you are interested, pick up a book on cryptography.)

There are several standards available for wireless network encryption, including the two most common ones:

■ **Wired Equivalent Privacy (WEP)**—Provides a simple and fairly effective means for keeping your information private and your network secure from those wishing to access it without your knowledge or approval.

   WEP is the most widely available encryption standard and is offered with several different key-lengths, including 64, 128, 152, and even 256 (bits). You may also see references to 40 and 104, but these are exactly the same as 64 and 128.

■ **Wi-Fi Protected Access (WPA)**—A newer and more sophisticated method of encryption. We recommend that you use WPA if it is available on your gear because it provides better protection than WEP. There are two common types of WPA: TKIP and AES, also referred to as WPA and WPA2, respectively. The AES version (known as WPA2) provides "business level" security for home networks.

The major difference between WEP and WPA is that with WEP your encryption key remains the same until you change it, while with WPA the network automatically changes the key periodically. Changing the key makes it more difficult for someone to discover the key, and even if they do the key is only useful for a very short time, because it will change again.

Some home networking products (wireless NICs and wireless routers) will support all of the encryption options, while others will support a smaller subset. This is important because both the NICs and routers need to be talking with the same encryption method and key to understand each other.

Table 11-1 summarizes the different encryption methods mentioned previously. It is important to note that these encryption methods typically can not be mixed together on the same network, so pick the highest level of security that all your wireless network devices can support.

Table 11-1   Available Wireless Encryption Methods

Encryption Method	Security	Recommendations
WPA2 (sometimes referred to as WPA-AES)	🔒🔒 🔒🔒	Adds a new encryption algorithm (AES) to WPA, which makes it even more secure. Not likely to be available for older devices.
WPA (sometimes referred to as WPA-TKIP)	🔒🔒 🔒	Adds a degree of security beyond WEP. The secret key is changed periodically to reduce the opportunity for "cracking." Typically available with a software upgrade for older devices.
128-bit WEP (sometimes referred to as 104-bit WEP)	🔒🔒	Very commonly used and offers a high degree of security. A professional hacker with enough money and time can "crack" the code, but this is secure enough for most people.
64-bit WEP (sometimes referred to as 40-bit WEP)	🔒	Minimum level of encryption. We recommend 128-bit WEP. However, if you have some older devices, they may only support 64-bit WEP.

Choosing an Encryption Key

So how do you choose an encryption key? There are two ways, one very simple, one not so simple. The simple way is to use the key generator that is built into the home networking products. (Linksys products offer this in every Wireless NIC and Router they sell.)

Essentially, you just create a "pass-phrase," that is like a password, enter it into the NIC or router, and click on a **Generate Key** button. Examples are shown later in the "How to Build It" section. The same rules apply to pass-phrase selection as passwords: Never use names, pets, or words. Make up a random series of 8 to 63 lowercase letters, uppercase letters, and numbers. Do *not* try to spell words or use clever encoded phrases such as "weLUVr2Dogs".

The key generator will take the pass-phrase and translate it into a series of numbers (0–9) and letters (A–F). Don't worry about understanding the number system, but this is the encryption key. Write down both the pass-phrase and generated key; we are going to need it several times.

VERY IMPORTANT: **We can't stress enough that anytime you create something such as an encryption pass code, password, or WEP key, you need to write it down in your notebook. If you lose it, you may have to reset the wireless router to the factory defaults and start over.**

The second way to choose an encryption key is make it up yourself using a random combination of numbers (0–9) and letters (A–F). You will need to create an exact number of numbers and letters depending on which key-length you are trying to create. For example, a 64-bit key will have 16 digits; a 128-bit key will have 32 digits; and so on.

If at all possible, use the built-in key generator from a pass-phrase. You will pull your hair out trying to create them by hand.

 A final note about WEP keys: Since the key is not rotated like with WPA, you should plan to periodically change your WEP key.

How to Build It: Securing Your Wireless Network

Here is an overview of the steps you'll go through in this section:

- Stop advertising your wireless network

- Enable wireless encryption

- Disable ad-hoc networking

Stop Advertising Your Wireless Network

By default, wireless routers are set up to "broadcast" their SSID to make it easy for NICs to "learn" the wireless network without having to know information in advance. Nice feature, bad security practice. Broadcasting the SSID of our wireless home network is entirely unnecessary. So the first step to securing our network is to shut it off.

Here's the configuration steps that we need to do:

Step 1   As we have done several times before, access the wireless router using your Internet browser.

Step 2   Click the **Wireless** tab.

Step 3   On the line labeled Wireless SSID Broadcast, checkmark **Disable** (see Figure 11-3).

Step 4   Click **Save Settings**. That's it!

There is nothing that needs to be done on the computers with wireless NICs. They should continue to be connected to the wireless network. Just by taking this simple step, you have made your wireless network relatively "invisible" to the outside world. Someone would have to know in advance the

SSID of your network (or use highly skilled hacking techniques) to be able to access it. More importantly, your wireless network will not show up on common scanner lists, like that demonstrated previously, so potential intruders will likely move on to the next easy target.

Figure 11-3   Disabling the SSID Broadcast

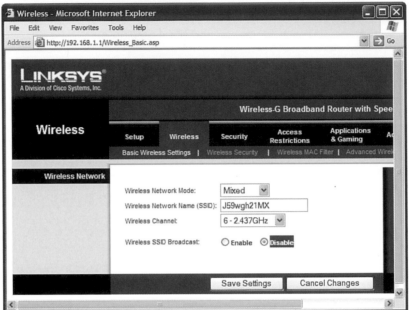

VERY IMPORTANT: As a reminder, *never* **use the default SSID that the wireless router is set up with (for Linksys products this is "linksys"). If the SSID is not being broadcast but is easily guessed by intruders, your wireless network is still vulnerable. Change the SSID to a random series of uppercase letters, lowercase letters, and numbers. Write it down.**

Enable Wireless Encryption

Even with reduced visibility to your wireless network, a more sophisticated eavesdropper still might be able to learn the SSID and try to obtain access, so you need more security.

The next step to securing the wireless network is to turn on encryption. Again, by default, encryption is disabled in wireless router products out-of-the-box. To turn on encryption, we make up a secret key (see the section, "Choosing an Encryption Key") that is known only by the wireless router and the wireless NICs in our wireless network. To communicate, this secret key must be known; otherwise, the conversation is unintelligible.

In general, both the wireless router and all wireless NICs in your network have to be running the same encryption method. However, depending on the age of the wireless product, they may not support all options listed in Table 11-1. The key then is to examine what each device (including the router) supports and use the highest level of encryption that all of them can handle. Meaning, start at the top of the table, if all your devices support WPA2, use it. If even one of the devices you plan to network does not, then you either need to replace it with one that does or go "down" in the table (for example, WPA or 128-bit WEP).

NOTE Keep in mind that even 128-bit WEP is pretty good and will defeat common intruders. WPA2 is approaching the level of wireless network security that large corporations rely on (and is implemented with much more expensive gear!). So don't necessarily be alarmed if your network "only" supports 128-bit WEP. That's reasonably difficult to defeat.

After you choose your method of encryption, you need to implement it on the wireless router and all wireless NICs in your network. Each device must be "told" what the super-secret key is to be able to join the conversation.

Enabling WEP Encryption on the Wireless Router

First, let's take an example of implementing 128-bit WEP encryption. We will pick a key-phrase of 64Gx3prY19fk2. Now, let's program the wireless router to use this WEP key.

VERY IMPORTANT: **It is good practice to always make any modifications to the settings on your wireless router from a computer that has a wired connection, not a wireless connection. This is especially true when changing the wireless settings, such as WEP encryption. If you make a mistake, you will likely cut off the limb you are standing on.**

Step 1   As we have done several times, access the wireless router using your Internet browser. Click the **Wireless** tab.

Step 2   Click the **Wireless Security** sub-tab (see Figure 11-4). On the line labeled **Wireless Security**, checkmark **Enable**. On the line labeled Security Mode, select **WEP**

Step 3   On the line labeled **Wireless Encryption Level**, select **128 bits**. On the line labeled Passphrase, enter the pass-phrase you made up. In our example, we chose 64Gx3prY19fk2 (see Figure 11-5). Click **Generate**. This translates the pass-phrase into the actual key to be used. Click **Save Settings**.

Figure 11-4   Select WEP as Your Security Mode

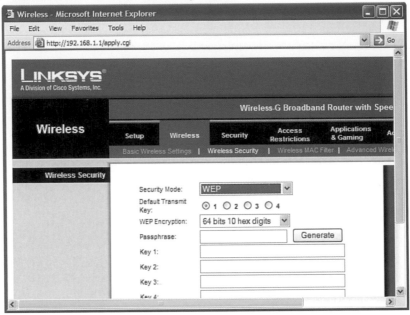

Figure 11-5   Generate the WEP Key

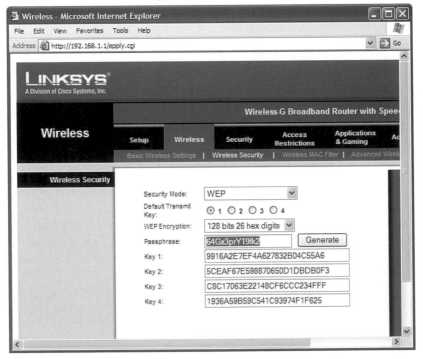

Immediately after clicking **Save Settings**, any computers that were connected with wireless NICs to the wireless router will lose connectivity. This is normal because we have just changed the way they are supposed to communicate with the wireless router, but we have not told them the super-secret password to use yet. Let's do that now for each wireless NIC.

Enabling WEP Encryption Using the NIC's Utility

In Chapter 10, "Going Wireless at Home," when we initially built the wireless network, we used two example NICs: a Windows 98 desktop computer with a USB-connected wireless NIC and a Windows XP laptop with a built-in wireless NIC. This section will demonstrate how to enable WEP encryption for the USB wireless NIC for the same computer we set up in Chapter 10. The next section will do the same for the XP laptop with built-in NIC.

Step 1   Launch the Linksys WLAN Monitor by double-clicking the ⬛ icon on the far right of your Windows taskbar. (The example shows a computer running Windows 98.)

If you don't see such an icon, try going through **Start > Programs > Instant Wireless > Instant Wireless LAN Monitor**. Notice there is no connection to the Wireless Router (in other words, Access Point). (See Figure 11-6.) Click the **Profiles** tab.

Figure 11-6   Launch the WLAN Monitor Utility

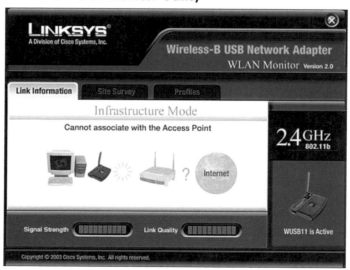

Step 2   Select the profile for the home network, and click **Edit** (see Figure 11-7).

Figure 11-7 Select and Edit the Wireless Profile

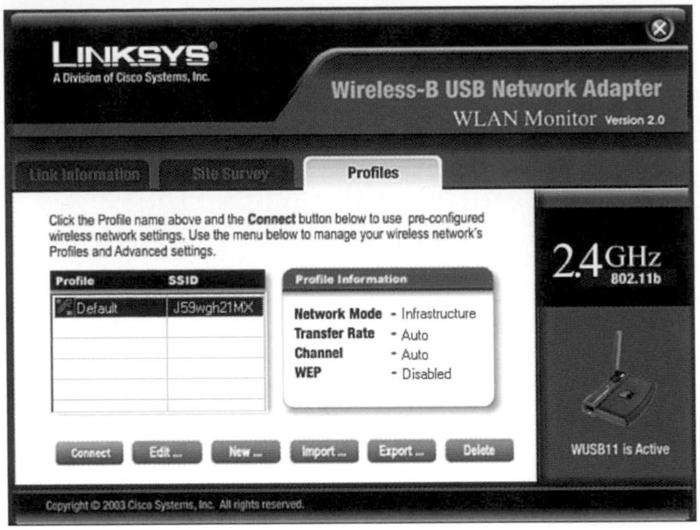

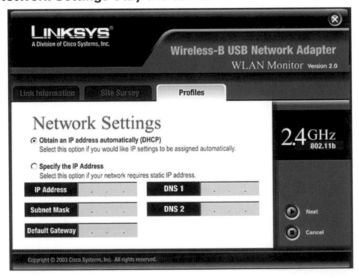

Step 3 No changes are needed to the Network Settings (see Figure 11-8). Click **Next**.

Figure 11-8 Network Settings Stay the Same

No changes are needed to the Network Mode (see Figure 11-9). Click **Next**. The Security Settings window appears.

Step 4 On the line labeled WEP, select **128-bit**. On the line labeled Passphrase, enter the passphrase you made up. In our example, we chose 64Gx3prY19fk2. (See Figure 11-10.) Leave the WEP Key and TX Key fields alone. Click **Next**.

Figure 11-9 Network Mode Stays the Same

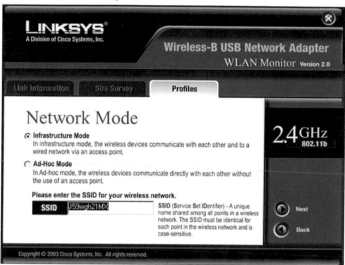

Figure 11-10 Generate the WEP Key

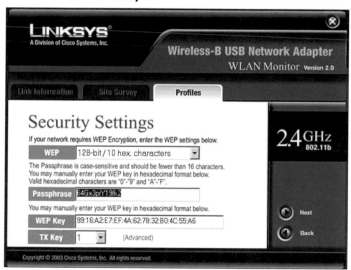

VERY IMPORTANT: **Make sure to enter the pass-phrase exactly as you did on the wireless router. Lowercase "a" is different from uppercase "A." The two keys (on the router and on the NIC) must be identical.**

Step 5 A confirmation window appears (see Figure 11-11). Double-check that WEP is set to 128-bit and click **Yes**.

Figure 11-11 Confirm the New Settings

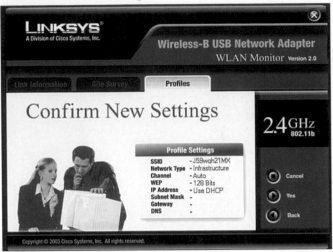

Step 6   Another confirmation window appears (see Figure 11-12). Click **Activate new settings now**.

Figure 11-12 Activate Your New Settings

Step 7   Click the **Link Information** tab. If you entered everything correctly, the Signal Strength and Link Quality should reappear as green bars (see Figure 11-13).

   NOTE The green bars may or may not be solid the whole way across. It depends on the strength of the wireless signal and how far away you are from the wireless router, much like a cell phone.

Figure 11-13 Success At Last!

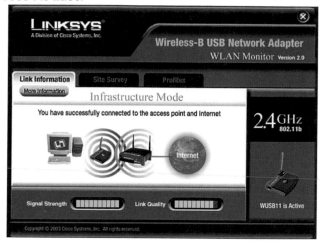

If not, you probably entered something incorrectly. See the "Troubleshooting Tips: Wireless Encryption" sidebar later in this chapter for help.

Enabling WEP Encryption Under Windows XP

Let's walk through the same thing on a built-in wireless NIC on a laptop computer running Windows XP:

Step 1   Select **Start > Control Panel > Network Connections**. Note the red X on the Wireless Network Connection icon. This is normal as we have lost communication with the wireless router. Click the **Wireless Network Connection** icon in the right section of the window, and then click **Change settings of the connection** on the left. (See Figure 11-14.)

Figure 11-14 Windows XP Network Connections

Step 2   Click the **Wireless Networks** tab (see Figure 11-15). In the Preferred Networks section, select the entry for your wireless home network and click the **Properties** button. (See Figure 11-15.)

Figure 11-15 Modify the Wireless Network Properties

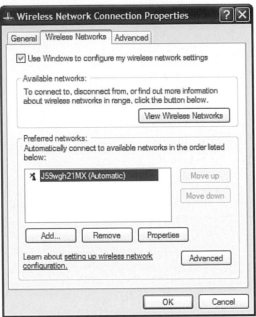

Step 3   Select **WEP** for data encryption (see Figure 11-16). In the box labeled Network key, enter the WEP key you generated using the wireless router. In our example, we chose 64Gx3prY19fk2 as the pass-phrase, which resulted in 9916A2E7EF4A627832B04C55A6 as the generated key. Enter the key, not the pass-phrase when using Windows XP to manage your wireless NICs.

VERY IMPORTANT: **Windows XP does not support pass-phrase WEP key generation. If you have Windows XP, you will have to enter the WEP key itself, not the pass-phrase. You should have the WEP key written down from when we enabled WEP encryption on the wireless router.**

If the "The key is provided for me automatically" box is checkmarked, uncheck it. (See Figure 11-16.) Click **OK**.

Figure 11-16 Enable WEP and Enter the Key

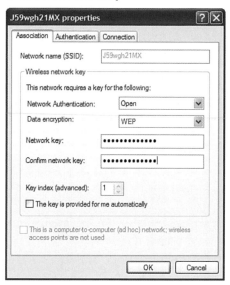

Step 4   You should now see the entry in the Preferred Networks section show a connection. (See Figure 11-17.) Click **OK**.

Figure 11-17   Communication Established Again

Step 5   Going back to the Network Connections window, the red X should now disappear from the Wireless Network Connection icon (see Figure 11-18). This means that you're all done.

Figure 11-18 Encryption Is Enabled and Working

WPA Encryption Example

To compare enabling WEP encryption to how WPA encryption is enabled, let's take an example of WPA. (This time, we will pick 8F37ahr43K as our example pass-phrase.) Enabling WPA encryption is a lot like enabling WEP encryption, except there's one additional decision we have to make: You must decide how long an encryption key will be allowed to be used before a new key is created by the network. The lower the value, the less time a hacker has to try and "crack" the key. For example, if we set the value to 1800 seconds (which is 30 minutes for you non-math majors), a key will be used for 30 minutes, and then the wireless router and wireless NIC will create a new key. If a hacker "cracks" the key within 30 minutes (which is pretty tough to do), the key will only be valuable for the remainder of the 30 minutes before it is switched to an entirely new key, and the hacker would have to start over.

Here's an example of setting up WPA, first on the wireless router:

Step 1   On the Wireless Security tab again (see Figure 11-19), select **Pre-Shared Key** on the line labeled Security Mode. (On some Linksys products, this is labeled WPA Pre-Shared Key.)

Figure 11-19 Enabling WPA Encryption on the Wireless Router

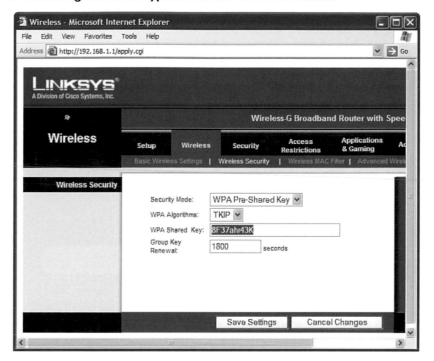

Step 2 Select either **TKIP** (for WPA 1) or **AES** (for WPA 2).

Step 3 On the line labeled WPA Shared Key, enter the pass-phrase you made up. (In our example, we chose 8F37ahr43K.)

Step 4 On the line labeled Group Key Renewal, enter the number of seconds that you want the key to be used before changing it (see Figure 11-19). We chose 1800 (which is 30 minutes) for this example. Click **Save Settings**.

With WPA, we also then need to tell the super-secret password to each of the wireless NICs so that they know how to decode the conversations with the wireless router. Here is an example for a Linksys WPC54GS Wireless-G PCMCIA laptop NIC:

Step 1 Launch the WLAN Monitor Utility, similar to the example earlier where we enabled WEP on a USB-connected wireless NIC.

Step 2 For the Encryption Method, choose **Pre-Shared Key** (see Figure 11-20). (On some Linksys products it is called WPA Pre-Shared Key.) Click **Next**.

Figure 11-20 Choose WPA Pre-Shared Key Encryption

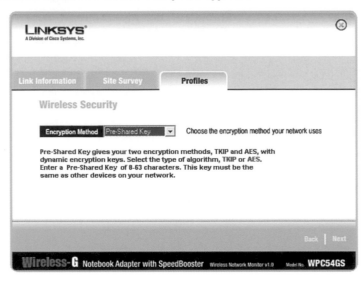

Step 3   On the line labeled Encryption, select **TKIP** (for WPA 1) or **AES** (for WPA 2). On the line labeled Passphrase, enter the key-phrase you made up (see Figure 11-21). In our example, we chose "8F37ahr43K." Click **Next**.

Figure 11-21 Enter the WPA Pass-Phrase

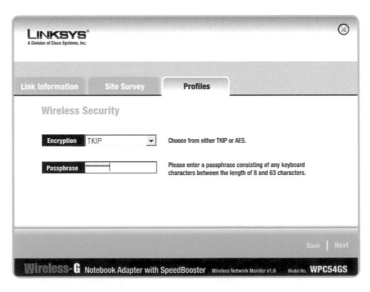

Step 4   In the confirmation window that appears, double-check that Encryption is set to Pre-Shared Key, and then click **Save** (see Figure 11-22).

Figure 11-22 Confirm New WPA Settings

Step 5 Click the **Link Information** tab. If we entered everything correctly, the Signal Strength and Link Quality should reappear as green bars (see Figure 11-23). If not, we probably entered something incorrectly.

Figure 11-23 You Are Successfully Connected!

Continue setting up each NIC with the super-secret password, each time checking to see if the connection is re-established to the wireless router.

Troubleshooting Tips: Wireless Encryption

If any of the computers do not re-establish communication, items to check are

- Make sure the encryption method chosen on both the wireless router and *all* wireless NICs is the *same*.

- Make sure the pass-phrase for WEP key generation (or WPA) is entered exactly the *same* on both the wireless router and *all* wireless NICs. The pass-phrase is case-sensitive, which means that "p" is different than "P." Take care to make sure the entered phrase matches *exactly,* including lowercase and uppercase letters.

- For Windows XP, make sure that the WEP key you entered (not the pass-phrase) exactly matches the WEP key generated.

- If all else fails, disable encryption on both the wireless router and all wireless network adapters, re-verify the connections without encryption turned on, and then start the encryption setup from scratch.

- Follow the instructions in the "Check Wireless Network Operation" section in the previous chapter.

- Read the Troubleshooting and Wireless Security chapters in the installation manuals that came with the Linksys wireless router and Linksys wireless NICs.

Disable Ad-Hoc Networking

As previously mentioned, we recommend for security reasons to operate your wireless home network in Infrastructure mode, meaning a wireless router provides the hub of the network and all wireless NICs communicate only with the hub, not to each other directly (which is called "ad-hoc").

This is a relatively low security risk, but there is a very small possibility someone sitting next to us in an airport or other public location can try to make an ad-hoc connection directly between their laptop and ours. Because we only ever plan to use our laptop computers connected to a wireless router in Infrastructure mode, we should disable ad-hoc networking mode so that it is not possible for another laptop computer to attempt to make a connection directly to our laptop at all.

Using the Linksys NIC management utilities (such as WLAN Monitor), we do this by selecting Infrastructure mode, as we have already done. When using Windows XP, the operating system manages most wireless NICs for us and an additional step is required. If your laptop or NIC does not support doing so, don't worry about it too much, but if it is supported, why not take advantage of it? Here's how to disable ad-hoc wireless networking in Windows XP for a built-in wireless NIC:

Step 1   Bring up the Properties of the wireless NIC. Click the **Wireless Networks** tab (see Figure 11-24). In the Preferred Networks section, click the **Advanced** button.

Figure 11-24 Wireless Networks Tab

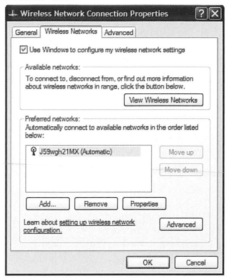

Step 2   Checkmark **Access point (infrastructure) networks only** (see Figure 11-25). Click
Close. Click **OK** (on the Properties dialog box).

Figure 11-25 Do Not Allow Ad-Hoc Connections

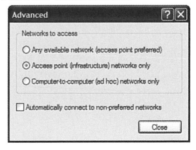

Now, if we encounter another computer with a wireless NIC that attempts to set up an ad-hoc connection, our wireless NIC will not respond to the attempt, keeping our wireless network (and laptop)
secure.

Wireless Security Checklist

Wireless networks are extremely beneficial, but you must take some simple steps to protect them.
Without taking the steps above, it's the equivalent of locking the front door, and leaving all windows

and back doors unlocked and standing open. It is pretty easy (and *so* critical) to add appropriate security. Here's a quick checklist to refer to:

❑ Change the password on the wireless router from the default (for example, "admin").

❑ Change the SSID from the default (for example, "linksys") to a random series of lowercase letters, uppercase letters, and numbers.

❑ Disable SSID "broadcast" on the wireless router.

❑ Enable WEP or WPA encryption on the wireless router and all wireless network adapters. Use the strongest encryption level that all devices support.

❑ Use a WEP or WPA "pass-phrase" that is a random series of lowercase letters, uppercase letters, and numbers.

❑ Periodically change the WEP key your network uses.

❑ Disable ad-hoc wireless networking on all network adapters (Windows XP).

Final Thoughts on Wireless Security

The steps in this chapter are really what most people need to keep their network secure in all but the most extreme cases. The fact is that your SSID can be guessed or discovered, encryption schemes can be cracked (especially WEP), and MAC addresses can be spoofed (via a method called MAC address cloning), but this takes a great deal of skill, time, and money. If you want more protection than this, you can get it, but if you are still worried about wireless security, your best solution may be to stick with a wired network.

One additional wireless security measure that can be taken that has not yet been discussed is MAC address locking. Because each wireless NIC has a unique MAC address, and we know what the MAC addresses are for all of our NICs, we could instruct the wireless router to only accept connections from our NICs and no one else's. This is called MAC address locking.

Turning on MAC address locking is not trivial and can be a bit of trouble. Remember, with every security measure enabled, you typically lose some flexibility. For example, with MAC address locking enabled, you need to change the configuration on the wireless router any time you buy a new wireless NIC or device. Also, if you have visitors who want temporary Internet access, you would have to grant them access by adding their MAC address to the permission table.

MAC address locking does provide an additional level of protection. If you want to enable it, see Appendix B, "MAC Address Locking for Wireless Security," which is located at ciscopress.com (http://www.ciscopress.com/1587201364).

One final thought for those of you who are really paranoid. We mentioned earlier that the only way to make your network 100 percent secure was to not turn it on. That was not just a snide remark on our part, and it is a viable security measure. Going to bed for the night? Leaving town for the weekend? Turn your network off. If your wireless router and your broadband modem are on the same power strip, you can completely secure you network with the flip of a switch. This will not affect anything at all on your network (unless you are running a server, of course) and gives you complete piece of mind while you are away from your network.

Wireless Away from Home

One of the biggest advantages of wireless technologies is the ability to easily take it on the road with you. Public Internet access was rare before the advent of WiFi mostly because of cost and convenience. Allowing patrons of a coffee shop, airport, or bookstore to access the Internet meant expensive cabling retrofits to put Ethernet ports in, and—even if a lease holder were willing to put up the expense—there are only so many ports you can put where patrons can get to them.

Wireless, of course, removes the need for network cabling and provides vendors the same flexibility as home users of wireless. With virtually no need to cable outside access and power, a shop owner can provide Internet access to every patron in the store and even those sitting outside. No cables and no expensive retrofits are needed. In most cases, the actual Internet access is provided by a regional or national service provider who charges individual users directly.

What Is a Hotspot?

A *hotspot* is an area served by a wireless access point to provide Internet service. Figure 12-1 shows the basic elements. A *hotspot provider* is the owner of the Internet service, and it can be a very large commercial operator, such as T-Mobile, or a small privately owned hotspot, such as a neighborhood shop. Depending on whether the service is a free or pay service (which requires a subscription), the hotspot provider may have a membership database, which contains information about who is permitted to use the service.

Figure 12-1   Hotspot and Its Basic Elements

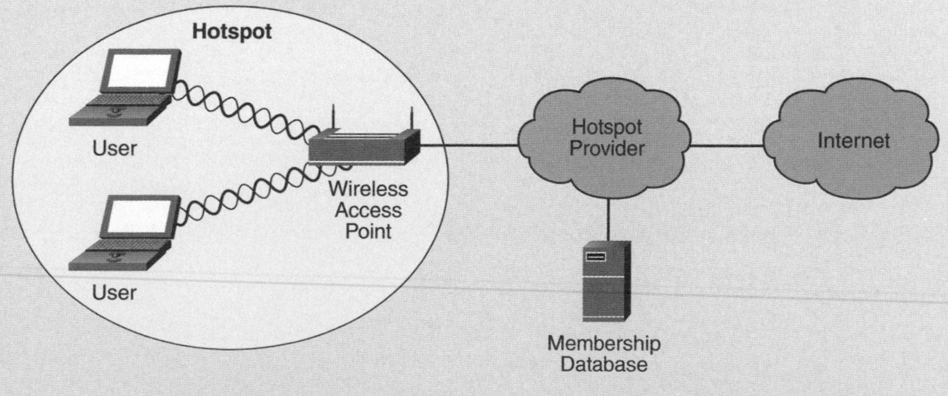

Connecting to wireless hotspot networks is similar to connecting to your wireless network at home, with some distinct differences:

- At home, we know the SSID of the wireless system; with a hotspot, we need to discover this crucial information. To make this easy, hotspots typically broadcast their SSID.

- For a home network, we want to provide access to *only* our computers, so we turn on very strong security measures. By their nature, hotspot networks are very open, using no encryption, otherwise how would we be able to connect?

- Our home network is free to access (but you still need to pay your ISP), while hotspot networks may be free or may require a membership or subscription to use.

- We know that our home network is our own and can be trusted. We have to be far more careful with hotspot networks as by their nature we may not always be certain who is operating them. Currently, no regulations exist regarding who can and cannot operate wireless hotspots.

- Having secured our home wireless network, we know the users are "friendly." On a hotspot network, we have no idea what other people are also using the hotspot, if they are "friendly," or are the source of a potential hack attack.

How to Find a Hotspot

The first step to using wireless access while you're away from home is to find a hotspot. Hotspots are relatively easy to find (and it gets easier every day). Hotspot networks are popping up in everyday places such as the corner coffee shops (Starbucks), fast-food chains (McDonald's and Schlotzsky's), book stores (Borders), and office services stores (FedEx Kinko's and UPS Store).

While traveling, hotspots are almost commonplace in airports and hotels as well. Many of these are owned or operated by a large wireless network provider, such as T-Mobile, Boingo, SBC, or Wayport.

There are a couple of different ways to find out where wireless hotspots are, including

- Doing an online search

- Downloading a list to your PC

- Scanning

If you know you will be looking for a hotspot before you leave your home or office, your best bet is to do an online search prior to heading out. There are several sites that allow you to enter an address, airport code, or even a ZIP or postal code. For example, the search tool at www.jiwire.com allows you to sort by proximity, location, or by service providers (who pay for preferred placement on the site). Here are a few sites for online hotspot searches:

- **JiWire**—http://www.jiwire.com/

- **WiFi Zone**—http://www.wi-fizone.org/

- **WiFi 411**—http://www.wifi411.com/

If you plan on using hotspots regularly, you may want to download a program to your laptop that contains a list of hotspots (regular updating is required). This can be of great benefit if you need to find a hotspot after you have already left home. A few examples of free downloadable hotspot lists are

- **Boingo**—http://www.boingo.com/download.html

- **JiWire**—http://www.jiwire.com/hotspot-locator-laptop.htm

- **T-Mobile Hotspot**—http://client.hotspot.t-mobile.com/

The T-Mobile hotspot locator will generally only show those networks that are owned or operated by T-Mobile, while the others (such as Boingo and JiWire) will generally show many more hotspots, no matter of ownership or affiliation.

A third option for finding a hotspot is to do a scan for a hotspot at the moment you need one. To do so, you need a program that will go out and "sniff" for a wireless signal. Depending on the wireless NIC that you are using in your laptop, it may come with a scan function in the NIC's management utility (the Linksys products do). Windows XP has this functionality built in to its wireless NIC management. You can use either of these, or there are also several programs available for free download with built-in scan capability, including

- **Boingo**—http://www.boingo.com/download.html

- **T-Mobile Hotspot**—http://client.hotspot.t-mobile.com/

Hotspot Options and Costs

In general, there are free sites and pay sites for hotspots:

- **Free sites** are typically offered by businesses such as hotels, coffee shops, and restaurants in order to attract customers.

- **Pay sites** are more numerous and widespread. Many business-like hotels are using them to extract an extra $10 from your wallet. Pay sites are also growing rapidly due to the entry of large wireless cell phone companies, such as T-Mobile, Cingular, SBC, and BellSouth.

Four basic types of hotspot services exist, as shown in Table 12-1.

Ironically, the initial popularity of wireless network hotspots was the idea of free Internet access. Despite attempts at an organized citizen-led mosaic of free hotspots, it seems inevitable that the sizeable market opportunity is just too attractive for the traditional telecommunications companies to pass up. The upside is that to make money, these companies will invest the cash to put hotspots everywhere you need them. Soon, any place that people can stand or sit for more than 60 seconds will be a hotspot.

One growing trend worth mentioning is many local communities are starting to invest in citywide wireless hotspot networks. Most rolling out have two aims: provide high-speed access for public sector agencies such as police, fire, and so on, and provide access to citizens themselves.

If you fall into the category of a regular hotspot user, and you can either pick the hotspot location where your preferred provider has an access point, or you can always access from the same locations (such as your local airport), your best bet may be to get a monthly or annual subscription. If you are a casual hotspotter, you will probably be better off with a per-day or other pay-per-use option.

Table 12-1   Types of Wireless Hotspot Services

Type	What Are They?	Where Are They Found?	Examples
Free	A free connect-and-go hotspot service, growing rare these days.	Small neighborhood businesses, public libraries; provided to attract customers	Public library, local communities (increasing trend)
Free with Registration	It's free, but you provide your name, address, e-mail address, and maybe answer a survey.	Hotels, coffee shops, restaurants; provided to attract customers	Schlotzsky's Deli, Bear Rock Cafe, Panera Bread, Holiday Inn Express
Subscription	You pay a monthly, annual, or per-usage fee to use the service, much like your cell phone.	Hotels, airports, coffee shops, restaurants, business service shops, planes (soon)	T-Mobile (at Starbucks, Borders, Kinkos), SBC (at UPS Store), Wayport (airports, McDonald's), Cingular (airports)
Roaming	Same as subscription service, except you are roaming on another provider who has an agreement with your provider.	Same as subscription	Same as subscription

NOTE Accessing a network that was unintentionally left open (such as your neighbor's) isn't very nice. On the other hand, there are many "unwired city" initiatives where local governments are providing free access. It's no problem to use free access when it is made available on purpose, but not when someone just forgot to set up security. It's usually easy to tell the difference.

How to Build It: Using Wireless Hotspots

Here's a brief overview of the steps we will go through:

- Discover and connect to a hotspot

- Pass the hotspot membership test

Discover and Connect to a Hotspot

As we discussed earlier, because hotspot locations want to advertise their willingness to accept your business, they broadcast their SSID and do not require an encryption key to connect. But you do need to discover or be told what the SSID is for the hotspot so that you can tell your wireless NIC how to connect to it.

There are several methods that can be used to discover the hotspot's SSID, depending on the Windows operating system you use, the capabilities of the wireless NIC in your laptop computer, and the hotspot service to which you want to connect. In general, Windows XP manages wireless NICs, so the ability to detect hotspots is built in to the operating system. For Windows 98, 2000, and Me, generally the manufacturer of the wireless NIC supplies a software program that manages the adapter.

Let's start with an example under Windows 2000 and a Linksys WPC54GS Wireless NIC. The following steps show how to find and connect to a hotspot:

Step 1   Launch the WLAN Monitor Utility by double-clicking the icon on the desktop or through **Start** > **Programs** > **Linksys** > **Wireless Notebook Adapter**. Click the **Site Survey** tab (see Figure 12-2). Click the **Refresh** button to perform a survey of what wireless networks are available.

Figure 12-2   Perform a Site Survey

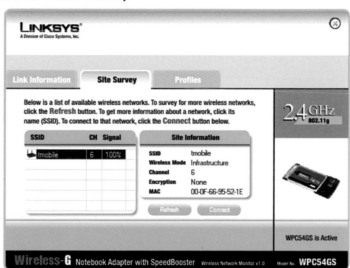

Step 2   Click the hotspot that you wish to connect to. In our example, we found a T-Mobile hotspot. Click **Connect**. You should see the connection made to the hotspot (Signal Strength and Signal Quality show green) (see Figure 12-3).

Step 3   You can save this hotspot into your profiles so the next time you use it, connection happens automatically. Click **More Information** > **Save to Profile** (see Figure 12-4).

Figure 12-3   Successful Connection to Hotspot

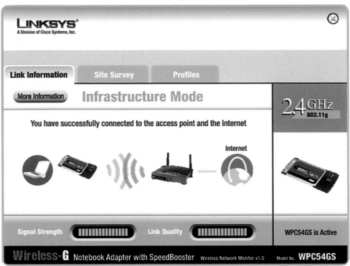

Figure 12-4   Save the Hotspot in Your Profile

NOTE A profile is a way to store information that can be used in the future to remember how to connect to the hotspot (or another wireless network). Think of a profile like adding a new key to your keychain to have access to a new lock. Information stored in a profile includes the SSID, encryption method (for example, WEP or WPA), and encryption key (although for hotspots it will usually just be the SSID).

Step 4   A dialog appears asking for a name for the new profile (see Figure 12-5). Enter a description you will remember, and click **OK**.

Figure 12-5   Enter a Name for the New Profile

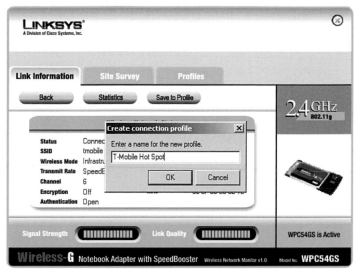

Step 5   The new profile just created will now appear in the Profiles list (see Figure 12-6). Now whenever you encounter a hotspot with this profile, the wireless network adapter will automatically connect to it.

Figure 12-6   New Profile Is Listed

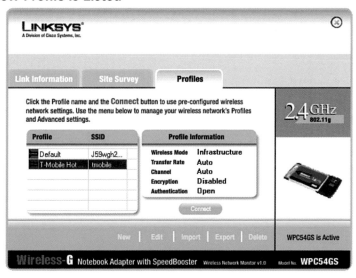

Let's walk through the same thing on a built-in wireless NIC on a laptop computer running Windows XP:

Step 1   Select **Start > Control Panel > Network Connections**. Note the red X on the Wireless Network Connection icon. This is normal as we have not yet established a connection to the wireless hotspot network.

Click the **Wireless Network Connection** icon in the right section of the window, and then click **View available wireless networks** on the left. (See Figure 12-7.)

Figure 12-7   Perform a Site Survey (with Windows XP)

Step 2   Click the hotspot that you want to connect to ("tmobile" in this example), and click **Connect** (see Figure 12-8).

Figure 12-8   Select an Available Hotspot

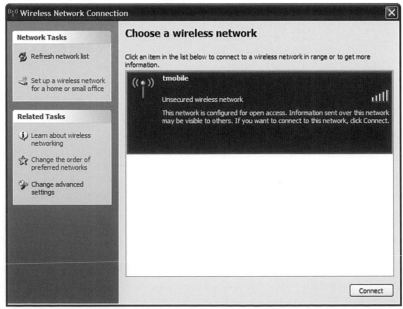

You may have to checkmark **Allow me to connect to the selected wireless network even though it is not secure**. This is normal because the hotspot is not running encryption such as WEP or WPA.

Step 3   Back on the Wireless Network Connection window, you can verify you are connected successfully to the hotspot. (See Figure 12-9.)

Figure 12-9   Successful Connection to the Hotspot

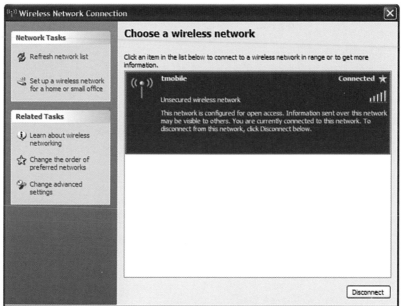

Step 4   Windows XP typically adds the hotspot to the Preferred Networks list upon successful connection. To check this, on the Network Connections window, click **Change settings for this connection** > **Wireless Networks**. You should see the hotspot in the Preferred Networks section (see Figure 12-10). Click **OK**.

A third possibility, which can generally be used on any of the Windows operating systems versions (98, 2000, Me, XP), is to use a Connection Manager software program that is provided by the hotspot system provider we have a membership with. For example, if you subscribed to a T-Mobile or Boingo hotspot service, using the provided Connection Manager software can make location and connection to hotspots literally just a click of a button. Boingo Wireless operates through a collaboration of many different hotspot providers who choose to affiliate with Boingo Wireless and list their hotspots in the Boingo database. Boingo provides a Connection Manager program (see Figure 12-11).

Figure 12-10 Verify Hotspot Is Added to Preferred Networks

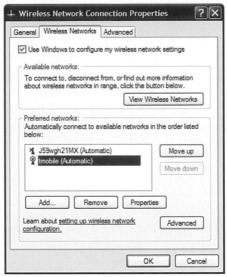

Figure 12-11 Boingo Connection Manager Program

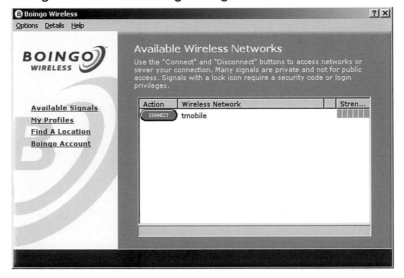

The Boingo application automatically detects wireless hotspots you encounter, and to connect, you simply click the **Connect** button for the hotspot network you choose. Boingo also provides a searchable database of hotspot locations. The Boingo application can be used whether you have a paid membership with Boingo, or it can also be used for free (limited functionality) as a general Connection Manager application, whether you are connecting to Boingo-affiliated hotspots or someone else's.

Pass the Hotspot Membership Test

At this point, you have accomplished getting your laptop to talk properly with the wireless hotspot access point. But you are not yet to the point of being able to access the Internet. The next step is the *membership test*.

Whether using a free site or pay site, the membership test is almost always started the same way: by launching your Internet Browser. When your browser first attempts to access the Internet, you will be re-directed to the membership page for that service. For free services, this web page may ask you to fill out some information about yourself and possibly hit you with a quick survey. For pay services, you typically must enter your user ID and password to prove that you have a valid subscription to their service.

The following is an example of using the hotspot service at a Bear Rock Cafe. In this example, access is free with registration. The registration process lets you create a user ID and password for easy repeat access in the future:

Step 1 Use your chosen Connection Manager program to connect to the hotspot. In this example, we used the Boingo free Connection Manager (see Figure 12-12). We can see that the SSID is wiresnap.

Figure 12-12 Using Boingo to Connect to the Hotspot

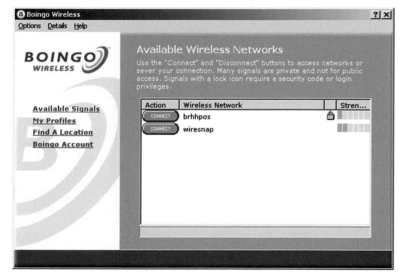

Step 2 Launch your Internet browser (such as Internet Explorer) and type in any web page address (see Figure 12-13).

Figure 12-13 Launch Internet Browser to Trigger the Redirect

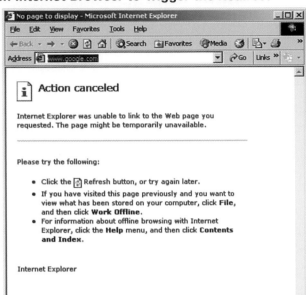

Step 3   You are redirected to the membership test page, prompting for the user ID and password (see Figure 12-14).

Figure 12-14 Hotspot Membership Login Page

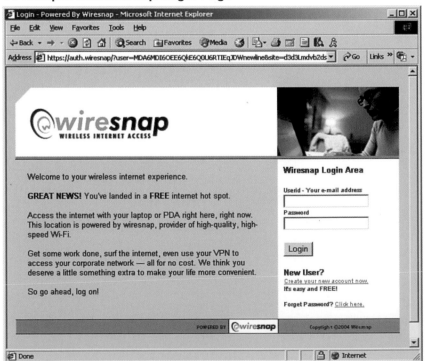

If you have already registered previously, you can enter the user ID and password and immediately login. If you have not already registered previously, you can click the **New User** button. To register for a free account, you provide your name, address, e-mail address, and age. You also create a user ID and password.

After logging in to the free service, you can then use the Internet.

The following is another example of using the hotspot service at a Borders store. In this example, T-Mobile owns and operates the Borders hotspots as a pay subscription service. (This example assumes you have already signed up for service with T-Mobile.)

 NOTE It is never a good idea to sign up for a new hotspot service over the hotspot. Remember, you are in a public location on a public network, and you do not want anyone to obtain your personal information or credit card number. Plan in advance where you are going, what hotspots you may want to use, and sign up from home or office.

Step 1   The Connection Manager program will indicate (with bars of service, much like a cell phone) when there is a T-Mobile hotspot in range.

Click **Connect**.

Figure 12-15 T-Mobile Connection Manager

Step 2   Launch your Internet browser (such as Internet Explorer) (see Figure 12-16) and type in any web page address.

Step 3   You are redirected to the membership test page, prompting for the T-Mobile login credentials (see Figure 12-17). Enter the user ID and password that you chose when you signed up for a T-Mobile HotSpot account.

Figure 12-16 Launch Your Internet Browser

Figure 12-17 T-Mobile Login Page

Step 4   A login confirmation box appears. Shrink this down to your taskbar and save it.

When you are ready to logoff, go back to this little box and click **Log off** or simply click **Disconnect** on the main T-Mobile Connection Manager dialog.

After you pass the membership test, you can finally move on to using the Internet. Make sure to read the following section, "What Not to Do When Using a Hotspot," for some important security tips.

What Not to Do When Using a Hotspot

Okay, so you never thought you would actually need to use a hotspot when you suddenly find that you need to take a cross country trip, or you go to visit family for a week and to your horror discover that they do not have broadband access in their home. We discuss how to deal with this so-called family of yours later, but in the mean time, you need to find a hotspot and reconnect.

Unfortunately for many people, this is pretty much how they start using hotspots, and it leaves them extremely vulnerable. Hotspots are convenient and kind of cool in a nerdy way, but you must protect yourself if you are going to use what is, by design, a very open and unsecure medium. Unlike a home or business network, a hotspot is wide open to allow maximum use through the provider's network. In this environment, security is second to access, so you need to take some precautions. Using a hotspot is a bit like being out in public at a bar: You don't go waving your credit card around, speaking loudly about a confidential topic, or handing out spare keys to your house.

Keep these common sense things in mind when using hotspots:

- Be aware of what hotspot you are connecting to. Use known, reputable services like those listed previously. Sometimes you get what you pay for; free sites are very attractive, but if they are provided by individuals and not businesses, you should eye these with great suspicion.

- It is *not* a good idea to be doing online shopping and entering your credit card information into websites over a hotspot connection.

- Exercise caution when reading e-mail, using instant messaging programs (chat), and other forms of personal communication. Assume everything you read or type might be read by others sitting next to you.

- If you use a pay hotspot service, change the password to your account frequently. Someone can grab the user ID and password "off the air," and then use your subscription on your dime.

- Turn off ad-hoc wireless networking. Chapter 11 discusses how to do this.

- If you have the need to use hotspots frequently, ask your provider about using a Virtual Private Network (VPN) software program. These programs encrypt all communications between your laptop, through the hotspot access point, and up to the Internet. Boingo Wireless provides a VPN service included with a pay subscription. Eventually, all service providers should do the same.

- If you already have access to a VPN service through your employer, use it!

- Make sure your laptop is running a Personal Firewall program (such as ZoneAlarm) and an antivirus program (such as Norton AntiVirus, McAfee VirusScan, Trend Micro PC-cillin). (Part IV, "Security of Home Networks," discusses security, including the use of some of these programs, in more detail.)

- When you use a hotspot, keep in mind that there are bad guys out there, so keep your guard up. When you are typing passwords, take a quick look around to make sure no one is looking over your shoulder (or over your fingers).

- Turn off all file sharing while using your computer in a public place. In the off chance that someone does access your computer, don't make it easy on them by sharing your entire C: drive. (You should never do this anywhere, ever.)

 Geek Squad One of the biggest security issues with PCs is laptop theft. If you are in a public place, treat your PC the same way you treat your wallet. Don't walk away from it, or it will walk away from you.

Following these simple steps should keep you plenty safe while using public hotspots, especially because the vast majority of folks don't do this, and hackers hit the easy targets first. We do realize that some of this might be a pain, but if you have ever lost data on a hard drive, or had your identity stolen (and had to deal with fixing your credit), you know that the pain of prevention is far, far less than the pain of getting burned by a hacker or thief.

So go out there and surf the Internet while sipping a cappuccino-coffee-hot milk thingy, you hip thing you—but protect yourself and your PC first.

From the Geek Squad Files

Wireless networking is a great convenience and for some people (roughly 45 percent of new users) its availability was the reason for getting access or at least switching to a high-speed connection. All knowledge from the known universe has been available for years on the Internet and what made it attractive to almost half of you out there was the ability to access it while on the toilet. Go figure.

As convenient as using wireless is, it does add a layer of complexity to your computing experience and we do see a few instances where people are confused and overwhelmed by it all. Here is a short list of things to think about. Don't be embarrassed if you have done one or more of these, you are not alone:

- Just because it says wireless Internet on the box of the router you buy does not mean you automatically get Internet access. You must subscribe to Internet service first.

- If you unplug the wireless router and put it in your closet, it is no longer functional.

- Putting the router in the corner of a concrete walled basement will severely limit the range of your wireless network. Read the box the router comes in to find out what the range is and then cut that in half. The numbers on the box are usually determined in an "ideal environment," which we have never actually seen in the field.

- Cat urine will destroy a router. This is rarely disclosed by the manufactures, who in all fairness probably did not assume that their products would be subjected to that and similar harsh environments, but we see it all the time. Treat your computer equipment just like you treat your television and you should get the same lifetime and repair costs.

- You do not always have to secure your router, and some people choose not to, allowing all their neighbors to have free Internet access. However, most people don't intend to provide a wide-open wireless system for themselves and all their neighbors. They simply are not aware they are doing so or have no idea what to do about it. It takes less than 2 minutes to provide better-than-average security to a wireless system, and most people never even bother. Think of this way: A $10 fire extinguisher can prevent a million-dollar home from burning to the ground, but only if it's in your house before the fire starts.

One final thought on wireless security: Many of our customers are surprised that their wireless systems are not secure because they "already have a firewall." Firewalls only prevent someone on the "outside" from getting "in." With a wide open wireless network, everyone within the broadcast range of the router is already "in." The firewall does not help for this. Know what you are getting into. If you still have questions, call the Geek Squad for help.

Protecting Your Network from Intruders

One of the characteristics of hight-speed broadband is that it is always on. Unlike dialup, your modem (unless it's physically turned off) is always connected and communicating with the Internet service provider (ISP). Although this is pretty convenient, it also means that your computer can be contacted, and possibly taken over by someone also connected to the Internet. To prevent others from gaining access to your network, in this part of the book, we learn how to turn on several important security tools, including a firewall, antivirus software, anti-adware/spyware, and several other tools to address numerous other security vulnerabilities of your computer network.

Although we primarily discuss firewalls in this chapter, it's helpful to introduce a number of computer and network protection options that we'll discuss throughout the rest of the book. So you can understand what kinds of threats exist and what tools are available for protection, here's a quick overview of the protective tools:

- **Firewall**—Simple firewalls block certain types of traffic. More sophisticated "stateful packet inspection" firewalls have the ability to tell good network traffic from malicious traffic based on very advanced programs (discussed in this chapter).

- **Personal Firewall**—Personal firewalls usually refer to a software firewall program that runs on a computer. Firewall without the word "personal" usually refers to a firewall device that is a "box" separate from the computer (discussed in this chapter).

- **Antivirus**—Viruses are malicious software programs that infect computers. Antivirus software are programs that run on computers to prevent them from catching viruses and Trojan horses (discussed much more in Chapter 15, "Viruses and Other Malicious Software").

- **Spam Blocking**—Spam is any e-mail you receive unsolicited, much like the thousands of junk advertisements you get in your house mailbox. Spam blockers try and help you filter your e-mail so that you only get the e-mail you want (discussed much more in Chapter 16, "Other Vulnerabilities [Spam, Cookies, Pop-Ups, Spyware, and Scams]").

- **Scam Blocking**—"Phishing" (pronounced *fishing*) is a type of scam (that arrives as spam) trying to trick you into going to a fake website and typing in your personal information, such as credit card numbers. Scam blockers try and prevent you from scams like phishing (discussed much more in Chapter 16).

Networking Nasties

Inside

Inside Jobs

Most security breeches originate inside the network that is under attack. Jobs include such things as password stealing (which can then be used or sold), industrial espionage, disgruntled employees looking to cause harm to their employers, or simple misuse.

Many of these security breeches can be thwarted by sound policy enforcement and observant employees who guard their passwords and PCs.

Viruses and Worms

Viruses and worms are self-replicating programs or code fragments that attach themselves to other programs (viruses) or machines (worms).

Both viruses and worms usually attempt to shut down networks by flooding them with massive amounts of bogus traffic, usually through e-mail.

Spyware

Spyware (SW) is hidden in programs such as Internet browsers. The SW keeps track of all site visits and reports back to privately owned research firms. Spyware can be dangerous because it can collect personal information that is then sold and resold to a variety of companies.

Open Access Points

Open access points are wireless routers that allow anyone within range of the router to get network access. In many cases, the name of the router is broadcast so that even a casual user (one with no hacking skills at all) can easily gain access. In businesses, these are called "rogue APs" and are typically set up by well-meaning employees who are not aware of the security risks they present.

Trojan Horses

This is the leading cause of all break ins. Trojan horses are attached to other programs. When downloaded, the hacked SW kicks off a virus, password gobbler, or remote-control SW that gives the hacker control of the PC.

Networking Natsies

Outside

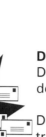

Denial of Service
Denial-of-service (DoS) attacks provide a means for bringing down a network without having to gain internal access.

DoS attacks work by flooding the access routers with bogus traffic (can be e-mail or TCP packets). Distributed DoS (DDoS) attacks are coordinated DoS attacks from multiple sources. DDOS is more difficult to block because the attacker uses multiple source IP addresses that are hard to keep track of.

Anarchists, Crackers, and Kiddies
So who are these people and why are they attacking your network?

Anarchists are people who just like to break stuff. They will usually exploit any target of opportunity.

Crackers are hobbyists or professionals who break passwords, develop Trojan horses, or other SW (called warez). They either use the SW themselves (for bragging rights) or sell it for profit.

Script kiddies are hacker wannabes. They have no real hacker skills, so they buy or download warez that they launch.

Sniffing/Spoofing
Sniffing refers to the act of intercepting TCP packets. This can be simple eavesdropping or something more sinister.

Spoofing is the act of sending an illegitimate packet with an expected ACK, which can be guessed, predicted, or obtained by snooping.

- **Spyware/Adware Blocking**—Spyware and Adware are software programs that are dropped onto your computer when you visit a website or download free stuff from the Internet. They track things like websites you visit or purchases you make and send data back to the originator. Spyware and Adware blockers try and prevent these little gifts from being put on your computer (discussed much more in Chapter 16).

- **Pop-Up Blocking**—Pop-ups are those annoying windows that appear out of nowhere onto your computer screen when you browse a website. Pop-up blockers aim to intercept these little devils and keep them from appearing on your screen (discussed much more in Chapter 16).

- **Parental Control**—The Internet is a wide open playground containing sites for everything from beloved purple stuffed dinosaurs to graphic pornography. Parental control lets you limit what your kids have access to on the Internet (discussed more in Chapter 17, "Keeping Your Family Safe on the Internet").

Introduction to Security Software

Implementing security for networks is kind of like trying to stop someone from stealing your DVD player out of your house. It's important to put as many safeguards and roadblocks between your DVD player and the guy who wants to steal it: locks on the doors and windows, an alarm system, a gated community, regular police patrols, and so on. In this section, you are going to get the benefit of what has taken many Fortune 1000 companies years (and literally billions of dollars) to learn about securing their networks: Layers are good.

Lines of Defense

Your ISP is your first line of defense. When you are selecting your high-speed broadband provider, consider the amount of integrated security they provide as part of your subscription. Many are now bundling in some level of protection. One unique offering worth pointing out is TotalAccess, a security offering from EarthLink, which has a built-in scam blocker, targeting protection against "phishing" (described in Chapter 16) schemes. Because each service provider is unique, it's not possible to cover all of them here, so we advise you to talk to your service provider directly about their role in your security.

The second line of defense is your home wireless router (or wired). Because the router is essentially the "heart" of your home network (brain is probably a stretch), it can offer a significant level of protection. It knows more information about your home network than the ISP, so it also knows better what is legitimate network traffic versus malicious. Expect security functionality to grow tremendously in the wireless router in the next couple of years. There is much untapped potential, for example, for the router to participate in antivirus, parental control, and scam blocking (you will learn much more about these terms as we move through this chapter and the others in Part IV, "Security of Home Networks").

Finally, the computers on your network are the final line of defense. After all, they are the bank vault holding your personal information, credit card numbers, as well as the computer itself, which can be compromised and used to attack other networks. Security products for the computer have gotten very sophisticated, protecting against a whole suite of threats.

Security Software "Bundles"

Before we rush into purchasing a whole collection of security programs, it's first helpful to take a look at what packages are available for securing your computers.

Previously, consumers like yourself had to piece together different solutions for each of these problems separately, and you got very little help from either your service provider or home networking equipment. Today, it is much easier. Not only are comprehensive solutions available on computers that provide protection against the vast majority of threats, help is also arising in the service provider and network itself.

For solving our computer security issues, there are several really great products for sale that are known as security "bundles," which provide a whole suite of tools to combat the threats listed previously. Table 14-1 compares several of these comprehensive solutions (because of heavy competition and technology advances, check with the vendors for the latest).

Table 14-1   Comparison of Security Software "Bundles"

Security Product Bundles	Personal Firewall	Antivirus	Spam Blocker	Scam Blocker	Spyware / Adware Blocker	Pop-Up Blocker	Parental Control
McAfee Internet Security Suite www.macafee.com	✓	✓	✓		✓	✓	✓
Symantec Norton Internet Security 2005 www.symantec.com	✓	✓	✓		✓	✓	✓
Trend Micro PC-cillin Internet Security www.trendmicro.com	✓	✓	✓		✓		✓
ZoneAlarm Security Suite www.zonealarm.com	✓	✓			✓	✓	✓

All these security "bundles" in Table 14-1 provide similar protection. You purchase the bundle at a one-time cost, and then pay an annual subscription fee. Expect to pay around $50–60 for the bundle, and another $20–60 for the annual subscription, and this cost is per computer on your network.

 GEEK SQUAD   At first look, it seems like an expensive proposition. We wish we could say that you don't really need these products, but unfortunately, because of the open nature of the Internet and the criminal elements in our society who are currently exploiting it, you need them. If you don't want to purchase these fine products, that's certainly your choice. But we can't stress enough the importance of protecting yourself against these types of security threats in one way or another.

The reason there is a subscription fee is that several of these security services, namely antivirus, spam blocker, and parental control rely on having a list of known viruses, spam sources, and adult-rated websites, respectively. These lists must be updated regularly and all these product vendors employ hundreds of people whose job it is to keep these lists current as the Internet changes and evolves. Each of these products has a built-in mechanism to go fetch the latest lists often.

All in all, we feel that for simplicity, insuring you always having the latest and greatest protection, and comprehensive coverage, we *highly* recommend you invest in one of these products or products like them. They truly are a good value for your money. By the way, it's getting more common for a trial version of one of these products to be pre-installed on any computer you purchase. As far as which product to choose, they all offer fairly equivalent functionality.

The TrendMicro product did not provide (at the time of this writing) a vendor-provided list for adult websites and instead expects you to manually type in websites to block. This is not really practical and we are quite certain by the time you pluck this book from the store shelf, this will no longer be the case. (But check to be sure.) McAfee seemed to offer the most robust user interface, with very straightforward defaults, visuals, and some pretty neat bells and whistles.

The bottom line: You need a security bundle, so compare prices, compare threats combated, and choose one or two. Then download a trial version, install it, and try it out. In the rest of this chapter and subsequent chapters in Part IV, we will show examples of how each of these security bundles handles the various security threats, which also may help you to choose, so read on.

 GEEK SQUAD Some people tend to over-buy on security, like installing every software firewall they can get their hands on, and then wonder why they can't get on the Internet. It's important to have a balance of usability and security.

Firewalls

A firewall protects a personal or corporate network from the outside world (the Internet). A firewall serves as a lock on the front (and back) door to your network so that not just anyone can get to the personal information stored on your network computers or servers. Firewalls were once primarily a corporate device and technology, but the wide available of "always on" Internet has made them a necessity for home networks.

How Firewalls Work

A firewall is typically placed between the Internet and the home network devices (routers and computers). The side of the firewall that connects to the Internet is the *dirty* side (which means that the traffic cannot be trusted), and the side of the firewall that connects to the home network is the *clean* side (the traffic can be trusted). A firewall has two primary functions:

- **Proxy**—The proxy function provides "perimeter security" by allowing you to communicate with the outside world through an intermediary device so that no one from the outside ever has direct contact with your computers.

- **Filtering**—The filter function provides traffic inspection and allows or denies traffic based on user criteria. This filtering can be set up to inspect Internet traffic going in either direction.

What Firewalls Protect You From

Here are some examples of the types of traffic a firewall can protect you from:

- **Passive Eavesdropping**—Attackers can use packet capture programs to glean sensitive information or steal username/password combinations.

- **IP Address Spoofing**—An attacker pretends to be a trusted computer by using the IP address within the accepted range of internal IP addresses.

- **Port Scans**—Servers "listen" for traffic on different ports. (A port in this case is a logical port on your computer assigned to different types of web traffic). Attackers find ways to infiltrate servers through individual server ports.

- **Denial-of-Service (DoS) Attack**—The attacker attempts to block valid users from accessing services by creating floods of bogus traffic. The additional traffic overwhelms the network.

- **Application-Layer Attack**—These attacks exploit the weaknesses of certain applications (such as Microsoft Outlook Express) to gain access to a network.

 GEEK SQUAD If you are walking down a dark alley at night alone, you up the odds of something happening to you. However, if you are walking down an alley with a professional body builder, you have less of a chance of something happening, but it could still happen. Same goes for a firewall; you are protected but something can still happen, it's not the end-all protection.

In general, firewalls observe traffic flowing through them and try to prevent malicious messages and transactions. In addition, firewalls also watch for certain known attack types to thwart them.

Another function firewalls can perform is to restrict access to the Internet, to the network, or to other resources. For example, a spyware program could attempt to access the Internet and be denied access because it has not been authorized through the firewall.

VERY IMPORTANT: **Stateful packet inspection (SPI) firewalls are preferred because they can observe whole protocols between your computer and the Internet and are able to tell when some part of the protocol is abnormal, out of order, or otherwise suspicious. The SPI firewall can then take action against the potentially malicious messages being transmitted.**

Firewall

Firewalls can protect your network from numerous attacks.

The three main types of traffic are described below. Your firewall will treat each of these traffic types differently.

To be safe, completely lock down your system, which means that all forms of externally initiated traffic should be blocked unless you have a specific reason to allow the traffic (for example, if you run a web server).

What to Do?
After you decide on what types of traffic to allow and what types of traffic to deny, you can set your firewall up to provide the most appropriate level of protection. You can also set up notifications if anyone attempts to access your network. Here are the typical options for a firewall:

Allow: Traffic that you specify is allowed through the firewall without further action.
Block: Some types of traffic are simply blocked and no further action is taken.
Block and notify: You can set up some firewalls so that you are notified when someone attempts to access your network. If you think that the attempts are illegal attempts to hack into your network, you can take action (such as notifying your service provider).

**Clean Net
(Your Home Network)**

Wireless Router

**Dirty Net
(The Internet)**

www.mywebsite.com

Traffic Flooding
Certain types of traffic are intended to shut down a router by creating more traffic than the router can process. One common version of this attack is called a denial-of-service (DOS) attack. (Think of this attack as making the router "drink from a fire hose.") DOS attacks can be mitigated by blocking traffic from certain IP addresses.

Legitimate Traffic
Legitimate traffic is typically confined to information that comes directly in response to a request originated inside a user's network, such as communication with a web site. The firewall determines both the protocol (HTTP for web traffic) and the originator. It is best to restrict everything but e-mail and user-originated web traffic to avoid becoming vulnerable. If you find that you need to allow different types of traffic, allow them on an "as needed" basis.

Remote Log-In Attempt
The biggest concern that you should have is a hacker gaining remote access and control of your network. This is especially a concern with "always on" connections, such cable or DSL. Hackers have numerous ways to attempt this, and firewalls protect against most attempts. As with wireless security, don't make it easy on the bad guys; make sure that your network is not wide open. Set up your firewall so that it blocks all attempts at remote login or protocols, such as FTP, that allows outsiders to get in. Only turn on these features if you specifically know that you need to use them, and then make sure you have a strong password that you change often.

Hiding Your Network Addresses

In Chapter 2, "Networking Fundamentals, "we mentioned that we were running out of usable IP addresses and the solution was Dynamic Host Configuration Protocol (DHCP). It turns out that DHCP can only do so much for us, especially given we've shown you how to add three, four, or five devices to your network (all requiring an IP address). Because your ISP will only give you one address, we need to find a way to make your one address work for many devices.

There are two methods for making a single IP address look like more than one, and both methods have the added advantage of hiding your real IP address from the outside world. This is good news because if a hacker does not know your "real" IP address, your PC is much harder to access and control. The two methods are Network Address Translation (NAT) and Port Address Translation (PAT)

NAT and PAT both work by using two different sets of IP addresses: The "outside" IP address is assigned by your ISP and is permanent. The "inside" IP address is allocated by you and can be changed as often as you like.

NAT and PAT are similar types of address translators. They both work by mapping an address (or port number) on your home network with an address (or port number) at your ISP. The ISP is unaware of your home network addresses. Your computers are unaware of your ISP addresses. The device providing the NAT/PAT service is the only one who knows both sides and acts as a translator.

This process accomplishes two things: One, it conserves IP addresses. Two, it provides you protection from outsiders knowing what your real IP addresses are. Efficiency and security, it's hard to beat that.

Now here is the really good news. To make this work, you do not need to do much at all. Your wired or wireless router does it for you.

NOTE Most wired or wireless routers will say they perform "NAT." These routers will almost always perform both NAT and PAT, although the box will rarely say it is a "PAT router." Don't go on a wild goose chase for a PAT router.

NOTE The reason for including this in this section is to demonstrate yet another benefit of using a router approach for the home network. If we have one (or more) computers directly connected to the Internet, it is less secure as we may not have our IP addresses "hidden."

How to Build It:
Protecting Your Network from Intruders

Here's a brief overview of the steps we will go through to protect your network from intruders:

- Turn on a firewall in the router

- Install a personal firewall in each computer

- Install a personal firewall in each computer. There are several possibilities including:

    — Install a professional firewall program (purchase)

    — Install a free personal firewall program (download)

    — Enabling the Windows firewall (built-in, starting with XP SP2)

- Keeping Windows security up to date

Turning on a Firewall in the Router

The router in your home network plays an important role in the security of your network. One of the most important functions it provides is a firewall. If possible, verify that the wireless router you purchase contains a stateful packet inspection (SPI) firewall. (Nearly all new Linksys wireless Routers have the SPI firewall included.)

Enabling the firewall functionality is pretty easy:

Step 1   Using your browser (for example, Internet Explorer), access the router like you have done in previous chapters. Click the **Security** tab.

Step 2   Make sure to checkmark **Enable** for Firewall Protection (see Figure 14-1). This enables the firewall (whether SPI or non-SPI). Click **Save Settings**.

Figure 14-1   Turn on the Firewall in the Router

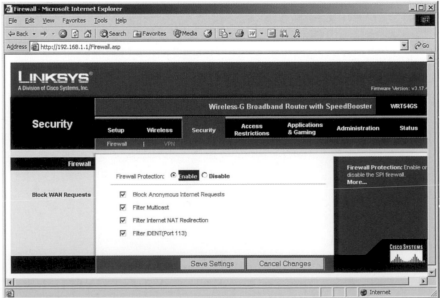

Figure 14-1   Turn on the Firewall in the Router

Other options that offer protection can also be set here:

- Checkmark **Block Anonymous Internet Requests** (on some Linksys routers, this is **Block WAN Requests**). This essentially blocks traffic from originating on the Internet "inbound" to your home network.

  Normally, you always originate actions to the Internet from a computer on your home network, whether you are browsing a website, sending e-mail, and so on. So any actions that originate from the Internet are usually suspect. Unless you are running a web service on your home network (which is out of the scope of this book), you should checkmark this option to block actions originated on the Internet.

- The other options including Filter Internet NAT Redirection, Filter Multicast, and Filter IDENT are other options to disallow particular types of behavior that have been exploited by hackers on some home networks. Go ahead and checkmark these options, and click **Save Settings**.

That's it. Pretty easy, and you just enabled quite a bit of protection for your home network, equivalent to what many corporations use to protect their networks.

Installing a Personal Firewall on Each Computer

Turning on the firewall in the wireless router in your network created an important line of defense. But to complete the protection of the end computers on your network, you need to enable them to act as a firewall as well. Although the firewall in the router protects against network intrusions, having a firewall on each of your computers will offer an additional layer of protection against intrusion, as well as a critical protection point against certain other types of programs that may find their way onto a computer and then try to access the Internet unbeknownst to you.

There are several alternatives for personal firewalls that you can choose from, including

- Professional firewall program (such as Symantec Norton Personal Firewall, McAfee Personal Firewall, ZoneAlarm Pro)

- Free firewall program (such as ZoneAlarm and Sygate Personal Firewall)

- Windows firewall, a new component of Windows XP starting with Service Pack 2 (SP2)

Which personal firewall program you choose depends to some degree on personal preference. Professional firewall programs and the Windows firewall probably get much better regular updates than a free firewall program. So if you are using Windows XP, the built-in firewall offers pretty good protection, and the price is right. If you are not using XP, you should consider either one of the free firewall programs or purchase one. The security software "bundles" described earlier (from McAfee, Symantec, Trend Micro, and Zone Labs) include a professional firewall. The next couple of sections show examples of each of the three types of firewall programs.

Installing a Professional Personal Firewall Program

Each of the security "bundle" products evaluated contains a personal firewall. All are pretty similar in the way they operate. You install them, they use pre-programmed defaults initially, and they get "smarter" over time by asking you whether to grant permission to new programs to access the Internet. We don't have enough room in this book to show you all four we evaluated, so we are going to arbitrarily pick screenshots of one of the products to make certain points.

 NOTE The first step is to install the security product bundle (not shown here).

After the security product bundle is installed and running, let's take a look at the personal firewall and make sure it is operating the way we want it to. Start by finding the new icon on the desktop for the security product "bundle" you just installed and double-click it to launch the central control window. Table 14-2 shows both the Symantec and McAfee products.

Table 14-2   Setting Up a Professional Firewall Program

Steps	Symantec Norton Internet Security 2005	McAfee Internet Security Suite
Step 1: Click the **Personal Firewall** tab. Verify that the status is On or Enabled. If not, enable it.	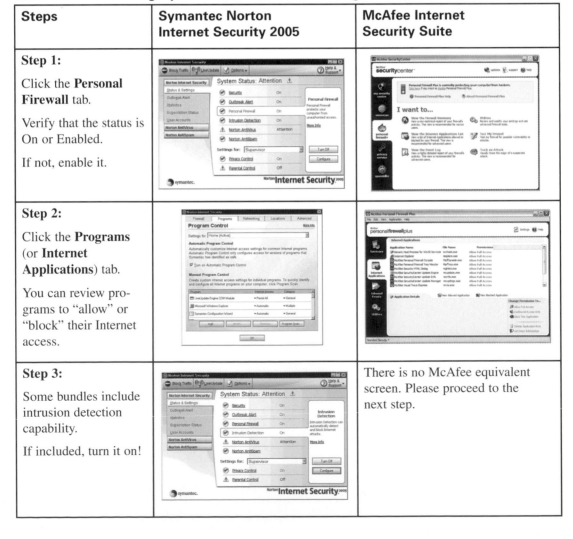	
Step 2: Click the **Programs** (or **Internet Applications**) tab. You can review programs to "allow" or "block" their Internet access.		
Step 3: Some bundles include intrusion detection capability. If included, turn it on!		There is no McAfee equivalent screen. Please proceed to the next step.

Table 14-2   Setting Up a Professional Firewall Program

Steps	Symantec Norton Internet Security 2005	McAfee Internet Security Suite
Step 4: Active programs will be auto configured to have appropriate Internet access. Others may prompt you for access permission.	*Norton Internet Security* **Program Control** ⚠ Low Risk Alert Assistant Nullsoft Winamp is attempting to access the Internet. Show Details What do you want to do? Automatically configure Internet access (Recommended) OK	*McAfee.com Personal Firewall Plus* **Application Wants to Access the Internet** The program **Outlook Express** is requesting access to the Internet. Do you want to allow it? **Path:** C:\Program Files\Outlook Express \msimn.exe ⚠ McAfee Recommends... Caution in allowing this application. Click here to learn more. ⊙ I want to... 🔓 Grant Access 🔒 Block All Access

Right after installation, and when new programs are installed, you are prompted to allow or block Internet access. Make sure you recognize the program asking permission before granting it. Also, make a note to periodically go and check the program access list (see Step 2) to make sure it only lists the programs you want to access the Internet. If you see programs you don't recognize or are obvious spyware or adware programs, block their access. If something stops working though (like you are no longer able to access the Internet with your browser), make sure you have not inadvertently blocked access to a necessary operating system program required for Internet access.

Congratulations, you have just put firewall protection on your home network!

Installing a Free Personal Firewall Program

ZoneAlarm offers a free personal firewall program that is extremely popular, and offers essential protection (you can upgrade for a fee to a professional version). Here is a link:

   http://www.zonelabs.com/store/content/catalog/products/sku_list_za.jsp

Follow the instructions to download and install the free firewall program. After the installation is complete, double-click the ZoneAlarm icon to launch the control panel (see Figure 14-2).

Similar to the professional firewall programs, the firewall keeps a list of programs which are permitted to access the Internet, and which are denied. Also, the ZoneAlarm firewall must "learn" which programs are permitted or denied access. You can modify the permissions by clicking on the **Program Control** button. Then you can permit or deny access as appropriate (see Figure 14-3).

A green checkmark indicates access is permitted, while a red X indicates access is denied.

The ZoneAlarm free personal firewall is a pretty good firewall, and again the price is right. So if you don't want to or can't invest in a professional program, there is still no excuse not to have personal firewall protection.

Figure 14-2 ZoneAlarm Firewall Control Panel

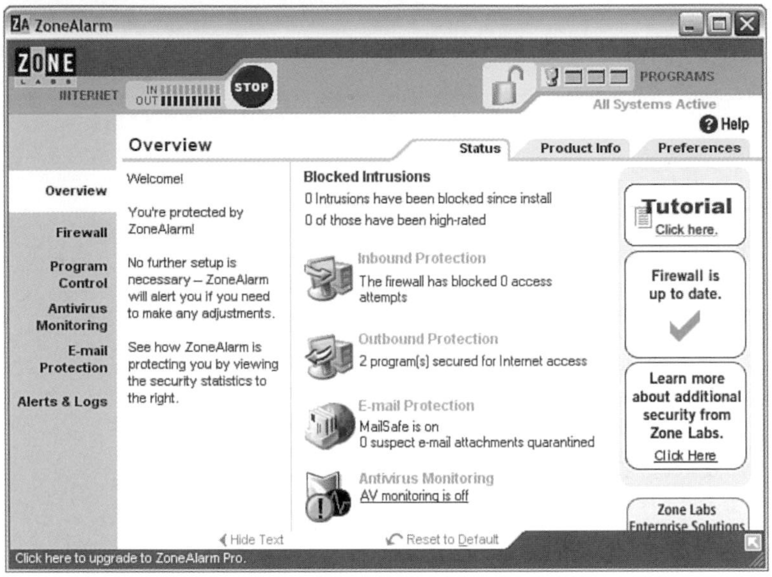

Figure 14-3 Modify the Program Access List

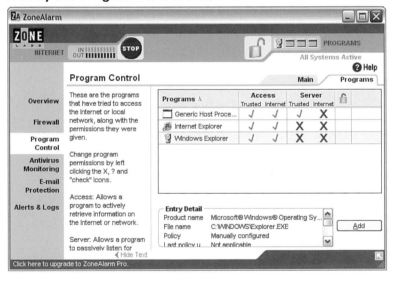

Enabling the Windows Firewall

Starting with Windows XP Service Pack 2 (SP2), a free personal firewall program is built in to the OS. If you are running Windows XP and have not yet installed SP2, here is a link to do so:

http://www.microsoft.com/windowsxp/sp2/default.mspx

Follow the instructions to download and install the Windows XP SP2 update. The Windows Security Center can be accessed to enable the firewall. Follow these steps:

Step 1 Click **Start** > **Control Panel** > **Security Center** to launch it (see Figure 14-4).

Figure 14-4   Windows Security Center

Step 2   If the Firewall status is OFF, click the **Recommendations** button (see Figure 14-4). Then click the **Enable Now** button to turn on the firewall (see Figure 14-5).

Figure 14-5   Enable Windows Firewall

The Firewall status should now show ON (see Figure 14-6). The Windows firewall is another pretty good firewall, and again the price is right. So if you don't want to or can't invest in a professional program, there is again no excuse not to have personal firewall protection.

Figure 14-6   Windows Firewall Is Now Enabled

Keeping Windows Security Up to Date

One thing to know about hackers is they are always trying to find new and creative ways to exploit security holes in products such as Microsoft Windows, Outlook, and Internet Explorer to gain access to networks or computers.

So just as important as installing a firewall program is to make sure that the Windows OS itself (and its various software components) are the latest versions. The folks at Microsoft continually release updates to improve functionality, but also to patch security holes that are found, so having the latest and greatest software is yet another critical security measure for your home network.

If you are running Windows XP, it has a built-in feature for fetching and installing the latest updates to itself from the Microsoft website. Make sure to turn on automatic updates, as you will not likely remember to do so yourself often enough.

For Windows XP SP2, the steps are easy:

Step 1   Click **Start** > **Control Panel** > **Security Center** to launch it (see Figure 14-7). If the Automatic Updates status is OFF, click the **Turn On Automatic Updates** button.

Step 2   The Automatic Updates status should now show ON (see Figure 14-8).

Now whenever your computer is running, and connected to the Internet, it will poll the Microsoft website for the latest and greatest software components and compare them with the versions you have installed on your computer. If a new security update is needed, you will be prompted that "Windows Updates are Ready to Install" and you can approve the installation.

For older versions of Windows, automatic updates may or may not be possible. For Windows 2000, you can install a similar Automatic Updates feature from here:

http://support.microsoft.com/kb/327850/EN-US/

Figure 14-7   Windows Security Center

Figure 14-8   Windows Automatic Updates Is Now Enabled

For Windows 98, Automatic Updates is not available, but Microsoft does offer a "Critical Update Notification" utility, available from here:

http://support.microsoft.com/kb/224420/EN-US/

At a minimum, you can update older versions of Windows manually by accessing the Microsoft website and performing the update. Here's how:

Step 1   Launch your web browser (such as Internet Explorer) and go to http://windowsupdate. microsoft.com. Click the **Scan for Updates** button (see Figure 14-9).

Figure 14-9   Windows Update Website

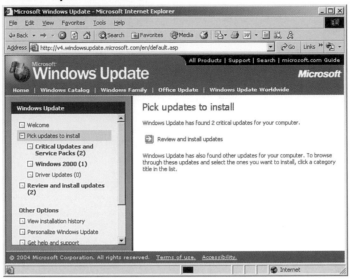

Step 2   After scanning is complete, click the **Review and Install Updates** button, and follow the instructions. The updates will be installed over the Internet to your computer (see Figure 14-10).

Figure 14-10 Windows Updates Will Begin Installing

Typically, you will need to reboot your computer after the updates are installed (especially if there are security updates included). Bottom line: Keep your Windows software up to date and automatically so if at all possible.

Where to Go for More Info

You can check out the effectiveness your security and firewalls by using an online security assessment. To do that, we recommend that you visit either of these sites:

http://grc.com/su-firewalls.htm

http://security.symantec.com

Viruses and Other Malicious Software

When people talk about computer and network security, they almost always mention computer viruses sooner or later. Even people who don't use computers very often have heard about viruses because of all the news hype that surrounds them. In this chapter, we will discuss viruses and other malicious code, including where they come from, what they do, how you can protect your computer against them, and how to get rid of them if you do get infected.

What Is a Virus?

The term "computer virus" tends to get used for any malicious code created with the intention of harming a computer or slowing network traffic, but a virus is actually a very specific type of program. The definition of a *computer virus* is a program that attaches itself to (or really within) another program (the host) so that it can replicate itself when the host program is run or executed. That's it. You may be surprised that this definition says nothing about removing data, crashing a system, or any other nasty effects. This is because a virus is defined by its replication behavior, not its effect on the host computer. That said, many viruses do harm data and systems (either intentionally or unintentionally) and any program activity that occurs on your computer or network without your knowledge or consent is a hostile attack against you and your property.

So what about the bad stuff, you ask? Although it is true that some viruses are designed to remove or replace data or corrupt computer systems, these types of viruses are exceptionally rare because they are extremely difficult to create. In fact, there are probably only a handful of people in the world who have the rare combination of skill, personality bent, and free time to create a virus. Of those folks who do, only a minority create viruses that maliciously destroy data or systems. That said though, when some people in that category are "successful," look out because the effects are devastating. Just as worrisome are the viruses created by people who are not skilled programmers, because their programs tend to be unpredictable, and in the off chance that a virus created by an unskilled programmer does replicate in the "wild" (on the Internet), there is really no telling what the program will do.

Where Viruses Live

There are a number of different places a virus can live and replicate, but we can lump them into three broad categories:

- **File viruses**—Hidden within other executable files. Typically, an executable file will have an extension (the three letter designation after the file name of .exe, .com, .sys, .bin). File viruses typically get to your computer when you download "free" programs off the Internet or open e-mail attachments.

- **Macro viruses**—A type of file virus, but they are launched through a data file containing a software subroutine called a *macro* (and thus break the rule above about file extensions). Macros are most often found in office applications, such as word processors or spreadsheet programs. When used as intended, macros can be very useful, but they offer an easily exploitable security hole for virus programmers. To help protect its customers, Microsoft products allow an option where the user is notified and given the option to disable macros when a file with a macro is opened. This allows you to open the file without risking exposure to the virus.

- **Boot sector viruses**—Live in the section of your computer's disk drive that controls the startup routine. If you get infected with a boot sector virus, it launches every time you start up your computer and, in some cases, will prevent you from starting up at all.

In addition to the main types of viruses, some variants have traits of several types (such as a file virus that replicates itself into the boot sector and then behaves like a boot sector virus).

Viruses may not always launch every time the infected file executes. Some may launch after a certain number of startups or after a certain date. It's also important to know that not all malicious viruses will have immediate devastating effects. Some viruses replace a single byte of data at a time slowly causing damage without the owner's knowledge until, like a home with termites, you find out after the damage is done.

 GEEK SQUAD Backing up your data is very important. If a virus does manage to infect your computer, sometimes important files can get eaten or lost.

Types of Computer Viruses

Viruses are files that attach themselves to other programs and replicate on "host" computers. In nearly all cases, this file replication occurs without the knowledge or consent of the computer's owner.

By definition, viruses do not destroy data or remove files (although some will take up all of your memory, which could cause you to lose saved work), but any actions taken on your computer should be considered hostile. Some computer viruses that are not meant to harm machines are so poorly written that they end up inadvertently destroying data. Here are the three most common types of viruses.

File Viruses
A file virus attaches itself to an executable file (anything with an extension of .exe, .com, .sys, or .bin). Many viruses get propagated via e-mail attachments. However, just opening an e-mail won't launch the virus; you must actually open the attached file, which many people do without giving it any thought.

Boot-Sector Viruses
A boot-sector virus attaches itself to the start-up routine of a computer. It usually launches when you turn on your computer, but it could have a delayed trigger so that it launches after a certain number of restarts or on a specific date, like the Michelangelo virus that launches on the artist's birthday.

Macro Viruses
A macro is a software subroutine that runs inside another program and is a ripe launching pad for viruses. Many Microsoft Office products allow macros, which are useful in most cases. To protect users, these programs now prompt you if a macro exists on a file and gives you the option to disable it if you are concerned about the source.

Other Nasty Stuff

As bad as viruses are, they are not the only programs out there that can cause your data and your network harm. The two types of programs that you should be most worried about (in addition to viruses) are worms and Trojan horses.

Worms

Worms are similar to viruses in that their defining characteristic is self-replication. Unlike viruses, however, a worm does not alter or remove files from computers. It just replicates, and replicates, and replicates.

Worms are also different from viruses in that they do not require an executable file. Worms exploit security holes in computer systems or software code that allows them to sort of just take off on their own after they are initially triggered (so they don't live inside other files). You may be thinking that simple replication without harming or removing files is not so bad, but worm growth is explosive to the point that the amount of network traffic they generate can crash routers, switches, and servers.

Trojan Horses

Trojan horses are probably the most unknown type of malicious program but are potentially the most devastating to those who launch them. Similar to viruses, Trojan horses are hidden within other executable files, usually inside "free" games, music files, or movies, and just like the horse from Homer's epic, a nasty surprise is waiting inside this gift.

Trojan horses are programs that give a hacker access to your computer. After the "gift" file is opened, the hacker's program is also opened and that's when the trouble starts.

Some of the more common programs are key stroke loggers or remote control programs:

- A key stroke logger collects everything you type on your keyboard (including passwords, usernames, and credit card numbers). After a certain amount of data is collected, the information is sent to the hacker (without your knowledge, of course).

- A remote control program allows the hacker to take over your machine, allowing them to go through your files and data, or use your machine to attack another computer. Imagine your embarrassment when the FBI knocks on your door to tell you your computer was used in an attempt to shut down a corporate or government network.

Worms and Trojan Horses

Worms and Trojan horses are often lumped with viruses, but their behavior and consequences are different and, as such, warrant a separate discussion.

Like viruses, both worms and Trojan horses launch without the knowledge or consent of the user, but that is about the only similarity.

Worms are dangerous because they tend to slow or shut down networks. Trojan horses are dangerous because they allow access or pass information to the hackers that launched them.

Trojan Horses
A Trojan horse is a program that a hacker places inside another program, usually a game or music/movie file. When a person downloads and executes the program, the hidden program also launches. The hidden programs can be used to collect passwords and information that are then sent back to the hacker without the owner's knowledge, or the program allows the hacker to remotely access and control the hacked computer to attack someone else.

Worms
A worm is a file that simply replicates itself and really does not do much more than that. It may not sound like much, but worm files tend to grow exponentially and can cause so much bogus traffic on a network that the network shuts down. Worms can also fill up a lot of disc space on your machine, which greatly slows performance and connection speeds.

Protecting Yourself Against Malicious Code

So now that you are good and terrified about all the bad programs out there that can crash your computer and steal your information, here is the good news: You can protect yourself with any number of easy-to-use programs and some common sense.

Common Sense

Here's one of the most powerful bits of advice that way too many people ignore: If something sounds too good to be true, it probably is. Any time you are about to download a program that claims to be "free," or open a file from someone you don't know, stop and think before you download or open it. Ask yourself these questions:

- Why is this being given away for free? After all, programming even a simple program takes a lot of time and effort. What's in it for the people giving it away?

- Is the file from a trusted source or site?

- Do you actually know the person who sent you an e-mail with the subject "pictures from the great party"? Was there really a party? Why weren't you invited?

With a few simple questions and a little healthy suspicion, we estimate that at least 9 out of 10 viruses and every Trojan horse would fail to propagate. Remember that, in nearly every case, a virus finds its way on to your computer because *you* put it there.

 NOTE If you have children who use the Internet from a computer at home, set a rule that all downloads should be approved by mom or dad. This is good advice for malicious software and for some topics discussed later in the book

Unfortunately, common sense does not save you from every malicious file, and anyone who has been using the Internet any period of time has likely been hit with a virus or worm. We've been hit. Everyone we know has been hit, and so has pretty much every company on the Fortune 1000. So, obviously, common sense is not enough. Fortunately, we have antivirus programs that are both affordable and effective.

Antivirus Programs

One of the reasons that common sense measures do not help with all viruses is that many of them propagate by sending a version of themselves to every address in an infected computer's e-mail program. After one person makes an error in judgment, many people they know get infected by opening an e-mail attachment from a person they know. The process is both insidious and brilliantly effective.

Another issue is that worms propagate without needing to be launched, so you could get affected by a worm without doing anything "wrong." Because of these cases, you really need to employ an antivirus program to protect your computers and your network. We recommend a few good ones in this section, show you how to set them up, and explain how they all pretty much work in the same way.

 GEEK SQUAD One of the reasons people get viruses is because they don't take proactive approaches to protect themselves. If you are out there visiting a lot of servers and websites without protection, it's only a matter of time before your system will become infected.

How Do Antivirus Programs Work?

Just about every antivirus program on the market today works by exploiting the signature inherent in all viruses. In this case, a signature refers to the unique sets of bit arrangements within the virus code.

After a new virus is discovered, teams of engineers begin working to identify the unique signature. The competition is fierce because the ability find the signature and distribute it to all subscribers is a point of competitive differentiation for the companies that provide antivirus software. But, all the major providers have very talented teams so over any given period, signature discovery and distribution is a wash.

After the signature is identified and distributed to everyone who purchased the antivirus software program, the program adds the signature to the list of what it looks for during the scanning process. When a match is found, an additional detailed comparison is made against the actual virus program to protect against false positives. If that comparison is positive, the program is flagged for removal from your computer.

It's important to remember a few things about your antivirus software:

- Always keep your antivirus software up to date. Typically, there is an option to have the program automatically check for updates. You should set this feature to check for new signatures at least once a week.

- Signatures only get identified *after* the virus has been launched (meaning someone had to have been infected).

What Happens with New Viruses?

One of the biggest problems today is that an Internet virus or worm can travel around the Internet faster than news about the virus or worm. So, even if the antivirus people start working on finding the signature as soon as the virus launches, by the time they find and distribute the signature, the virus could have gone around the world. In most cases, this is exactly what happens. Because of this, the antivirus people are under pressure to protect their customers from being affected by worms or viruses before a "cure" is found. Their answer to this is heuristic detection.

Heuristic detection looks at behavior patterns of files and executables on your machine. If a program launches and starts behaving oddly or in a virus/worm-like way, the program is flagged and the user is notified. Unlike signature-based detection, heuristic detection will notice and flag remote control behavior and key stroke loggers, offering protection against the most common Trojan horse attacks.

Although heuristic detection greatly improves your *day-zero* (the early moments of a virus or worm explosion) defense, there are some limitations:

- There is a high occurrence of false positives (flagging events that are not virus or worm related). This can get annoying for some folks, who then might just turn the feature off.

- Some virus programmers out there can spoof or fake out the behavior of their software and get around the defense that the antivirus programs provide.

Even with these limitations, though, behavior-based protection software is worth enabling.

All four of the antivirus programs we evaluated and are included in the security software bundles (McAfee, Symantec, Trend Micro, and Zone Labs) include heuristics in their products.

Virus Inoculation

Several products are available today that scan for and remove viruses and other malicious programs. Look for a program that performs signature-based inoculations and behavior-based (called heuristic) inoculations. Also, look for a service that updates signatures often.

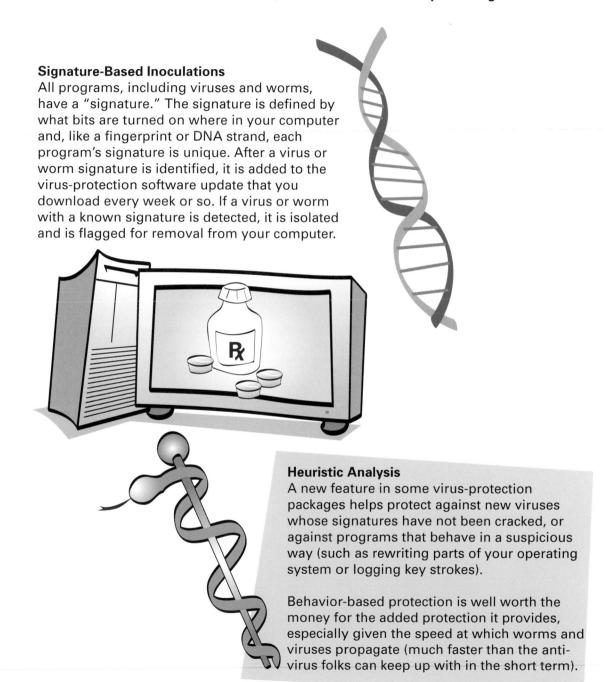

Signature-Based Inoculations

All programs, including viruses and worms, have a "signature." The signature is defined by what bits are turned on where in your computer and, like a fingerprint or DNA strand, each program's signature is unique. After a virus or worm signature is identified, it is added to the virus-protection software update that you download every week or so. If a virus or worm with a known signature is detected, it is isolated and is flagged for removal from your computer.

Heuristic Analysis

A new feature in some virus-protection packages helps protect against new viruses whose signatures have not been cracked, or against programs that behave in a suspicious way (such as rewriting parts of your operating system or logging key strokes).

Behavior-based protection is well worth the money for the added protection it provides, especially given the speed at which worms and viruses propagate (much faster than the anti-virus folks can keep up with in the short term).

How to Build It: Preventing Viruses and Other Malicious Software from Infecting Your Network

There are numerous antivirus products on the market. Because of the intense effort involved to keep antivirus programs up to date with the latest signatures, we are not aware of any really good free products. So there are two possibilities:

- Purchase a standalone antivirus program

- Purchase a security software bundle containing an antivirus program

For just a little more money than an antivirus program, you can typically buy the whole security software bundle, so look for the bargains.

In Chapter 14, "Protecting Your Network from Intruders," all the same security bundle products we evaluated also contain an antivirus program. So, in this chapter, we will continue showing how to enable the antivirus functions of those same security "bundles." But understand that the standalone versions of those programs work pretty much the same way.

Let's start by understanding the fundamental components of antivirus programs (intentionally over-simplified as we really don't need to understand everything about how these complex programs work). First, a virus "scanner" program (shown in orange) regularly examines every file on the hard drives of the computer to see if they have become infected by a virus. This program uses a large list of virus signatures that is provided by the antivirus program vendor. If a virus is found, the file can be "cleaned" or deleted. Scanners are usually set up to run automatically once a week.

Figure 15-1   Components of an Antivirus Program

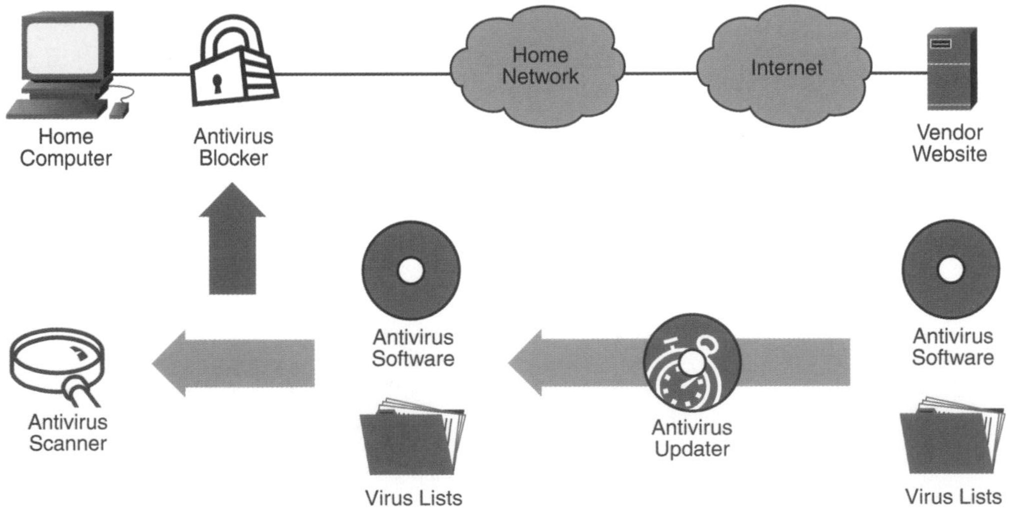

However, if we only look for viruses on the hard drive, it's a little like walking around barefoot with a blindfold on through a field full of cow patties: It's only a matter of time until you step in it. The antivirus "blocker" is like having a little gnome sitting on your shoulder with binoculars as you walk through the field: When you are about to step on one, the little guy can call out "stop, go right!," avoiding the…well, you know…splat.

Whereas the scanner runs periodically, the blocker runs all the time, constantly examining incoming e-mail, web pages, and files for virus infections. When one is located (notice we say when, not if, because it is inevitable you *will* hit one), you have the option to "clean," "quarantine," or "delete" the infected information.

Finally, the problem with viruses is that there are new ones every day. Virus "authors" are some of the most creative and prolific people on the planet. It's a shame we can't harness their powers for good. So, we need to very regularly update the antivirus scanner and blocker with the latest virus list information so that they can have the best chance to recognize all the most recent viruses, kind of like sending our little gnome friend to school to stay sharp on what cow patties look like (okay, this analogy is wearing thin). The antivirus "updater" runs automatically, usually once a week, to go out to the antivirus vendor's website and download the latest software and virus list.

 GEEK SQUAD Windows updates are an important part of antivirus protection. You need to keep on top of them and do them periodically.

Here's an overview of the steps we are going to go through to protect our network from intruders:

- Turn on antivirus protection at your service provider (if available)

- Set up antivirus protection on your home computers

- Make sure automatic updating is working

- Perform an initial virus scan

Turn on Antivirus Protection at Your Service Provider

Many service providers offer built-in antivirus protection within their e-mail service. Check with your service provider to see whether this is an option. If it is, it's certainly something you should take advantage of. Many, many viruses multiply themselves by using e-mail to "grow" the infection to other computers. Detecting and stopping these viruses inside the e-mail system of the service provider is preferable to waiting until they are on their way into your home network.

How to enable antivirus protection with your service provider will vary widely and depend entirely on how they have chosen to set up their services. Enabling the protection is very easy. We'll use EarthLink as an example:

Step 1 Log in to the EarthLink My Account page using your account user ID and password.

Step 2 Click **Turn On Virus Blocker** (see Figure 15-2).

Figure 15-2   Enabling Virus Blocker with EarthLink

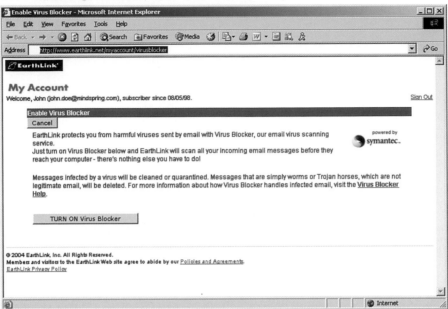

That's it. Now when new e-mail arrives to your mailbox at EarthLink, it is scanned for viruses. If it's found to be infected, the e-mail is routed to a special quarantine folder so that it will never be downloaded to your computer's e-mail.

Set up Antivirus Protection on Your Home Computers

Having set up a first line of antivirus defense in the service provider network, we now need to enable protection on each of the computers in your home network. It is assumed that you already installed the security product bundle you have selected. The example shown in Table 15-1 shows the process for enabling antivirus protection on both the Symantec and McAfee products. The other two bundles are similar.

Table 15-1   Enabling Antivirus Protection

Steps	Symantec Norton Internet Security 2005	McAfee Internet Security Suite
Step 1: Click the **Anti-Virus** tab. Verify that the status is On or Enabled. If not, enable it.		
Step 2: For Symantec: Click **Options > Norton AntiVirus > Threat Categories** For McAfee: Click **Configure VirusScan Options**. Verify that antivirus will check for all types of threats. Click **OK**.		

One additional feature we want to make sure is enabled is the heuristics scanning (looking for future viruses and worms). This will be a bit different for each antivirus program. Here is an example for the Symantec program:

Step 1   Click **Options > Norton AntiVirus**.

Step 2   Click **Auto Protect > Bloodhound**. Make sure **Enable** is checkmarked (see Figure 15-3).

Figure 15-3   Enabling Antivirus Heuristics

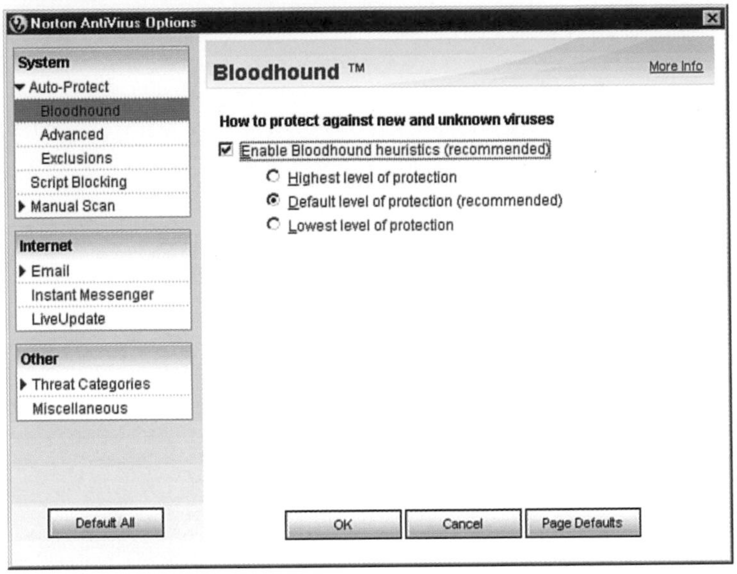

Make Sure Automatic Updating Is Working

Right after installing antivirus protection, it's important to trigger an automatic update of the software and virus lists. Some products will do this automatically when you install them, although others may need to be triggered manually or will wait for the first weekly update.

Table 15-2 shows the process for updating antivirus protection on both the Symantec and McAfee products. The other bundles are very similar to this process.

Table 15-2   Setting Up Automatic Update

Steps	Symantec Norton Internet Security 2005	McAfee Internet Security Suite
Step 1: Click the **Anti-Virus** tab. For Norton: Click **Automatic Live Update > Turn On**. For McAfee: Click **Updates**.		
Step 2: Make sure you are connected to the Internet. For Norton: Click **Next** and follow the instructions. For McAfee: Click **Check Now**.		
Step 3: You should see successful completion of the update.		

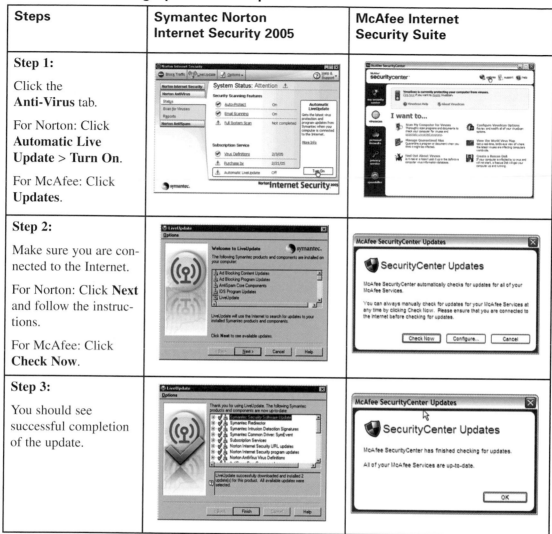

Troubleshooting Tips: Updating Antivirus

The update should complete successfully. If it does not, try the following:

- Make sure the Internet connection is working. Use your Internet browser (such as Internet Explorer) and try to connect to a website you know should work (such as a news or weather website).

- Make sure the security bundle subscription is valid. If you do not have a valid, paid subscription, it will not work. Verify that you entered the correct subscription key.

- Read the troubleshooting guide for the particular security product you are working with.

Perform an Initial Virus Scan

The next important step to complete after you install antivirus protection is to perform a complete virus scan on your computer. Some products do this automatically when you install them, although others may need to be triggered manually or will wait for the first weekly scan.

Table 15-3 shows the process for performing a manual virus scan on both the Symantec and McAfee products. The other bundles are very similar.

Table 15-3   Performing a Virus Scan

Steps	Symantec Norton Internet Security 2005	McAfee Internet Security Suite
Step 1: Click the **Anti-Virus** tab. For Norton: click **Full System Scan > Scan Now**. For McAfee: click **Scan My Computer > Scan**.		
Step 2: When the scan completes, a list of viruses and other security threats are displayed. Click **Fix** or **Delete** to clear any infected files found.		

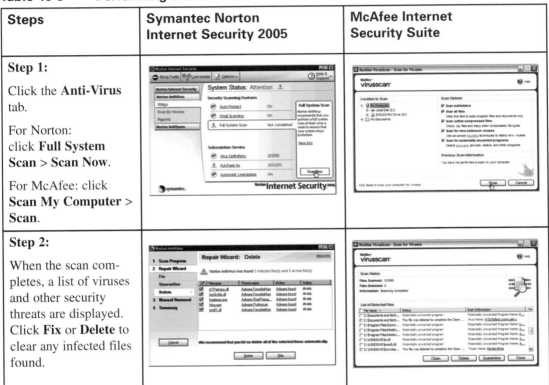

The antivirus scanner will recommend what to do with the infected files (fix, delete, or quarantine them). Most infections can be automatically repaired by the antivirus software. Severe infections may require more work.

In general, choosing the **Fix** (for Norton) or **Clean** (for McAfee) buttons tells the antivirus software to attempt to repair the file to its original state; choosing **Delete** tells the software to trash the file; and choosing **Quarantine** tells the software to isolate the file from the rest of your files by placing it in a special holding area. Try to clean (or fix) the file first, and if that fails, quarantine or delete the file.

All the major antivirus vendors provide information on their websites about how to remedy severe infections. Some infections may be so severe that irreversible damage is done to the operating system. This may require reloading the operating system from scratch. If you encounter a severe infection that the antivirus software cannot automatically repair, and you are not comfortable repairing it yourself, get help from someone who knows what they are doing, like the Geek Squad.

Now that the computer has had its first "cleaning," the antivirus blocker in each security bundle will hopefully keep the computer virus-free from this point. What is critical, is to make sure to maintain your subscription with the antivirus vendor to continue to receive regular updates to the virus lists, otherwise you can become infected with new viruses, worms, and Trojan horses that are created.

Congratulations, you have protected your home network from viruses!

Where to Go for More Info

These sites are helpful if you happen to have a severe computer infection and need to download a virus removal tool:

- http://securityresponse.symantec.com/avcenter/tools.list.html

- http://us.mcafee.com/virusInfo/default.asp?id=vrt

Other Vulnerabilities (Spam, Cookies, Pop-Ups, Spyware, and Scams)

In addition to viruses and worms, there are some other annoying programs and files out there that you need to protect your home network from. This chapter focuses on spam, cookies, spyware, and scams—what they are, how they work, and how to get rid of or at least control them. For the most part, these types of files are not as dangerous as the others we discussed in Chapter 15, "Viruses and Other Malicious Software"—none of them will remove or destroy data for example—but they are still common, extremely annoying, and in some cases, they can do things without you knowing about it.

Spam

Spam is the common name for unsolicited commercial e-mail and it is a problem that is rampant on the Internet today. Because of spam, a whole sub-industry of spam blockers has cropped up and is a major concern of Internet service providers (ISPs). Major service providers claim that they block on the order of 2 billion (yes, billion) unsolicited e-mails every day and have put the effort to stop spam at the top of their priority lists. One of the reasons that spam is so widespread is that it is extremely easy to send out millions and millions of e-mails with little cost.

How Spam Works

Spammers do their dirty work by purchasing or creating giant e-mail lists and automated mailing tools called *spambots*. The lists are usually compiled from web pages where people provide their e-mail address as part of a registration process. Usually, there is a box that is checked "yes" by default saying something along the lines of "Yes, please share my e-mail with your sponsors for related offers." If you agree, by leaving the box checked, you have just given the site permission to sell and resell your e-mail address to spammers. Although most spam gets caught by filters or deleted by the recipient, some of it is answered and that is why the spammers keep at it. It is really a matter of odds. Even if the response rate is 0.5%, it cost next to nothing to send spam to upward of 10 million e-mail addresses. At that rate, the spammer just pulled in 50,000 new customers.

 GEEK SQUAD Spammers also collect e-mails from web page "guest books" and message boards. Be careful where you leave your e-mail address. If you are lonely, this is a great way to make sure you always have new mail in your inbox.

Spam

Spam is unsolicited commercial e-mail, and it is a huge problem. Some large ISPs claim that they block over one billion e-mails a day and some still gets through. Here is one example of how spammers get their info.

1 Larry registers on a web page and leaves the "I want to know more" box checked.

Web-Page Registration

E-mail: LarryRoux@ping.com

X Yes, I would like to know about other offers from your partners.

Register

Web Server

2 The web page's owner creates a giant list of e-mail addresses, which is sold to multiple spammers.

4-Sale

3 A spammer collects millions of e-mail addresses from multiple sources and starts sending e-mails.

Address List

Larry's PC

Larry's E-Mail Client

Subject	From
Girls for Larry!	*Candi 123*
Viagra	*a friend*
Free Degree	*Becky*
Viagra	*sally*
More Viagra	*herman*
Refinance!	*Alice 111*
Date Me	*Esque*

ISP

4 Despite your ISP's efforts to block spam, it still comes through in droves. Be careful with whom you share your address.

How to Block Spam

There is a good chance that your ISP has some sort of spam-blocking feature available and, if spam is a problem for you, we suggest starting there. Your ISP probably uses some basic filters such as looking for keywords or multiple (100,000+) instances of an e-mail from the same source IP address. Unfortunately, spammers (those who create and send spam) are pretty good at staying ahead of the ISPs by using random or misspelled words or by constantly changing IP addresses as they send e-mails. (There is also talk of anti-spam legislation, but spammers can easily set up shop in countries with looser laws.) If the ISP filters are not blocking enough spam, you can purchase or download software that will provide a second layer of protection on your system. Typically, these programs use advanced algorithms to recognize and block spam but they are not perfect because sometimes spam gets through the filter, and sometimes legitimate e-mail gets blocked (essentially a false positive). You can modify the options in this program so that the blocking rules are customized. Be sure to check the folder that the spam blocker drops trash e-mail into every once in a while to make sure you don't miss "real" e-mail.

We recommend that in addition to using the ISP and commercial blockers that you set up a *dirty* e-mail address. What we mean by dirty e-mail address is an e-mail address that is only used for the purpose of registering on web pages. Given that most ISPs will allow several e-mail aliases with a standard account, you can reserve one for this purpose and still have plenty for the legitimate users in the home.

After you do this, only give your "real" e-mail out to people you know and use the dirty one for everything else. If you find that you do want some of the e-mail that comes into the dirty account, you can notify the sender to use your real e-mail address. Keep in mind that most legitimate commercial sites will not resell or share your e-mail address without your permission, but it's up to you to make sure that you read the fine print and uncheck any boxes that were pre-populated. This is always a red flag.

 GEEK SQUAD Just in case you are wondering, replying to a spam e-mail does not stop it from coming. In fact, such replies are used by the spammers to confirm "live" e-mail addresses, which then get put on a verified list. After this happens, you might as well retire the e-mail address.

Cookies

Cookies are small text files that web pages place on your computer when you visit a web page. The text file contains information that helps web pages track users and allows site preferences so that when you re-enter a page, it's unique to your custom settings or has "one-click" purchase options.

How Cookies Work

When you visit a website that tracks user data in this way, the site "drops a cookie" and creates a text file on your machine if it is your first visit, or updates a file that it left on your machine from a previous visit. The website does not change anything on your computer other than the file and, in all but the rarest of cases, the cookie does not contain any private information such as credit card numbers or home addresses and phone number. Most often, the cookie contains only the name of the web page and a unique identifier that the web page uses to pull information from a secure database where the private information about you is kept. This helps prevent problems associated with different people sharing the same machine, or a single user who switches between machines. It also allows web pages to keep track of users even when they have deleted all their cookie files.

Cookies

Cookies are text files that websites place on your computer to help them keep track of visitors and customized settings. Most of the time, cookies are harmless, but you should set your privacy settings to at least "Medium High" to avoid cookies from sites that share your information with others.

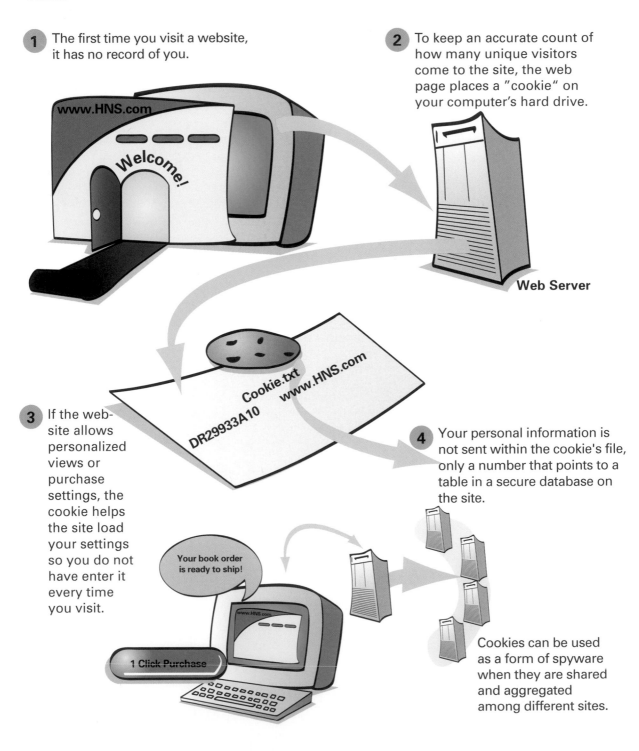

1 The first time you visit a website, it has no record of you.

2 To keep an accurate count of how many unique visitors come to the site, the web page places a "cookie" on your computer's hard drive.

www.HNS.com

Welcome!

Web Server

Cookie.txt   www.HNS.com
DR29933A10

3 If the web-site allows personalized views or purchase settings, the cookie helps the site load your settings so you do not have enter it every time you visit.

4 Your personal information is not sent within the cookie's file, only a number that points to a table in a secure database on the site.

Your book order is ready to ship!

www.HNS.com

1 Click Purchase

Cookies can be used as a form of spyware when they are shared and aggregated among different sites.

Bad Cookies

Not all cookies are bad things. For example, http://www.weather.com may place a cookie on your computer to store your ZIP code so that each time you return to its website, it can immediately bring up the local weather for your location.

However, one of the main issues with cookies is that marketing companies often use information about what you buy and where you click on a web page to better target you for advertising and spam. Some cookies are tracked across multiple sites by third-party companies. This is considered a privacy or security violation by many users. To protect your personal information, you can set your Internet browser to one of various privacy settings ranging from accept all cookies to block all cookies. Both these options are a bit impractical because accepting all will greatly increase security risks and blocking all will make it very difficult to browse many private and commercial websites (the pages will fail to load).

On Internet Explorer, we recommend a setting of Medium High as Figure 16-1 shows. (The screen is found by selecting the Privacy tab on the Internet Options dialog box, which is found under the Tools drop-down menu on the top of the browser.)

Figure 16-1   Setting Your Privacy to Medium High in Internet Explorer

If you are worried about the cookies you have previously accepted, you can delete all cookies by selecting the Delete Cookies button on the General screen of the window shown in Figure 16-1. If you had your privacy setting set to anything below Medium High, you should probably do this when you reset your settings.

Pop-Ups

Pop-ups refer to windows that are displayed on your computer screen for the purposes of advertising. Pop-ups occur when you browse certain websites. Some websites are funded by selling advertising space, some of which decide to hawk their wares by flooding your computer screen with clever ads.

How Pop-Ups Work

Pop-ups work using the same mechanism built in to web browsers, such as Internet Explorer, to open a URL in a new window. Sometimes this can be a useful function; for example, http://www.weather.com may use a pop-up window to display an urgent weather bulletin. But, in general, they are an annoying waste of your time.

 GEEK SQUAD Our favorite pop-ups are the ones that insist your computer is vulnerable to pop-up ads and try and sell you pop-up blocking software.

How to Get Rid of Pop-Ups

Just like spam and other scams, pop-ups get a response rate or else companies would not use them any longer. So, first and foremost, stop clicking on them. Your PC will not run faster, you will not win free money by clicking on the monkey, and a pop-up IQ test is pretty ironic actually.

Second, get a pop-up blocker. Microsoft Internet Explorer 6 Service Pack 1 (SP1) running under Windows XP SP2 now has a built-in pop-up blocker. Turn it on by clicking **Tools** > **Pop-Up Blocker** in Internet Explorer.

If you are not running this version of Windows or Internet Explorer, download any number of free pop-up blockers and use it.

Spyware/Adware

Spyware or *adware* refers to programs that are installed on your machine for the express purpose of tracking your online movements. Spyware is typically installed without your knowledge. It can become a real problem by slowing down your machine's performance and slowing down your online activity because the network connection is being shared by the programs that are sending information back to the third-party vendors who paid to place the programs on your machine.

How Spyware or Adware Works

Spyware or adware is installed on your machine in a number of different ways:

- The most common by far is through the installation of programs that hide the spyware file within the main program.

- Through peer-to-peer sharing programs (such as Morpheus), certain websites install spyware programs.

- Some forms of cookies are considered spyware as well.

One company called Double-Click created a version of spyware by connecting cookies from tens of thousands of websites. This information is used to "spy" on you while you surf the Internet. Although this ploy was bad, it still only spied on your Internet browsing. Other more aggressive forms of spyware can and do collect personal information on you by scanning files, e-mails, and e-mail address books.

How to Get Rid of Spyware and Adware

Although some ISPs provide spyware blockers, we strongly recommend the purchase of a commercial spyware sweeper. If you have been using the Internet for any amount of time and have not run a spyware blocker on your machine, you will likely be shocked by the number of spyware files found on your machine when you first install the sweeper.

We found one site that has a nice comparison of various spyware sweepers called Adawarereport.com. You may also want to do some research by going to http://www.google.com and doing a search on spyware blockers.

Ultimately, your willingness to put up with spyware is a matter of your personal tolerance, but keep in mind that after the information leaves your machine, there is no telling where it goes or who sees it. You really should err on the side of caution.

 GEEK SQUAD Almost everything we get called for on viruses and spyware is very preventable. Run a spyware blocker and, for goodness sake, don't ever click YES on pop-ups that say you have won free money.

Additional Scams

The Internet provides the perfect playground for scam artists, and by using the same principle as spammers, they figure that if they try a scam on enough people, sooner or later, someone will take the bait.

Phishing

In some cases, spam is actually used for the scam. One of the newest scams to make the news is *phishing*. In this scam, the target is sent a *very* official-looking e-mail from what they think is their bank or credit card company. A short note describes the "bank's" concern about identity theft and asks you to click a link so that they can confirm your account number. The link takes you to a very convincing website, complete with company's logo and trademarks and, in some cases, a 1-800 number. The site is bogus, however, and is operated by the actual identity thieves. The 1-800 number goes to them as well so if you call, everything seems legitimate. Figure 16-2 shows an example of a phishing e-mail (assuming that Pangea National Bank is an actual bank). Take a look at how official this looks and reads. However, clicking on the web link provided sends you to a website in China.

Figure 16-2   Sample Phishing E-Mail

Dear Pangea National Bank customer,

Recently there have been a large number of identity theft attempts targeting Pangea National Bank customers. In order to safeguard your account, we require that you confirm you banking details.

This process is mandatory, and if not completed within the nearest time, you account may be subject to temporary suspension

To securely confirm your Pangea National Bank account details, please go to:

https://web.da-us.pangeanationalbank.com/signin/scripts/login/user_setup.jsp

Thank you for your prompt attention to this matter and thank you for using Pangea National Bank!

Pangea National Bank
Identity Theft Solutions

Do not reply to this e-mail as it is an unmonitored alias

Rest assured that any bank or credit card company that you deal with knows what your account number is. It is their business to know it, especially if you hold a balance on your credit card. If you get an e-mail like the one just described, you should immediately do these things:

- Report the scam to the Federal Trade Commission—Forward the e-mail you received to spam@uce.gov and identify that you believe it to be a phishing scam.

- Call your credit card company to notify them of the scam—Use the phone number on the back of your credit card or the one printed on your monthly bill, not the one in the text of the e-mail or on the scam page.

- Notify your ISP—You can reach most ISPs by sending an e-mail to the abuse reporting address for your domain. For example, if you subscribe to EarthLink, the e-mail would be abuse@earthlink.net. There will usually be a fraud alert link on the provider's main page as well.

As always, think before you act when it comes to giving out your personal information or responding to official looking e-mails. Phishing scams do not necessarily have to have money involved, it could just as easily be your e-mail account itself. To spammers and hackers, even an e-mail account is of value. Educate your friends, family, and strangers on the street about what you have just learned.

Phishing Scam Example

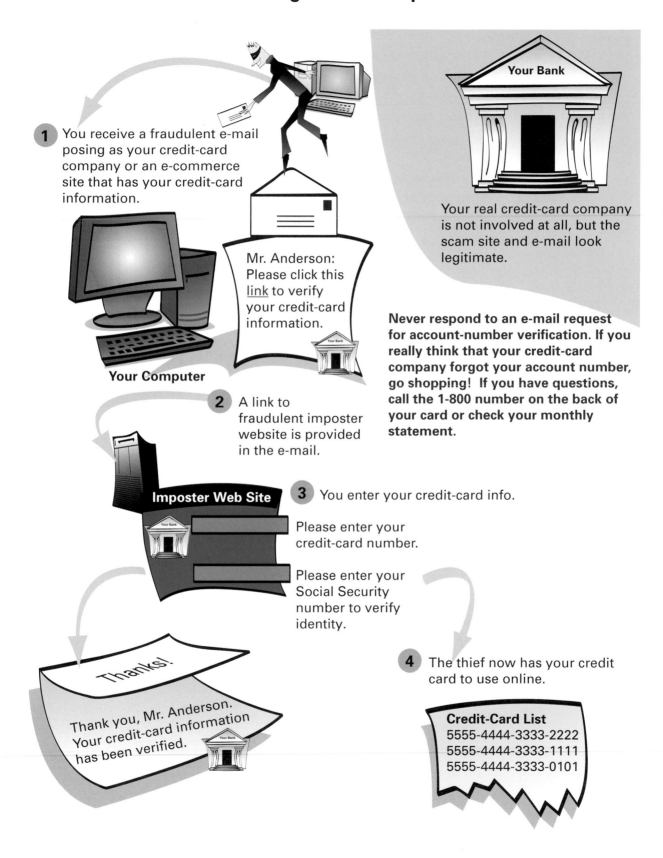

1 You receive a fraudulent e-mail posing as your credit-card company or an e-commerce site that has your credit-card information.

Your Computer

Mr. Anderson: Please click this link to verify your credit-card information.

Your real credit-card company is not involved at all, but the scam site and e-mail look legitimate.

Never respond to an e-mail request for account-number verification. If you really think that your credit-card company forgot your account number, go shopping! If you have questions, call the 1-800 number on the back of your card or check your monthly statement.

2 A link to fraudulent imposter website is provided in the e-mail.

Imposter Web Site

3 You enter your credit-card info.

Please enter your credit-card number.

Please enter your Social Security number to verify identity.

Thanks!.

Thank you, Mr. Anderson. Your credit-card information has been verified.

4 The thief now has your credit card to use online.

Credit-Card List
5555-4444-3333-2222
5555-4444-3333-1111
5555-4444-3333-0101

Urban Legends

The urban legend e-mail is also a popular Internet scam. An *urban legend* is one of those amazing or scary stories—you know, like the one about the couple that went to lover's lane and then found the bloody hook of the one-armed mass murderer on the passenger-side door.

If you get an e-mail about an incredible story, amazing opportunity, or terrible injustice that compels you to copy everyone in your address book: *Don't do it*! To our knowledge, terrorists are not buying UPS uniforms, Bill Gates is not giving away stock or money, there is no top-secret Neiman Marcus cookie recipe, and no one—not one person—has ever been slipped a mickey in his drink and then woke up in a hotel bathtub filled with ice, missing one of his kidneys.

 GEEK SQUAD Our favorite variant was when the story was changed to say the person woke up missing a liver. Still someone forwarded it on.

Although some of these stories are amusing, they are nearly always false. To avoid annoying your friends, family, and colleagues, and to save yourself some embarrassment, check out the facts first. There are a number of sites that debunk these claims. http://www.scambusters.org covers urban legends, e-mail scams, and a lot more. http://www.scopes.com is also a winner. Take a quick look there before you forward that "Warning to All" e-mail.

How to Build It: Preventing Network Vulnerabilities

It would take an entire book to cover this area properly, so do not take the steps outlined in this section as the all-encompassing solution to online privacy. However, we do cover a few of the major issues, namely spam, phishing, spyware (including adware), and pop-ups.

We cover a few of these topics because the problems are very common, and because most people don't seem to have good information on where to start.

Here is an overview of the steps you follow to decrease your network's vulnerabilities:

- Turn on spam blocking at your service provider

- Set up spam blocking on your home computers

- Avoid phishing scams

- Set up spyware and adware blocking on your home computers

- Set up pop-up blocking on your home computers

Turn on Spam Blocking at Your Service Provider

How to enable spam blocking with your service provider will vary highly and depend entirely on how the ISP has chosen to set up its services.

Enabling the protection is very easy. Just follow these steps (in this example, EarthLink is the ISP):

Step 1   Log in to the EarthLink My Account page using your account user ID and password.

Step 2   Click **Spam Blocker**. Choose the blocking setting that is appropriate (see Figure 16-3).

Figure 16-3   Enable Spam Blocking at Your ISP

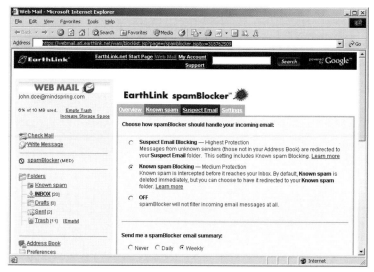

There are three possible setting levels that we will take a moment to explain as they will also apply to spam blocking on home computers (which we will set up next). The three settings and how they operate are

- **Off**—All e-mail is forwarded; no spam checking is performed.

- **Medium**—E-mail is checked against known spammer lists, and matches are discarded.

- **High**—In addition to checks against known spammer lists, you create a list of e-mail senders that are in your address book. Matches against the known spammer list are discarded. Matches from your address book are forwarded to your inbox. If the sender is unknown (in neither list), the e-mail is held as "suspected" spam. You then have to go in periodically and sort out acceptable e-mail from spam.

If you receive e-mail from only a few known e-mail addresses (friends and relatives), put them in the address book and turn the spam blocker on High. If you receive considerable e-mail from new sources, you probably need to go with the Medium setting.

If your kids have e-mail accounts, we would *highly* recommend the High setting (no pun intended). Kids should never receive e-mail from sources that you don't go in and specifically authorize.

Set Up Spam Blocking on Your Home Computers

If possible, set up a first line of spam defense in the service provider network. This may be enough, so we recommend trying the ISP route first, and then see if you need additional protection.

If you need to enable blocking on each of the computers in your home network, as mentioned earlier, most security bundles contain a spam blocking component. This section shows the steps to enable this service.

First, it's helpful to understand a bit about how a spam blocker works. Spam-blocker vendors maintain lists of known spammers, which can be automatically updated on your home computers by the security bundle software. Figure 16-4 shows the components of a typical spam blocker.

Figure 16-4   Spam Blocker Components

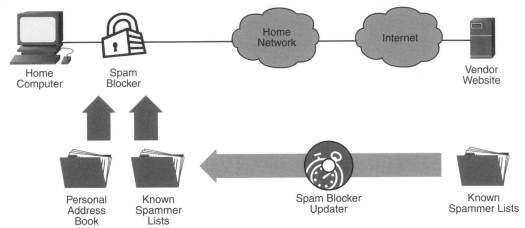

The spam blocker works much like the description in the previous section on service provider spam blockers. There is typically a setting (like Medium) that discards e-mail matching known spammer lists, and a higher setting (like High) that additionally compares against a personal address book that you provide and maintain.

It is assumed that you already installed the security product bundle you have selected. Table 16-1 shows the process for enabling spam blocking on both the Symantec and McAfee products.

With the spam blocker enabled, you should see considerably less spam e-mail. We suggest starting off with a Medium setting, and moving up to a higher setting if you are not satisfied with the reduction in spam.

Table 16-1   Enabling Spam Blocking

Steps	Symantec Norton Internet Security 2005	McAfee Internet Security Suite
Step 1: For Norton: click **AntiSpam**. For McAfee: click **SpamKiller**.		

Table 16-1   **Enabling Spam Blocking** *(Continued)*

Steps	Symantec Norton Internet Security 2005	McAfee Internet Security Suite
Step 2: Set the level of blocking. Start with the Medium or High setting. Click **OK**.		
Step 3: (This step may occur automatically during install.) It's possible to import address books from other e-mail programs. Click **OK**.		
Step 4: You can also add "friendly" addresses manually to your allowed list. Click **Add** to add new addresses.		

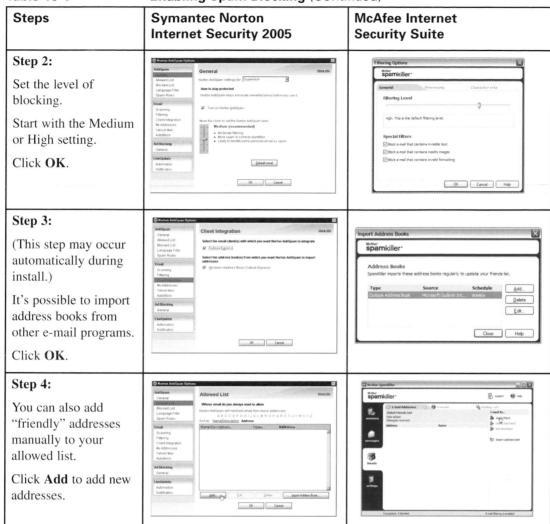

Avoid Phishing Scams

It's surprising that the security bundles, which so far have done just about everything for us, do not have specific tools to combat phishing scams. They *do* provide spam blocking, which would undoubtedly filter most if not all of them. But it is still surprising that this opportunity has not yet become apparent to the security software vendors.

On the other hand, at least one ISP (EarthLink) is hot on the trail. EarthLink provides a service they call ScamBlocker, which claims to be able to stop phishing scams in their tracks. The way it works is you have to download a web portal tool called EarthLink TotalAccess, which inserts functions into your Internet browser.

Figure 16-5 takes a quick look at the tool. (Note, however, that we did not actually test it with a real phishing scam to see if the claim is true.)

Notice the ScamBlocker icon on the toolbar after we have installed the service. We would expect the security product bundles to quickly incorporate specific scam blocking functions. (By the time this book is published and you read it, it's possible this will be a standard function, so check with your security bundle vendor.)

Figure 16-5   EarthLink ScamBlocker Toolbar

Set Up Spyware and Adware Blocking on Your Home Computers

So far, we have mitigated very serious security risks. We have set up firewalls, antivirus protection, and spam blockers. Now onward to some less serious threats, but nonetheless irritating. Fortunately, the security product bundles we have been talking much about do incorporate protection for spyware and adware also.

It is assumed that you already installed the security product bundle you have selected. Table 16-2 shows the process for enabling spyware and adware blocking on both the Symantec and McAfee products.

Table 16-2   Enabling Spyware and Adware Blocking

Step	Symantec Norton Internet Security 2005	McAfee Internet Security Suite
Symantec: Click **Options > Norton AntiVirus > Threat Categories.** McAfee: Click **Privacy Service > Configure Privacy Service Options** Checkmark **Prevention** of **Spyware**, **Adware**, and **Pop-Up Ads**. Click **OK**.		

To see if your computer contains spyware or adware, we highly recommend the Spybot Search & Destroy program, which is available here:

http://www.safer-networking.org/en/download/index.html

After installation, you can run a scan of your computer by double-clicking on the Spybot S&D icon, and then clicking **Check for Problems** (see Figure 16-6).

Figure 16-6   Using Spybot Search & Destroy

When the scan completes, click **Fix Selected Problems** to erase the spyware or adware.

Set Up Pop-Up Blocking on Home Computers

Blocking pop-up ads can be accomplished three ways:

- Enable built-in Internet Explorer pop-up blocker (Windows XP SP2 with IE 6 SP1)

- Install free pop-up blocker (such as the Pop-Up Stopper from Panicware)

- Enable pop-up blocking in the security software bundle you purchased

We trialed the pop-up blocking in the security software bundles and found them more difficult to disable temporarily when needed than the other two methods. So we recommend either the built-in IE approach or the free pop-up stopper program.

Figure 16-7 shows how to enable the pop-up blocker built in to Windows XP SP2. In Internet Explorer, click **Tools > Pop-Up Blocker > Turn On Pop-Up Blocker**

Alternatively, if you are not running XP, we recommend installing Pop-Up Stopper Free Edition from Panicware, available here:

http://www.panicware.com/product_psfree_download.html

After installation, a small white hand icon will appear in the lower left of your Windows toolbar. Right-click on the white hand and you can toggle the pop-up blocking function on and off very easily (see Figure 16-8).

Figure 16-7   Enable Windows XP Built-In Pop-Up Blocking

Figure 16-8   Using the Pop-Up Stopper from Panicware

Note that there are web pages that do use pop-up windows to convey legitimate information that you ask for. So, sometimes, pop-up windows are good. There is no easy answer to this problem except you can either disable pop-up blocking and endure the annoyance, or enable it and when you run into issues with some websites, disable it temporarily.

Where to Go for More Info

Visit these websites for more information on online privacy:

http://www.symantec.com/homecomputing/library/library.html

http://www.ftc.gov/bcp/menu-internet.htm

Keeping Your Family Safe on the Internet

 NOTE This chapter is intended for adults as it covers some fairly sensitive topics. Although there is nothing explicit written in this chapter, we recommend that you as a parent read this first, even if you are delegating the build out and maintenance of your home network to your teenager.

If you have children and access to the Internet, you need to educate and arm yourself to protect them against the many dangers that they can and likely will encounter. The Internet is a particular danger to children because often times the kids know more about the technology than the parents. This leads to situations where the parent is either unaware of the dangers or where the parent takes some steps to protect the children, which are easily circumvented by a tech-savvy kid.

The natural curiosity and rebellious nature of kids, combined with greater technical knowledge means parents are at a disadvantage. Unlike other forms of rebellion, like partying in the basement or sneaking out at night, you do not have the benefit of having tried these tricks and getting caught by your parents. The Internet is an entirely new game, and your children are the first generation of kids to have access to it.

What Are the Online Dangers?

This chapter outlines some of the dangers or inappropriate web activity kids (or spouses) may encounter and steps that you can take to protect them. Most of the tips we will provide will be known, but some of these solutions can be considered an invasion of privacy because the child or spouse will not be able to detect the monitoring tools used. It is always best to be up front with your children and spouse, but in cases where someone is knowingly violating household rules, we believe that it is your right to take action.

The next sections outline just some of the dangers of letting your family access the Internet.

Pornography

The number-one Internet concern for many parents and spouses is easy access to websites containing sexually explicit or graphically violent material.

This is especially a concern when many sites containing pornography have website addresses that are common misspellings for other popular sites. Even more insidious are porn sites that use common misspellings of children's television shows.

Much of this type of activity has been curtailed by the Truth in Domain Names Act, which makes misleading web page names illegal (in the United States). Some of these sites get around the law by showing a front page that advises viewers that they are about to enter a site with adult material. This is great for little kids who do not intend to view adult material, but it does nothing to keep a teenager from entering the site.

Predators

One of the most frightening dangers on the Internet is the possibility of a child being contacted and then stalked by sexual predators who roam chat rooms. (If you don't think this is a real danger just go to a chat room where kids would be, log in, and wait.)

A favorite tactic used by predators is to pose as another kid and then lure the victim into a private chat room. That's usually when the predator turns on his or her web cam. There is also a danger that a child can inadvertently provide a sexual predator with personal information, such as home address, school name, phone number, or parents' work schedule. Take it seriously and report it if you find out about this happening. Sexually enticing a minor online is a crime.

By the way, there is a site called http://www.pervertedjustice.com that tracks online sexual predators. (This website is only intended for adults.) The site posts their names, addresses, pictures, and sends the log files to local and federal authorities.

Gambling

There are tens of thousands of gambling sites on the Internet, both legal and illegal. Whether legitimate or a scam site, it is doubtful that most parents would allow their underage kids to visit gambling sites. There are some reports of kids "borrowing" their parents' credit card and racking up serious debt in no time at all. If this happens, parents may actually be liable for the debt their children run up.

Hacking

We mentioned hacker programs that reside inside other, often "free" or shareware programs. Kids tend to be more vulnerable than adults because most do not have the financial wherewithal to purchase software programs on their own. Be suspicious of any free program targeted at children.

Hacking may not look like an immediate danger to your family; however, it is illegal and, therefore, you can be held liable for any damages done by your child.

Illegal Peer-to-Peer Sharing

Peer-to-peer sites are often used to illegally trade copyrighted material. In addition to being a favorite cover for people distributing viruses and spyware, sharing copyrighted material (songs, movies, and so on) is punishable by law in the United States and many other countries. As with gambling sites, parents can be held financially responsible if a child is found guilty of copyright infringement. Lawsuits brought by the music industry (RIAA) against people sharing music illegally on the Internet are typically resulting in thousands of dollars per family in settlements.

Protecting Your Family from Online Dangers

Now that we have scared you, you're probably thinking it might be a good idea to never ever let your kids use the Internet. Well, that's probably not such a good idea because

- It puts them at a serious disadvantage in school and socially.

- If they don't use the Internet at home, they will access it somewhere else. It's too big and too easy to get access to.

 GEEK SQUAD A rule of thumb: If kids are under 12 or so, most of the time they access adult content by accidentally clicking the wrong link or ad. But, if you find that a teenager has accessed an adult site, it's time to start asking them questions.

Given that, you can do a number of things to keep your kids out of danger— to protect children who do not know better and to prevent children and spouses from breaking the rules:

- **Educate yourself**—The fact that you are reading this a big step in the right direction, but it should not end here. Keep up to date with new threats, scams, and solutions.

- **Browse in plain sight**—Only allow your children to be online in a public part of the house where you can see them and the computer screen by just passing by. Kids are much less likely to be lured into inappropriate websites or chat rooms if you are monitoring their online activity.

- **Use a parental control program**—Numerous programs are available that allow you to block inappropriate online content. We will walk through a couple of programs that we found very useful in the section "How to Build It: Making the Internet Safe."

  A number of ISP-supported options can block inappropriate content. The best programs allow you to choose specific types of material to block based on what you think is inappropriate for your child. Some even allow tiers for different age ranges. The various filters are enabled based on the user login (each of your children gets a login ID and password) so you can have different settings for different age children.

You definitely want to choose a program that has automatic updates from the vendor and one that uses a combination of manually entered URLs and behavior logic to actively scan sites for inappropriate content. Chat recorders are also a good feature to look for, but make sure you get one that records both sides of the chat. Avoid programs that require you to enter all the URLs (addresses) you want to block. You could do nothing but enter porn URLs every minute for the rest of your life and still not catch even half of them.

- **Log and monitor (as a last resort)**—If you have a child (or spouse) who, despite your rules, keeps attempting to view adult material, you can buy a program that allows you to record everything that appears on a computer screen. They work like a VCR for your computer screen and can be played back later.

    The best ones operate in "stealth mode," meaning their operation is nearly impossible to detect even by savvy computer users. Some programs even send screen captures to a website that allow you to view the screen remotely. These programs are a bit more expensive than the typical filter programs mentioned and are usually used as a last resort.

For all the good that the Internet provides, it can be a dangerous place for kids. For the most part the good outweighs the bad and, although the adult sites and chat rooms and online gambling halls are fine for adults who want visit them, you need to protect your kids from visiting them whether they simply mistype a popular web address or if their curiosity gets the best of them.

 GEEK SQUAD As a starting point, try these three steps and if they don't work, go on to something more restrictive:

- Use Windows or parental control programs to put time restrictions on computer usage.

- Use the built-in parental controls on a Linksys router or at the ISP.

- Move the computers to common areas, such as a kitchen or living room.

How to Build It: Making the Internet Safe

Here is the overview of the steps you go through to make surfing the Internet safe for your family:

- Decide which parental controls are right for you

- Enable parental controls at your ISP

- Enable parental controls using your home router

- Enable parental controls on home computers

Decide Which Parental Controls Are Right for You

The first step in enabling parental controls on your home network is to make two decisions:

- What types of controls do you need?

- Where will you put your enforcement point(s)?

Parental controls we can enable include a number of possibilities, not just blocking website access. Most parental control programs include features to

- Restrict website access by site (in other words, block URLs)

- Restrict website access by content (in other words, scan pages for non-blocked URLs for inappropriate content)

- Restrict which programs can be used (such as web browser, e-mail, chat, instant messaging (IM), music sharing)

- Enforce time limits and hours of usage

So you need to decide what Internet usage framework you are going to provide for your child. Some things are pretty clear cut, for example, pornography. But, there are grey areas, such as medical or biology sites and graphic news reports. Time limits also seem straightforward, just limit to one hour a day and never between the hours of 10 p.m. and 7 a.m., right? Well, yes and no. The Internet is a fantastic resource for homework and research. One hour a day could be restricting how well your kids do at school. We know, it makes your head spin.

Most parental control programs start with a recommended profile for many of these options, based on age group. We recommend starting with those and then make exceptions as situations arise.

Second, there are now a number of possibilities for where you put your enforcement point (in other words, where is the traffic cop that controls access). Possible enforcement points are

- In the ISP network

- In your router

- On each computer in your home network

- Any of the above

Each has advantages and disadvantages. For example, it may seem intuitive to only place parental control on a child's computer. However, is it possible they could access your computer and bypass the controls? Still, applying parental controls on every computer in your home network could be cost-prohibitive (depends how many computers you have to protect). It could also be a little cumbersome to make updates to several computers if you need to change access rules. For these reasons, parental control provided by the router or the ISP may be a better option as it provides a single, central enforcement point, and this is an increasingly popular way to go.

If you are really, really concerned, another possibility is to apply parental control in layers (like security), with a central router/ISP-based enforcement point coupled with parental control software on the child's PC.

The sections that follow show how to enable each of these options: ISP-based, router-based, and computer-based parental control.

Enable Parental Controls at Your ISP

Many service providers offer built-in parental control as part of their service. Check with your service provider to see whether this is an option. Most of the bundled parental services work by installing an Internet browser that is specific to the service (for example, AOL, EarthLink, MSN) and then only using that browser for accessing the Internet.

This type of protection will work in preventing the completely inadvertent access into adult content, such as making a typo in a website and your child ends up on a porn site staring at unmentionables on the screen, probably to their horror as much as yours. Just keep in mind, though, that the controls are only as good as the willingness to use their modified Internet browser. Most kids beyond the age of eight can quite easily figure out how to circumvent the controls.

Turning on parental control at your service provider will vary highly and depend entirely on how they have chosen to set up their services. Follow these steps to set up your services (we use EarthLink here as an example):

Step 1   Log in to your ISP account. Under Profile Management, find the Parental Control setting for the child's account. Set it to On. Click **Profile Settings**. With this particular service, you can specify the child's age, and the access controls are set accordingly see Figure 17-1). Click **Save**.

Figure 17-1   Example of EarthLink's Parental Control

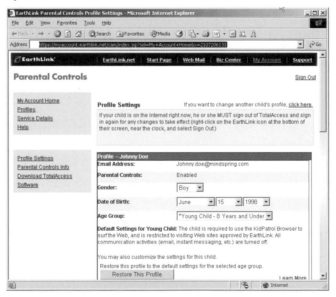

Step 2   Click **Web Browsing Settings** (see Figure 17-2).

The options have been set appropriately to the child's age (eight, for our example):

- Must use KidPatrol browser

- Mask all inappropriate website content

- Allow access to approved websites only

Click **Save**.

Figure 17-2   Setting Your Child's Profile

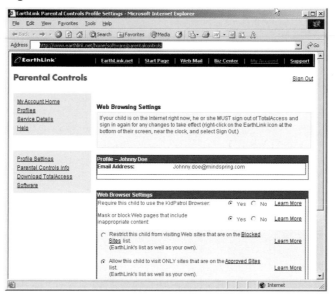

To take advantage of the parental controls with this service, everyone must use the specially provided EarthLink TotalAccess browser with integrated security functions. Then each family user must log in with their user ID and password. Access privileges are set according to each person.

Again, this type of protection is adequate against inadvertent access to adult content, but probably not that difficult to circumvent. For example, someone wanting to access adult material may be able to download a different browser.

Enable Parental Controls Using Your Home Router

Another (more recent) option is to use your home network router as the parental control enforcement point. Linksys has partnered with Netopia to offer a service where the Linksys router works in conjunction with a centralized service to provide parental control. The service requires an annual subscription for $40 ($3.33 per month seems like a bargain to us!). Here's a website with more information:

http://www.linksys.com/pcsvc/info.asp

The model is similar to the ISP model, in that each user logs in with a user ID when they access the Internet. Based on the account, privileges are enforced by the router. A major advantage of this approach is that the enforcement is provided for your entire home network, regardless of the computer used to access the Internet. Another major advantage of this approach is that it is not dependent on the web browser being used; enforcement occurs regardless.

If you want to go with this type of parental control, you need to make sure the wireless router you buy supports the feature. At the time the book was written, the WRT54GS—Wireless-G SpeedBooster Router model was the first to support the feature.

Follow these steps to set up parental control (on Linksys WRT54GS):

Step 1   Access the wireless router using a web browser. Click **Access Restrictions > Parental Control** (see Figure 17-3). Click **Enable** to activate the feature on the router. If you have not done so already, click on **Sign Up for Parental Control Service** to create a service account. Click **Save Settings**.

Figure 17-3   Enable Linksys Parental Control

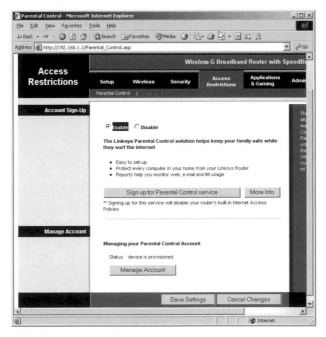

Step 2   Click **Manage Account**. Click **Family Settings > New Family Member** (see Figure 17-4). Create an account for each person in your family that will use the Internet, specifying their age. Write down the account user IDs and passwords. Click **I'm Done**.

Figure 17-4   Setting Up Family User IDs and Profiles

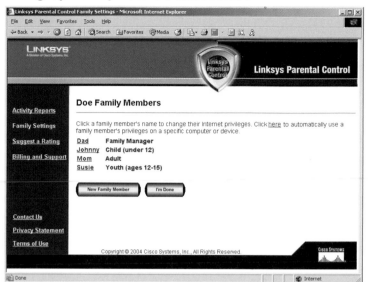

    NOTE We dodged a bullet by being able to specify that our spouse is simply an "Adult" instead of specifying his or her age. Sensitive subject in many households.

Step 3   Click on the child's new user ID (**Susie** in our example) to change their usage settings. Click the appropriate areas to change settings, including access times, web restrictions, and e-mail and IM restrictions(see Figure 17-5). Click **Save**.

Figure 17-5   Modifying User Privileges and Settings

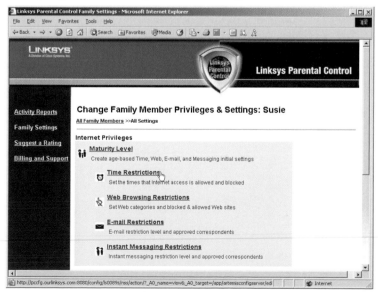

Now whenever someone in your house attempts to access the Internet, the router is going to prompt them for their user ID and password (see Figure 17-6).

Figure 17-6   Log In to Obtain Internet Access

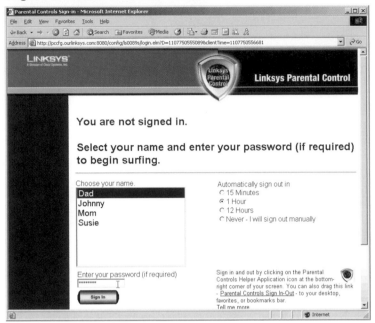

Because the enforcement point is the router, not a computer, it is not possible to circumvent the controls by changing computers or downloading a different web browser.

Another fantastic feature of this service is the ability to periodically look at usage logs and reports to do a little proactive monitoring to see if the rules you have set are doing their job (see Figure 17-7).

Figure 17-7   Checking Activity Reports

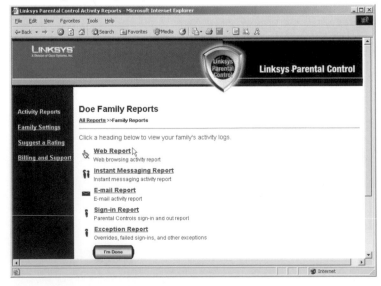

In our opinion, this is the model for the future of parental control. It makes a lot of sense.

Enable Parental Controls on Home Computers

Still another possible enforcement point for parental control is on the computer itself. Parental control software works in a similar model to other software we have discussed, such as antivirus and spam blocking. With the software you purchase, you get an annual subscription that includes periodic downloading of the latest lists of known adult content on the Internet.

Security Bundle Parental Control Option

Again, the software security bundles we evaluated all support some form of parental controls. The following steps show the process for enabling parental control with the Symantec product. The other security bundles are similar:

Step 1   Double-click the Norton Internet Security icon on the desktop. Click **Parental Control**. If it's set to Off (default), click **Turn On** (see Figure 17-8).

Figure 17-8   Turn On Parental Control

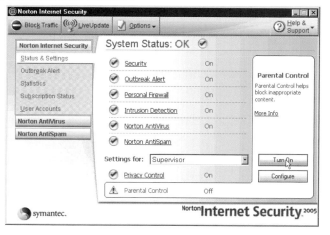

Step 2   Click **Configure**. With most products, you can set up different profiles for each user of a shared computer.

Select the user you want to set the Parental Control settings for, and then click each of the tabs, **Sites**, **Programs**, **Newsgroups**, and **Defaults**, to customize the restrictions you want to enforce (see Figure 17-9).

Figure 17-9   Customize Restrictions for Each User

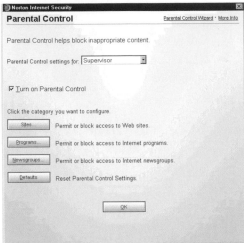

To test the parental controls, launch your Internet browser and enter a URL that is likely to be blocked (http:www.sexsite.com, for example). You should see a rejection like what's shown in Figure 17-10.

Figure 17-10 Example of Restricted URL Being Blocked

The parental control in the software security product bundles seem to work well. We tested out a number of websites hosting adult content, including "grey" area sites that are not all adult material, but have some adult material. All in all, the products seem to perform pretty well, and as far as we can tell are pretty difficult to circumvent (nothing is impossible to circumvent given enough time, energy, and cleverness, and teens are full of all three).

The disadvantage of this approach is that every computer on your home network must have parental control installed and maintained.

GEEK SQUAD We once had a boy offer to pay us what probably amounted to a year's pay from his paper route to clean up traces of porn on his parent's computer, which he had accumulated while his parents were away on vacation.

NetNanny Option

Looking for a much more software restrictive level of control? You might have a look at other products that are specifically focused on parental controls. There are numerous products. Check parenting magazines and consumer guides for recommendations. One such product that we evaluated is NetNanny.

NetNanny installation is like any other software installation, so we skip that part and go straight to setting up the rules. There are numerous features and controls in NetNanny, we only scratch the surface.

Double-click the NetNanny icon on the desktop to bring up the control window. Here, you can set the level of restriction to 1, 2, 3, or 4 for website blocking (see Figure 17-11). Set the level that is appropriate for your family.

Figure 17-11 Setting Level of Restriction in NetNanny

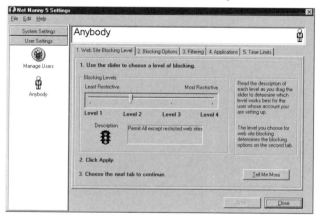

You can then proceed through the different settings to provide your rules for programs which can and cannot be used, whether to scan pages for objectionable content, and so on.

One nice feature to point out is the ability to limit usage to certain days and times, or provide a daily limit to time spent on the Internet (see Figure 17-12). No more 2 a.m. IM sessions!

By the way, we installed NetNanny "on top of" Symantec Norton Internet Security 2005 and the two worked together. The parental control provided by the Symantec product caught a lot of attempts to access what were clearly adult content sites. NetNanny tended to be more restrictive, jumping in where Symantec left off.

 NOTE What's neat about NetNanny is you can tailor the message displayed in the NetNanny Violation dialog box, so you can give your kids the hairy eyeball, so to speak: "Johnny, Mommy knows what you are doing and does not approve!"

Figure 17-12 Setting Internet Access Time Limits

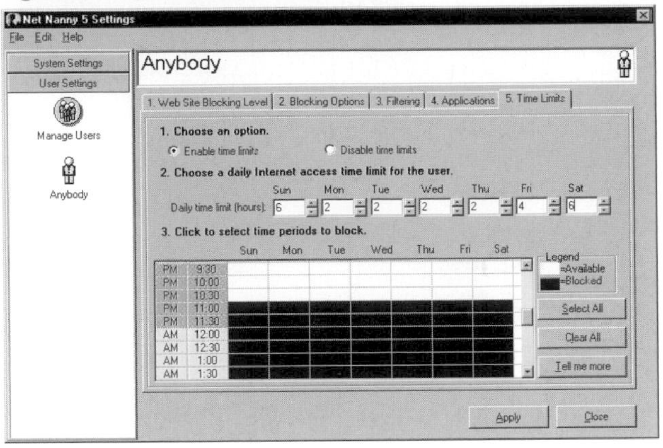

How to Track Internet Activity

If you reach the point where you believe a child is not playing by your rules; for example, you think they may have dark circles under their eyes from instant messaging with their friends at 2 a.m. each night, and you have exhausted all other measures, it's probably time to try some Internet activity tracking and logging.

Here are a couple of Internet-tracking programs that are recommended by various computer magazines:

■ **Activity Logger**—http://www.softactivity.com/

■ **AceSpy**—http://www.internet-pc-spy.com

■ **Spector**—http://www.spectorsoft.com/

These programs can also be useful for monitoring spouses who may be doing some stuff online that is…how should we put it…not exactly conducive to the marriage. Now the authors are not marriage counselors, and if a spouse will seek out these venues on the Internet, chances are there are serious problems in the relationship, anyway. As the saying goes: Where there is a will, there is a way. But this section would not be complete without mentioning that the same Internet activity logger tools, which can be used to track what a child is doing on the Internet, are also just as useful for tracking spouses. Enough said.

Each monitoring program is different, and we obviously can't cover them all here. So we chose one named Activity Logger because the name is easy to remember, and they had a free trial download. The installation of Activity Logger is straightforward, so in the interest of space (which our publisher keeps hounding us about), we skip it. It is worth, however, pointing out that during installation, several options are presented related to how "hidden" the program is in the computer. Hidden is good. In general, you want to follow these guidelines:

■ **Do not** create any icons for the logger. If a new icon appears on the desktop or the Windows toolbar, you are busted.

■ **Do not** have the running program show up on the Windows toolbar as a running task.

■ **Do not** have the program show up under the Add/Remove Programs function in Windows.

■ **Do** have the program start when Windows starts. You want the program to always be running when the computer is being used.

You can set the logging options you want by accessing the program's setup function (because it's hidden, you probably have to launch this directly from the installation directory on the hard disk). Set up whatever logging options you want (see Figure 17-13). Set the log file size to be large enough for how much usage time you want to capture.

Figure 17-13 Configure Your Logging Engine

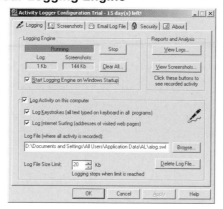

Now that you have the program set up to log and hidden, time to sit back and let it do its magic. After some period of time (overnight or whatever makes sense), you can go view the logs. Figure 17-14 shows a sample Activity Logger log.

From Figure 17-14, we can tell that someone used the computer around 10:21 p.m. First, they used Internet Explorer to go to Yahoo! Personals. Next, they started an AOL IM session to someone with an IM nickname of "SassyChick573." So, right there we know something is up.

Here's another pretty cool feature of Activity Logger (and other programs have it as well): It can take full-screen snapshots at intervals, so you can see exactly what was being displayed on the computer screen while the person was using it. Figure 17-15 shows a sample of a tracked session.

Figure 17-14 Sample Activity Logger Log

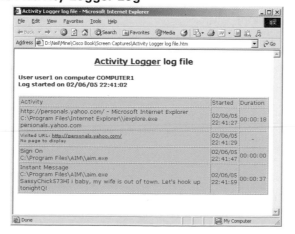

Figure 17-15 Sample Screen Shot of a Tracked Internet Session

Now we can actually see what the person was doing on Yahoo! Personals. Much harder to claim, "Oh I just landed on that page by accident" if you have screenshots of the person doing searches and interacting with people. We can also see the actual text being typed on both sides of the IM conversation. In this example, the originator typed, "Hi baby, my wife is out of town tonight. Let's hook up!" Yikes, let's see someone explain that away.

 NOTE We are pretty sure that using the programs discussed in this chapter is legal when you are monitoring your kids, but not sure what the laws are regarding tracking of spouses. Check the laws in your state. We are not lawyers, trust us, neither of us had the attention span to sit through law school.

Where to Go for More Info

These websites offer lots of great information on parental control:

http://www.getnetwise.org

http://www.safekids.com

http://www.netopia.com/products/pc/

 # From the Geek Squad Files

This part of the book accounted for a pretty big percentage of our agent calls: security, viruses/spyware, and porn. Each is worth a separate look but all are related:

- **Security**—Having some level of security on your network is a must, and not having any security is a really bad idea. This seems simple enough, but here's the catch: Just because you have some security on your network it does not mean you can stop using your brain. New programs and new hacks come along all the time, so don't dare anyone by downloading programs, posting your passwords in a chat room, or giving your credit card number out so that your account can be "verified." Stop and think before you click.

- **Viruses and spyware**—A virus that you download and launch (usually not on purpose) has already penetrated your firewall. We get calls on this all the time. Do not open files from people you do not know, and scan your system at regular intervals. Spyware is not usually damaging to your files, but it can significantly slow down your computer. At the risk of sounding pessimistic, *nothing on the Internet is free*. There is almost always a program or a piece of spyware attached to "free programs." One of the newest scams is to send popup windows that claim to rid you of viruses or spyware. When you click them, they launch a virus or attach a spyware tag. Classic.

- **Porn**—The authors do not cover this much in this book, but if you had not noticed (like if you have never used the Internet), there is quite a bit of porn on it. Before we tell you how to get rid of it, we want to point out that regardless of your views on the material, the industry as a whole has driven a great deal of the technological innovations on the web including streaming media, compression, secure downloads, and online commerce. Never underestimate what some people will do for dirty pictures.

Back to the topic at hand, content downloaded from adult sites (particularly "free" adult sites) is infected with viruses and spyware. Beware, if you are not willing to pay for the material that has been swept for viruses (no pun intended) the suppliers of this material are guessing (probably correctly) that you are hiding this material from a parent or significant other and are probably not willing to fess up on how a virus got on your PC in the first place. Have no fear, though, you can call the Geek Squad. We will clean your files and we never compute and tell.

In the spirit of being good sports, though, here are some tips for the suspicious parent or partner:

■ In the history of the Internet, pornography has never "spontaneously appeared" on anyone's machine. If you find adult material on a computer, someone put it there...on purpose.

■ It is exceptionally rare that the person who did put the adult material on the computer was the teenager computer geek down the street trying to frame someone in your house. We are not saying it could not happen, we have just never seen it.

■ If you suspect someone has put porn on a computer and that they are trying to hide it from you, look in the computer folders that are named in such a way that you would never look there. For example

— Baseball Statistics 1932-1954

— Important Military Documents

— German Chemist Trivia

— Mars Lander Transcripts

It's a good bet that these folders contain some dirty pictures.

Now that you've read how and why to properly secure your network, your head may be spinning from the length of your to-do list. Relax; it's not that bad! To help you in your quest for security, just use this checklist, which gives you the nitty-gritty of what you need to do to protect your network.

General

❏ Choose passwords using a random series of lowercase letters, uppercase letters, and numbers.

❏ Install a router (wired or wireless) between your broadband connection and home network.

❏ Change the router administrator password from the default (admin) to a new password, and write it down.

❏ Change the administrator password for any wired or wireless device you add to your network, and write it down.

❏ Download and install the latest updates to the Windows operating system regularly. Enable automatic updates if provided (Windows XP).

❏ NEVER respond to an e-mail requesting you to confirm a credit card number or confirm and enter your user ID and password. Similarly, never call a phone number in an e-mail and give them credit card numbers or user ID and password over the phone. Call your bank or credit card number directly from a number in the phone book.

File and Printer Sharing

❏ Do not share the entire C:\ drive from your computer on the home network.

❏ Always disable Windows File and Printer Sharing on dialup NICs.

❏ If you use a computer as a gateway to the broadband Internet connection for other computers, always disable Windows File and Printer Sharing on the NIC that's connected to the broadband service.

❏ Do not share files or folders containing sensitive information (such as credit card numbers and bank account information).

Firewalls

❏ Enable the firewall feature on your router, preferably a stateful packet inspection (SPI) firewall.

❏ Make sure your computers are running a personal firewall program, such as ZoneAlarm or the Windows XP built-in firewall.

Antivirus

❏ If your Internet service provider offers an antivirus service for your e-mail, enable it.

❏ Make sure your computers are running an antivirus program, such as Symantec Norton AntiVirus or McAfee VirusScan.

❏ Keep your antivirus software up to date with the latest virus signatures, enabling automatic updates if possible.

Spam

❏ Set your Internet Explorer Privacy setting to Medium High to prevent certain cookies from being stored on your computer.

❏ If your Internet service provider offers an anti-spam feature for your e-mail, enable it.

❏ Create a dirty e-mail address that you use for online registrations and to provide to companies. Free e-mail services, such as Hotmail or Yahoo! Mail, work well.

❏ Optionally, set up an anti-spam program on your computer, which should be integrated with your e-mail program.

❏ Never respond to any unsolicited e-mail, even to remove yourself from their distribution list.

Cookies, Adware, Pop-Ups, Phishing, and Other Threats

❏ Never respond to pop-up ads.

❏ Install a pop-up blocking software program, such as Panicware's Pop-Up Stopper or the pop-up blocker built in to Windows, as of XP SP2 and Internet Explorer 6 SP1.

❏ Never respond to phishing scams. Report them immediately to the company being impersonated, the Federal Trade Commission (FTC), and your Internet service provider.

❏ Install a spyware and adware sweeper program, such as Spybot Search & Destroy.

❏ Do not forward e-mail that sounds too incredible to be believable (such as urban legends).

Wireless Networks

❏ Change the SSID from the default (for example, linksys) to a random series of lowercase letters, uppercase letters, and numbers.

❏ Disable SSID broadcasting.

❏ Enable WEP or WPA encryption on the wireless router and all wireless NICs. Use the strongest encryption level that all devices support.

❏ Use a WEP or WPA pass-phrase, which is a random series of lowercase letters, uppercase letters, and numbers.

❏ Disable ad-hoc wireless networking on all NICs.

Wireless Hotspots

❏ Know the hotspot you are connecting to; beware of free hotspots that might be a potential "man-in-the-middle" attack trying to obtain your personal information.

❏ Use caution sending confidential information (including e-mail, chat, and online purchases) when connected to a wireless hotspot.

❏ Use a VPN client to encrypt traffic, if possible.

Parental Controls

❏ Install some form of parental control at your ISP using your home network router or on each computer in your network.

❏ Set guidelines for Internet usage and discuss openly with your children.

❏ Set up computers preferably in non-private locations in your home (such as the kitchen or living room) to discourage family members from visiting a site they shouldn't be visiting.

❏ Enforce time limits and time of day usage restrictions. Kids have no business being on the Internet at 2 a.m.

Wireless Print Servers:
The Cure for Joy

In previous chapters, we described how to set up your home network, including how to use Windows File and Printer Sharing to be able to print to printers that are attached to a different computer on your home network. Figure 19-1 shows an example of this setup, where we have three computers on one home network. The two desktops (Computer 1 and Computer 2) each have a printer attached and share them with the other computers via the network connection.

Figure 19-1   Wired Printer Sharing

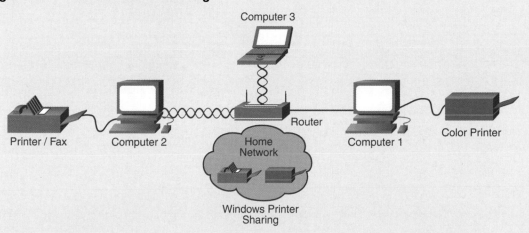

Although this setup works effectively, there are several disadvantages, including

- For the laptop (Computer 3) to print to the color printer attached to Computer 1, Computer 1 must be turned on. When Computer 1 is turned off, the printer attached to it is inaccessible.

- Changing a printer's location potentially requires modification of the network layout. For example, if the color printer shown in Figure 19-1 is swapped with the printer/fax device, the printer sharing must be completely changed, and each computer must be updated with the new location on the network.

- Printers can clutter a desk or working space. Wouldn't it be nice to get them off the kids' homework desk and off your desk? Why not put them in a central location in your house (like an unused nook in a hallway or the corner of a room)?

A wireless printer server solves these disadvantages. As Figure 19-2 shows, a wireless printer server connects to a wireless home network, and then connects with one or two home printers. The wireless printer server makes the printers it "owns" available to the entire home network. Each computer on the home network thinks that it has one or more printers attached to it. Furthermore, the printers can now be placed anywhere that suits your needs within your home.

Figure 19-2   Wireless Printer Sharing

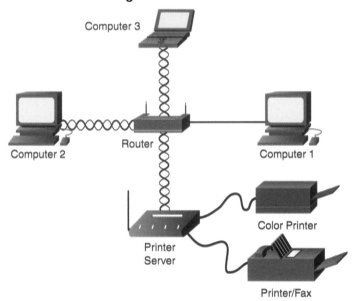

You may be wondering why the chapter title includes the phrase "The Cure for Joy." For very good reason: Everyone we spoke with had trouble getting wireless print servers to work properly. So we hope this chapter will make it easier.

Table 19-1 shows the wireless printer server products from Linksys that we recommend.

Table 19-1   Linksys Wireless Print Server Products

Model	Printer Ports	Works with Wireless Standards	Wireless Encryption Supported
WPS54G	1 USB	802.11b 802.11g	64-bit WEP 128-bit WEP WPA
WPS54GU2	1 USB 1 parallel	802.11b 802.11g	64-bit WEP 128-bit WEP
WPS11	1 parallel	802.11b 802.11g	64-bit WEP 128-bit WEP

Wireless print server products were fairly expensive (approximately $150) until recently, but these products have fallen in price to the point where they are not much more expensive than a wireless router or NIC.

VERY IMPORTANT: **Keep in mind that when you purchase a wireless product like those mentioned previously, you need to check two things:**

- **Does the product support the wireless standard you are running (for example, 802.11b, 802.11g, and so on)?**

- **Does the product support the wireless security you are running (for example, 128-bit WEP, WPA, and so on)?**

See the discussion in Chapter 9, "ABGs of Wireless," and Chapter 10, "Going Wireless at Home," on wireless NIC compatibility with wireless Routers, and Chapter 11, "Securing Your Wireless Network," on wireless security.

Consider any wireless device you will connect to your network like you would a wireless NIC.

How to Build It: Wireless Print Server

In this section, we install a wireless printer server on your home network. Here's an overview of the major steps:

- Set up the wireless print server for your wireless network

- Connect printers to the wireless print server

- Install the wireless print server driver on each computer

- Print a test page

Set Up the Wireless Print Server for Your Wireless Network

First, you need to configure the wireless print server so it can communicate with your wireless home network. Just like any other computer you've added, you must tell the wireless printer server how it can communicate to your wireless network. Here are the steps to do this (we use the WPS54GU2 product as an example):

Step 1   Connect the Linksys wireless print server to the Linksys wireless router using an Ethernet cable (ordinary, not crossover), and plug in the power adapter (see Figure 19-3).

The LAN LED light on the front should light up.

Figure 19-3   Connect the Printer Server to the Wireless Router

Step 2   Put the CD that came with the Linksys printer server into a computer on the network (one that is wired is preferred). The setup utility should start automatically (see Figure 19-4). If not, use My Computer to browse the CD and double-click **Setup.exe**. Click **Setup Wizard**.

Figure 19-4   Linksys Wireless Print Server Setup Wizard

Step 3   The setup utility searches for the new wireless print server on the network (see Figure 19-5).If it does not show up, try clicking **Refresh**. If it still does not show up, check your cabling.Click on the entry for the print server, and click **Next**.

Figure 19-5   New Wireless Print Server Found

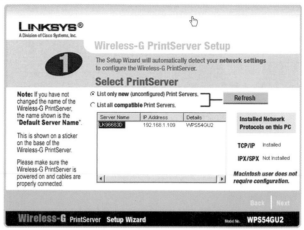

Step 4   Enter the default password, **admin**, and click **Enter** (see Figure 19-6).

Figure 19-6   Enter the Default Password

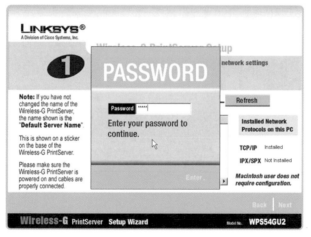

Step 5   Enter a device name for the wireless print server. (We used "Print_Server" in this example.) Enter the domain name you used when you installed Windows networking ("HOME" in this example). See Figure 19-7. Click **Next**.

Figure 19-7   Choose a Device Name and a Domain Name

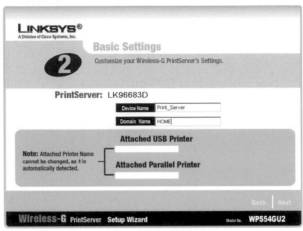

Step 6   Checkmark **Automatically obtain an IP address (DHCP)** (see Figure 19-8), and click **Next.**

Figure 19-8   Automatically Obtain an IP Address

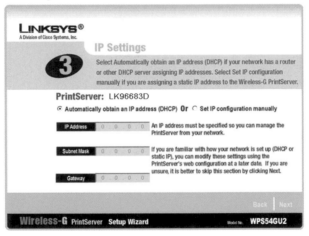

Step 7   Change the password from the default (admin) to a random series of uppercase letters, lowercase letters, and numbers. (See Figure 19-9.) Write it down somewhere safe for keeping. Click **Next**.

Figure 19-9   Change the Administrator Password

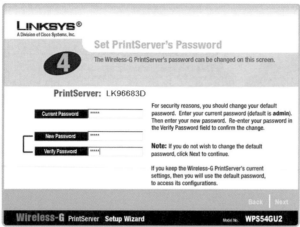

Step 8   Enter the SSID for your wireless network (in this example, it's "J59wgh21MX"). (See Figure 19-10.) Channel is not important; let it default to **6**. Set the Network Type to **Infrastructure**. Click **Next**.

Figure 19-10 Enter the SSID of Your Wireless Network

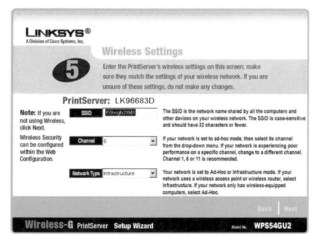

Step 9   Set the wireless security setting to **128 Bit Keys** (or the encryption you are using). Enter the pass-phrase you have been using for your wireless network (in this example, "64Gx3prY19fk2"). (See Figure 19-11.) Click **Next**.

Figure 19-11 Enter Your Wireless Security Settings

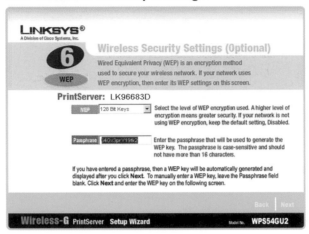

Step 10 Check the WEP key to ensure it matches the key being used on the wireless router. (See Figure 19-12.) Do not modify the key! Click **Next**.

Figure 19-12 Confirm the Generated WEP Key

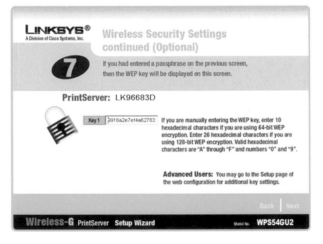

 NOTE If the two keys do not match, modify the key value to match what is being used on the wireless router. Normally, the keys will match as long as the print server and router are both Linksys products.

Step 11 The setup utility then displays a summary of the new settings (see Figure 19-13). Click **Yes**.

Figure 19-13 Settings Confirmation

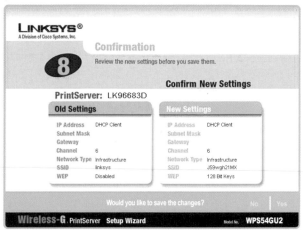

Step 12   You're all done (see Figure 19-14). Leave the setup utility for now because we come back to it later. Unplug the Ethernet cable from the wireless print server, power it off, and then power it back on.

Figure 19-14 You're All Finished!

The WLAN LED indicator light on the front of the wireless printer server should now be lit.

Troubleshooting Tips: Wireless Print Server

If, after you complete these steps, the WLAN LED indicator light on the front of the wireless printer server is still not lit, try the following:

- Make sure the wireless router is powered on and functioning normally. Test by making sure you can access the Internet from one of your computers that is connected by a wireless NIC.

- If you are running a personal firewall program, such as ZoneAlarm, it may be preventing the Linksys print server installation utility from accessing the network. Temporarily disable the firewall, or grant the utility access to the network.

- Reconnect the Ethernet cable between the wireless router and the wireless printer server. Restart the setup utility and repeat Steps 1–12. Pay close attention to the wireless settings: SSID, WEP key length, and WEP key pass-phrase. They must be entered identically to your wireless network, including uppercase and lowercase letters.

- Check on the wireless router to see if the wireless printer server is getting assigned an address on the home network: Use an Internet browser to access the router; click **Status > Local Network > DHCP Client Table**. You should see the wireless printer server with an address on the network (see Figure 19-15, which uses the Print_Server example).

Figure 19-15 Verifying the Print Server Is Getting an IP Address

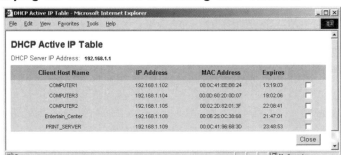

- If you implemented MAC address blocking on your wireless router (see Chapter 11, "Securing Your Wireless Network"), double-check that you permitted the new wireless device's MAC address to access your wireless network.

- Read the "Troubleshooting" chapter in the installation manual that came with the Linksys wireless print server.

Connect Printers to the Wireless Printer Server

After you verify that the wireless printer server is properly communicating with your wireless network, you can set up the rest of the service:

Step 1   Unplug the Ethernet cable to the wireless printer server (if it's still connected).

Step 2   Move the wireless printer server to wherever you want the printers to be.

   Because it's wireless, you can put it anywhere in your house near an electrical outlet.

Step 3   Plug your printers into the appropriate port on the back of the wireless print server (see Figure 19-16 for an example).

Figure 19-16 Plug Your Printers into the Wireless Print Server

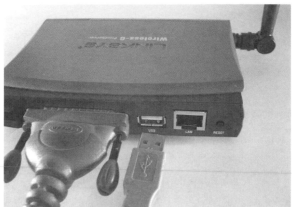

Remember to connect the power cable to the wireless print server. After connecting the cables to both the print server and the printers, also remember to plug in the printers to the electrical outlet.

After the printer finishes booting, you should see the corresponding parallel or USB LED lights light up on the front of the wireless print server. If not, check the cabling and try powering off and on the wireless print server and printers.

Install the Wireless Print Server Driver on Each Computer

We can now install a print server driver on each computer on the network. The *print server driver* is a software program that knows how to "talk" to the wireless print server over your network. Its job is to make sure your computers are able to communicate with the printers over the network as if they were physically attached to the computer itself.

Here's how you install the printer server driver:

Step 1   Insert the CD that came with the Linksys printer server into your computer. The setup utility should start automatically (see Figure 19-17). If not, use My Computer to browse the CD and double-click **Setup.exe**. Click **User Install**.

Step 2   The driver install program starts (see Figure 19-18). Click **Next** and follow the standard installation steps for software (such as which directory, do you want desktop icons, and so on).

Figure 19-17　Linksys Wireless Print Server Driver Setup Wizard

Figure 19-18　Print Server Driver Install Program

Step 3　After the install is finished, a dialog appears acknowledging that the print server driver has been installed. Checkmark **Configure Print Driver now** (see Figure 19-19). Click **Finish**.

Figure 19-19　Print Server Driver Is Installed

Step 4   You should see one or both of the printers that are connected to the wireless print server. Click the printer you want to install printing service to (in this example the Officejet 500 on port 1, the parallel port). (See Figure 19-20.) Click **Next**.

Figure 19-20 Printer Port Setup

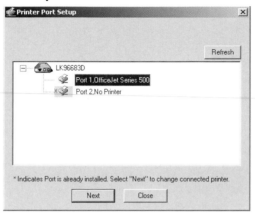

 NOTE If you have multiple printers you want to install print service to, you must do one at a time. *Do not select both printers simultaneously or bad things may happen.*

Step 5   Click **Add New Printer** (see Figure 19-21). The Windows Printer Wizard starts.

Figure 19-21 Add Printer to the Wireless Print Service

Step 6   If the printer was previously connected to the same computer, it should appear in the Printers list. If not, click **Have Disk** and insert the CD that came with the printer (see Figure 19-22).

Figure 19-22 Windows Add Printer Wizard

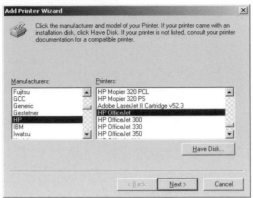

Step 7 Here's an example of pointing to the printer manufacturer's CD. Locate the appropriate driver on the CD, and then click **OK** (see Figure 19-23).

Figure 19-23 Locate the Printer Driver on the Printer Manufacturer's CD

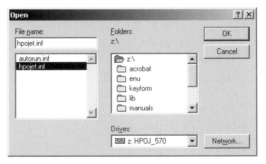

Step 8 After installing the printer drivers, Windows asks for a printer name (see Figure 19-24). Checkmark **Yes** if you want this to be your default printer. Click **Finish**.

Figure 19-24 Give the Printer a Name

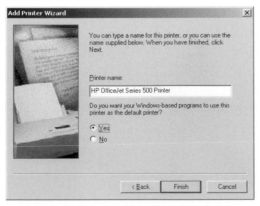

Step 9   The printer you just installed should now appear in the list. Click the printer to select it, and then click **Connect** (see Figure 19-25).

Figure 19-25 Mapping the Printer to a Print Server Port

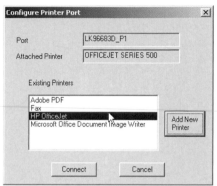

Step 10   The Printer Wizard ends and you are returned to the setup dialog for the print server driver. You should see the printer you just added now appear highlighted in yellow, which indicates that it is active (see Figure 19-26). Click **Close**.

Figure 19-26 Your Printer Is Now Active

You need to perform these steps on each computer on your network from which side you want to be able to use the network printers. If you have more than one printer connected to the wireless printer server, you will need to perform the previous steps for each printer on each computer. Although, before you spend your time doing that, it's highly recommended that you verify the installation on the first computer by printing a test page.

NOTE The Linksys Wireless Print Server setup wizard has an option for installing a Bi-Admin component. This component is only for network administrators who may need to perform detailed management of multiple wireless print servers in a business environment. Ignore it for your purposes.

Print a Test Page

At this point, the computer should recognize the printer and be able to print to it. Try a test page by following these steps:

Step 1   Open any document with Microsoft Word (or whatever document editor you use).

Step 2   Select **File > Print**. The new printer should show up in the selection list (see Figure 19-27).

Figure 19-27 Microsoft Word Recognizes the Wireless Printer

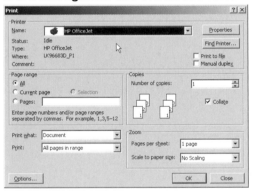

Step 3   Click **OK**. Verify that you actually get a printout.

Troubleshooting Tips: Print a Test Page

If your printer fails to print out a test page, try the following:

- If the printer was previously installed on the computer, try deleting the printer first. Restart the setup utility and repeat Steps 1–10 in the "Install the Wireless Print Server Driver on Each Computer" section.

- Read the "Troubleshooting" chapter in the installation manual that came with the Linksys wireless print server.

CHAPTER 20

Video Surveillance

Earlier in this book, we mentioned that the network capacity (or bandwidth) within your home network was much greater (three times or more) than the fastest upload/download speeds you will get from your high-speed connection to the Internet. So why does all this excess capacity exist on your home network? There are actually many in-home applications that require more bandwidth; we discuss many of them in this chapter (and a few more in the following chapters). The first of these applications is video surveillance.

Once limited to very expensive closed-circuit television (CCTV) systems, video surveillance is now affordable and, if you already have a wireless network in your home, a decent video surveillance system only costs you a hundred dollars or so. (We say *only* because a basic CCTV system costs more than $1000.)

Video surveillance systems have all sorts of practical uses: from home security to nanny cams to naughty amateur…well, you get the point; they have lots of uses. Regardless of the specifics, video surveillance systems fall into two broad categories:

- **Passive surveillance**—Refers to a camera that constantly transmits video information. As long as there is power to the system, whatever passes in front of the camera is transmitted to an external monitor or recording device. Web cams are probably the most common type of passive surveillance, but other types include nanny cams and latchkey cams.

- **Active surveillance**—Refers to cameras that begin recording when a sensor detects movement within view of the camera lens. This type of system is usually used for security purposes, but you can use this for any type of surveillance (including as nanny and latchkey cams). If you are storing the video files on a hard drive and you are unable to turn the camera on and off as needed to capture the footage you want, you may want to consider a motion-activated camera. They typically cost a bit more but it's a trade-off with the expense of a hard drive that can store many gigabits of information. (Video consumes much more disk storage space.)

How to Build It: Wireless Internet Video Cameras

Video cameras that attach to computers are very common, usually used for communicating with other people that have similar video cameras. Also popular recently have been very inexpensive wireless cameras that can be placed anywhere in your house. The ability to use either of these video cameras for live surveillance while you are not at home is limited. However, newer products like the Linksys wireless Internet video cameras have several distinct advantages:

■ No computer is required for them to operate, so they can be located anywhere in your house (or outside, for that matter) where there is an electrical outlet.

■ Images from the camera are viewable with any computer from inside your house, or from anywhere outside your house where there is Internet service.

In Figure 20-1, we placed a wireless Internet video camera in a house with a view of the front door.

Figure 20-1   Home Surveillance with Wireless Internet Video Cameras

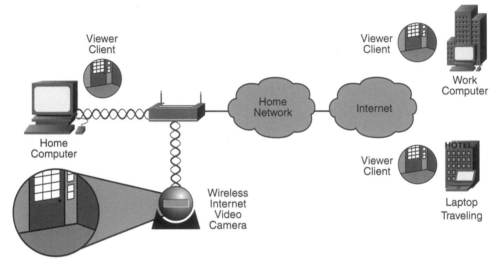

Now, we can use a viewer client to view the real-time video feed. So from upstairs, we could check who is at the front door. We could also use the viewer client on a computer at work to periodically check the residence, to see that the kids got home at the expected time from school. In a similar way, you could even use your laptop to check on the house while traveling on business. To avoid the need for constant surveillance, you can set up the camera to act as an automated sentry, and notify you only when there is something worth seeing.

As shown in Figure 20-2, you can program the camera to send a signal to a pager, cell phone, or e-mail to notify you if motion has been detected. You can even have the camera send you a video clip that it captures of the event. In this example, when little Susie arrives home, the camera detects the motion of her entering the front door. It then can send a notification e-mail (including a video clip) so you can verify that it is her. Or the camera could send a text message to your cell phone (via Short Message Service [SMS]) or to your pager (alphanumeric) with a message such as "Susie is Home."

Linksys offers a couple of different camera products. Table 20-1 shows the wireless printer server products from Linksys that we recommend.

Figure 20-2 Notification of a Latchkey Kid Arriving Home

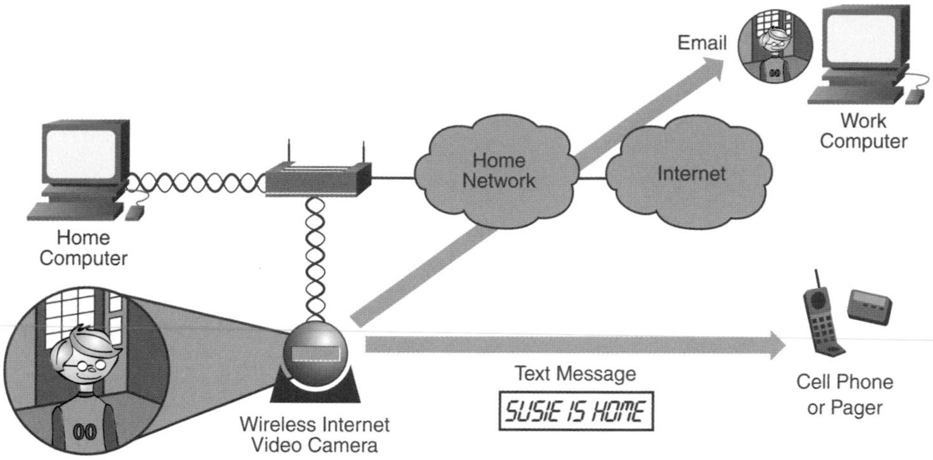

Email

Work
Computer

Home
Network

Internet

Home
Computer

Text Message
SUSIE IS HOME

Cell Phone
or Pager

Wireless Internet
Video Camera

Table 20-1 Linksys Wireless Internet Video Cameras

Model	Capability	Works with Wireless Standards	Wireless Encryption Supported
WVC54G	Audio, Video, and Motion Detection	802.11b 802.11g	64-bit WEP 128-bit WEP
WVC11B	Video and Motion Detection	802.11b 802.11g	64-bit WEP 128-bit WEP

The Linksys Wireless Internet Video Camera products listed here are not meant for outdoor installation and are not weatherproof.

The next few sections go through the steps to install a wireless Internet video camera on your home network. Here's an overview of the steps we will go through:

- Set up the wireless Internet video camera for your wireless network
- Configure the video camera security
- View video from your house
- View video over the Internet
- Use the camera as a motion detector

Set Up the Wireless Internet Video Camera for Your Wireless Network

The first step is to set up the wireless Internet video camera so that it can communicate with the wireless home network. Similar to the wireless print server we added in Chapter 19, "Wireless Print Servers: The Cure for Joy," you must tell the video camera how it can communicate with your wireless network.

One major difference is going to be the IP addressing we choose. For almost every other device or computer we add to the network, it's advantageous to let the wireless router choose and manage the IP addresses for the network. IP addresses can be assigned as needed, and the actual addresses assigned are not important to us. However, for the wireless Internet video camera, it will be necessary for us to assign a fixed IP address, so that we may access the camera images via the Internet.

The steps to install the wireless Internet video camera are as follows (the example shown is for the WVC11B Wireless-B video camera):

Step 1   Connect the Linksys wireless Internet video camera to the wireless router using an Ethernet cable (ordinary, not crossover), and plug in the power adapter. (See Figure 20-3.)

The LAN LED light on the front should light up.

Figure 20-3   Connect the Camera to the Router

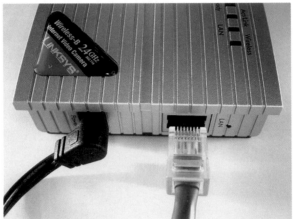

Step 2   Put the CD that came with the Linksys video camera into a computer on the network (one that is wired is preferred). The setup utility should start automatically (see Figure 20-4). If not, use My Computer to browse the CD and double-click **Setup.exe**. Click **Setup**.

Step 3   The setup utility instructs you to connect the video camera to the wireless router (see Figure 20-5). Click **Next**.

Figure 20-4   Linksys Wireless Video Camera Setup Wizard

Figure 20-5   Connect the Video Camera to the Router

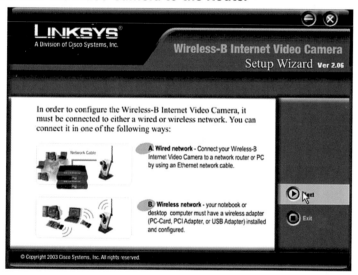

Step 4   The setup utility searches for the new video camera on the network (see Figure 20-6). Click **Next**. If it does not locate the camera, try clicking **Search Again**. If it still does not show up, check your cabling. Make sure the LAN LED light is lit on the video camera.

Figure 20-6   The Setup Wizard Searches for and Finds the New Video Camera

Step 5   Enter **admin** for both the Administrator Name and Administrator Password (see Figure 20-7). Click **OK**.

Figure 20-7   Enter Default Name and Password

Step 6   Enter a network name for the video camera (we used "Camera_1" in this example). (See Figure 20-8.) Enter the **Time Zone**, **Date**, and **Time**. Click **Next**.

Step 7   Check mark **Static IP address**, and then click **Next** (see Figure 20-9).

The setup wizard recommends choosing **Automatic Configuration—DHCP** if you are connecting the camera to a router. However, if you want to access the camera over the Internet, you need a fixed (static) IP address.

Figure 20-8   Enter the Basic Settings

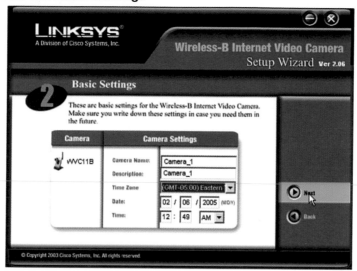

Figure 20-9   Choose Static IP Address

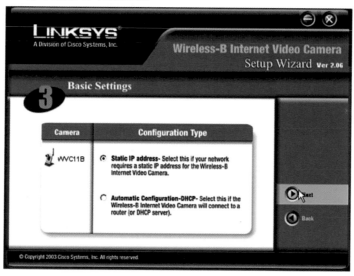

Step 8   Enter an IP address that is unlikely to be assigned on your network by the wireless router (for example, 192.168.1.140). (See Figure 20-10.) The subnet mask will be 255.255.255.0. The gateway will be 192.168.1.1. For the primary DNS and secondary DNS, enter the addresses listed on the sheet of paper you received from your ISP when you subscribed. If you can't find them, access the wireless router using an Internet browser and click **Status**. Click **Next**.

Figure 20-10 Configure the IP Address Settings

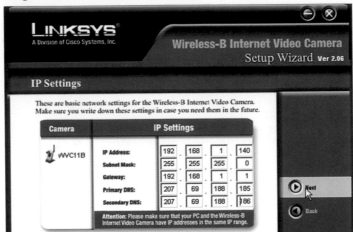

 NOTE The IP address you choose needs to be in the range of IP addresses for your home network. In Chapter 6, "Sharing Network Resources," we set up the router to use address range 192.168.1.2 through 192.168.1.254 for our home network (.0, .1, and .255 are reserved). In addition, we set up the router to dynamically assign IP addresses in the range 192.168.1.100 through 192.168.1.149 to computers and devices requesting an address. So we can assign the camera to an address:

- Between 192.168.1.2 and 192.168.1.99

- Between 192.168.1.150 and 192.168.1.254

- At the high-end of the dynamic IP address range (between 192.168.1.140 and 192.168.1.149)

It just needs to be unique on the network and within one of these ranges. We chose 192.168.1.140 for this example. Whatever address you choose, write it down, because this will be the address needed when accessing the camera. If you forget the address, you probably have to do a factory reset and start over.

Step 9   Check mark **Infrastructure** (see Figure 20-11). Click **Next**.

Step 10   Enter the SSID for your wireless network (see Figure 20-12). (For the continuing example, this is J59wgh21MX.) Click **Next**.

Figure 20-11 Select Wireless Network Type—Infrastructure

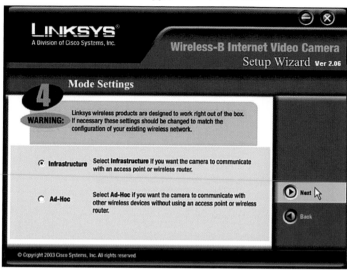

Figure 20-12 Enter the SSID for Your Wireless Network

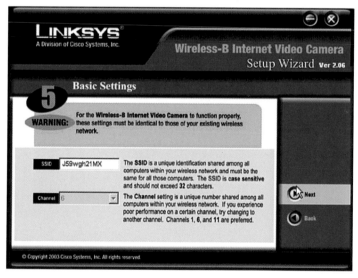

Step 11   Set the wireless security setting to "WEP 128-bit Keys" (or the encryption you are using). (See Figure 20-13.) Enter the pass-phrase you have been using for your wireless network (in this example, it's "64Gx3prY19fk2"). Click **Next**.

Figure 20-13 Enter the Wireless Encryption Settings

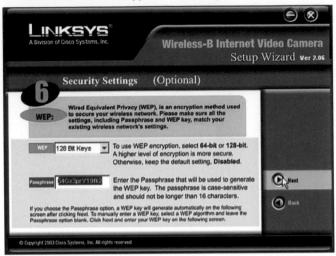

Step 12   Check the WEP key to ensure it matches the key being used on the wireless router (see Figure 20-14). Do not modify the key! Click **Next**.

Figure 20-14 Confirm the Generated WEP Key

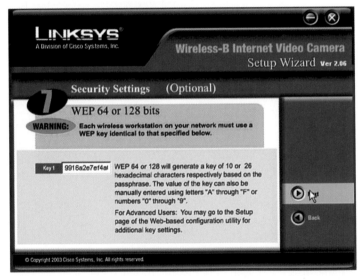

 NOTE If the two keys do not match, modify the key value to match what is being used on the wireless router. Normally, the keys will match as long as the wireless video camera and router are both Linksys products.

Step 13   The setup utility then displays a summary of the new settings. Click **Save**. Click **OK** on the double-confirmation dialog that appears next. (See Figure 20-15.)

Figure 20-15 Settings Confirmation

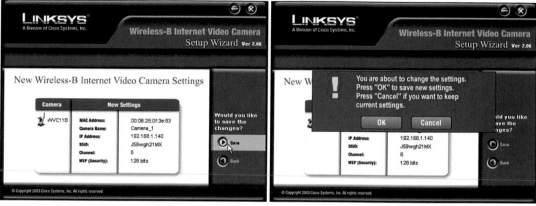

Step 14 You're all done (see Figure 20-16). Leave the setup utility for now. We have to come back to it later.

Figure 20-16 Video Camera Is Successfully Configured

Unplug the Ethernet cable from the video camera, power it off, and then back on. After you complete these steps, the WLAN LED indicator light on the front of the wireless Internet video camera should be lit. Congratulations, you just installed a wireless video camera!

You can now unplug the video camera and move it to the location of your choice.

Troubleshooting Tips: Setting Up Your Video Camera for Your Wireless Network

If it's not working, try the following:

- Reconnect the Ethernet cable between the wireless router and the wireless video camera. Restart the setup utility and repeat Steps 1–14. Pay close attention to the wireless settings: SSID, WEP key length, and WEP key pass-phrase. They must be entered identically to your wireless network, including uppercase and lowercase letters!

- Make sure the wireless router is powered on and functioning normally. Test by making sure you can access the Internet from one of your computers that is connected by a wireless NIC.

- If you are running a personal firewall program, such as ZoneAlarm, it may be preventing the wireless video camera installation utility from accessing the network. Temporarily disable the firewall, or grant the utility access to the network.

- If you implemented MAC address blocking on your wireless router (see Chapter 11, "Securing Your Wireless Network"), double-check that you permitted the new wireless device's MAC address to access your wireless network. Check to see if a device on the network is already using the IP address that you chose to assign to the video camera. Try a different address, such as 192.168.1.160 or 192.168.1.200.

- Read the "Troubleshooting" chapter in the installation manual that came with the Linksys wireless Internet video camera.

Configure the Video Camera Security

Now that the wireless Internet video camera is communicating properly with the wireless network, you need to perform a few steps to finish setting up the security for the camera:

Step 1 Open your Internet browser and type in the IP address that you selected for the video camera (for example, 192.168.1.140). (See Figure 20-17.) Click **Enter**.

Step 2 The main menu for the video camera should appear (see Figure 20-18).

If it does not appear, go back to the installation steps in the previous section.

Step 3 Click **Setup > Status**. Nothing here is all that interesting, but you just want to check the system log to make sure there are no error messages. The message "Wireless is activated" tells you that the video camera is properly communicating with the wireless network (see Figure 20-19).

Figure 20-17 Type the Video Camera's IP Address in the Browser

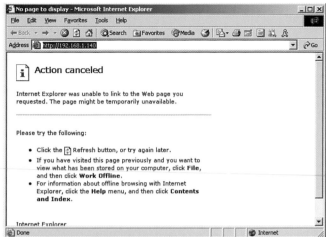

Figure 20-18 Video Camera's Main Menu

Step 4 Click **Image**. Here, you can change the quality of the video image (see Figure 20-20). (Keep in mind: The higher the quality, the more of your broadband link is used if you are accessing the camera over the Internet.) We set the quality to Normal. If you are bandwidth-challenged, try lowering the image quality. Check mark **Enable** beside Time Stamp if you want the date and time to appear on the camera image. Click **Apply**.

Figure 20-19 Checking the Camera's Status

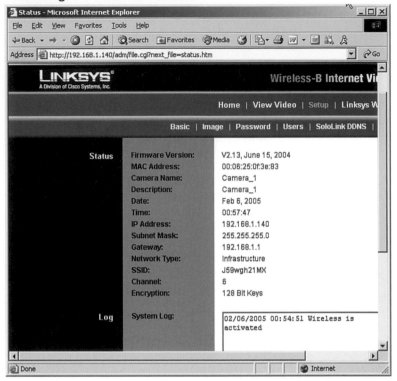

Figure 20-20 Adjust the Video Settings

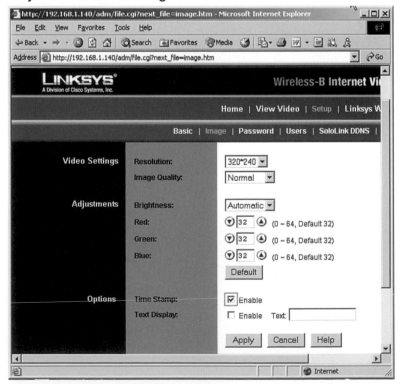

Step 5 Click **Password**. Enter a new password on both the Password and Verify Password lines (see Figure 20-21). Write it down somewhere. Click **Apply**.

Figure 20-21 Change the Default Administrator Password

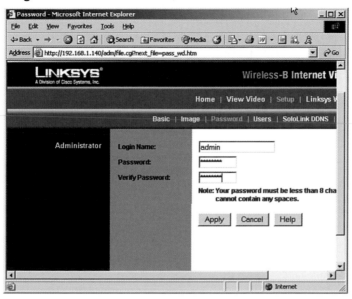

Step 6 Immediately, the video camera will re-authenticate (see Figure 20-22). Enter **admin** for the user ID and the new password you created. Click **OK**.

Figure 20-22 Re-Authenticating with the New Password

Step 7 Click **Users**. It's possible to set up video camera users that only have viewing privileges, not the authority to modify the video camera itself (see Figure 20-23). *Never* give out the master administration password. Click **Add**.

Figure 20-23 List of Authorized Camera Users

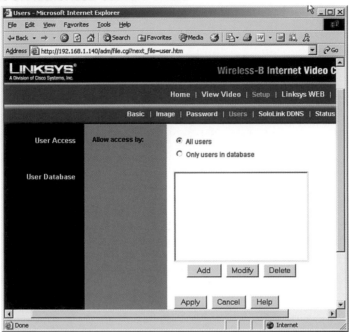

Step 8   Enter a user name and corresponding password (see Figure 20-24). Do *not* use the same password as the administrator. Click **Apply**. Repeat this step for as many user accounts as you want. Click **Close** when you're finished.

Figure 20-24 Add New Users

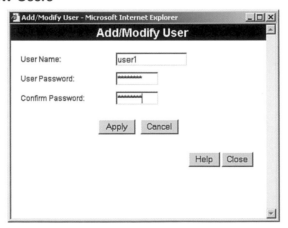

Step 9   THIS STEP IS CRITICAL! UNLESS YOU COMPLETE IT, ANYONE WHO TRIES TO ACCESS YOUR VIDEO CAMERA OVER THE INTERNET WILL BE GRANTED ACCESS! Check mark **Only users in database** (see Figure 20-25). Click **Apply**.

Figure 20-25 Restrict the Camera to Users in the List

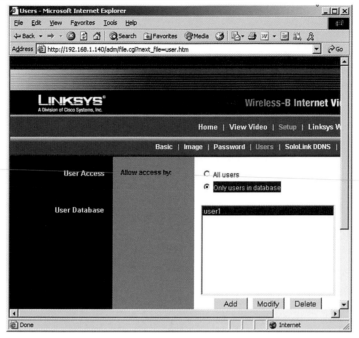

Now the wireless Internet video camera is installed, set up, and ready for use.

Viewing Video from Within Your House

Now that the wireless Internet video camera is set up completely, we can start using it to view video images. There are two ways to view video:

- **Internet Browser**—More involved than the Viewer Client, but it can be used on any computer with an Internet browser, which is useful when trying to check your camera from a friend's house or from a public computer. (Extra steps are required for viewing the camera from outside your home network. See the section "Viewing Video over the Internet.") With the Internet browser you can access the other administrative features of the camera, such as setting up motion detection.

- **Viewer Client**—The Viewer Client is software provided on the CD that came with the camera. It is easier than using the Internet browser and offers a recording feature. However, the Client must be installed on every computer you wish to view the video feed from. The Linksys Viewer Client software only works on computers running Windows XP or 2000, not Windows 98.

Viewing Images with an Internet Browser

Let's first look at viewing the video image using an Internet browser:

Step 1   Point an Internet browser to the video camera by entering the IP address (for example, 192.168.1.140) in the address field of the browser. (See Figure 20-26.) The main camera dialog appears.

Figure 20-26 Access the Camera Using a Browser

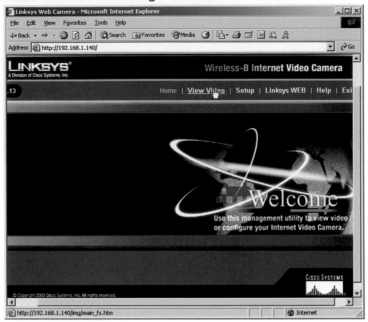

Step 2   Click **View Video**. Enter a user name and password that you created with viewing privileges (see Figure 20-27).

Figure 20-27 Enter Viewer User ID and Password

Step 3   The first time you want to view video with your browser, a special "plug-in" is downloaded automatically and installed into the Internet browser. You'll see the dialog box shown in Figure 20-28. Click **Yes**.

Step 4   It works! (See Figure 20-29.) Isn't she beautiful? Now, you're all done.

Figure 20-28 Plug-In Is Automatically Downloaded

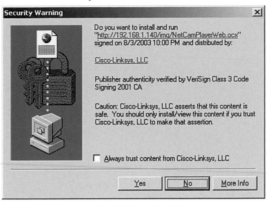

Figure 20-29 Viewing a Video Image

At this point, you can do a couple of things to save yourself some time in the future:

- Add the Video Viewer to your Favorites list by bookmarking the URL. The next time you use the Internet browser, you can then simply go to the Video Camera in the "Favorites" list instead of remembering the IP address.

- Create a shortcut on the Windows Desktop. While still in the Viewer mode, click **File > Send To > Desktop Shortcut** in the Internet browser menu. This puts an icon on the desktop of your computer that you can simply double-click to jump into the Video Viewer mode.

NOTE Keep in mind that accessing the camera with the IP address we assigned for the home network (for example, 192.168.1.140) will only work when we are within the home network. This IP address will not work for accessing the camera over the Internet.

The reason is—remember our discussion in Chapter 14, "Protecting Your Network from Intruders," about Network Address Translation (NAT)? It applies here, because the camera's IP address is not known beyond the wireless router. The Router "hides" the private network addresses on the home network and translates them to an Internet IP address.

This is great for security purposes, but it will cause a little difficulty for us trying to access the camera from outside the house. This is discussed more in the section "Problems with Viewing Video over the Internet."

Installing and Viewing Images with the Viewer Client

Now, let's look at using the Linksys Viewer Client. We need to install the Viewer Client on each computer we want to view video from. Here's how to install the Viewer Client:

Step 1   Put the CD that came with the Linksys wireless video camera into your computer. The setup utility starts automatically (see Figure 20-30). If not, use My Computer to browse the CD and double-click **Setup.exe**.

Figure 20-30 Linksys Wireless Internet Video Camera Setup Wizard

Step 2   Click **Install Viewer & Recorder Utility**. The Client install program starts. Click **Next** (see Figure 20-31).

Figure 20-31 Viewer Client Install Program

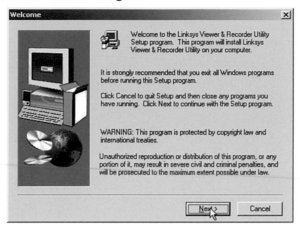

Step 3   Select the appropriate installation options, such as installation directory, and click **Next**. After the install is finished, a dialog appears acknowledging the installation (see Figure 20-32). Click **OK**.

Figure 20-32 Installation Is Complete

Step 4   Double-click the **Linksys Viewer & Recorder** icon on the computer desktop (see Figure 20-33).

Figure 20-33 Linksys Video Camera Viewer Client

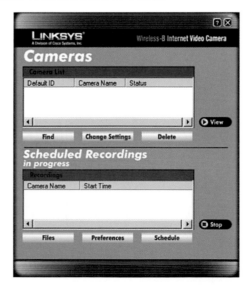

Step 5   Click **Find.** The utility searches for video cameras on the network. It should locate the camera (see Figure 20-34).

Figure 20-34 Viewer Finds the Camera

Step 6   Enter a login name and password that you created with viewing privileges (see Figure 20-35). Click **Add** > **X** to close.

Figure 20-35 Enter Viewer Name and Password

Step 7   An entry should now appear for the video camera (see Figure 20-36).

Figure 20-36 Select Your Video Camera

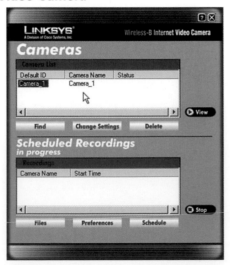

Step 8   Click the video camera that you just added, and then click **View**.

It works! (See Figure 20-37.) Click **X** to terminate the viewer.

Figure 20-37 You Can Now View the Video

 NOTE You need to install the Linksys Video Viewer Client on each computer you want to use to view the video images (assuming the Internet browser method is not sufficient for whatever you want to do).

Viewing Video over the Internet

Viewing video from within you home network (which we did in the previous section) is fairly straightforward. Viewing video over the Internet is a bit trickier. First, your home network is set up for access from inside-out, not from outside-in. Second, the actual IP address of your broadband service most likely changes over time (which is normal). It's a little like trying to deliver mail to someone whose address changes each week. Fortunately, there are a couple slick solutions to these potential problems.

First, let's tackle the inside-out/outside-in problem. How do you provide outside-in access to the video camera without compromising the security of your home network? Further, how do you reach the video camera, whose IP address on the home network is unknown to you? From the Internet's perspective, the video camera's IP address of 192.168.1.140 is not accessible. Remember, from Chapter 14, this is by design.

The trick is to use a feature on the Linksys wireless router called *port forwarding*. It can recognize incoming attempts to access the video camera, and can forward those requests directly to the video camera.

Here's how to set up port forwarding:

Step 1   Point an Internet browser to the video camera, by entering the IP address (for example, "192.168.1.140"). When prompted, enter **admin** and the administrator password. Click **Setup > Advanced**. Check mark **Enable Alternate Port for HTTP connections** (see Figure 20-38). Choose an IP port number that you want the camera to use (for example, "63333"). Click **Apply**.

Figure 20-38 Assign the Camera an IP Port Number

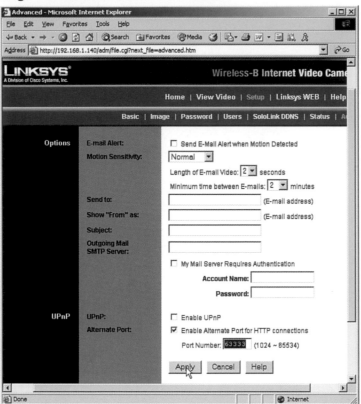

NOTE We have not discussed IP port numbers very much. An IP port number is a number from 1 through 65535 that is used by applications (such as an Internet browser) to access the network. If an IP address is like your home address, think of an IP port number like a room of your house; it's adding another level of detail to the address.

Applications such as Internet Browsers and e-mail programs use particular IP port numbers. We want to assign the camera to an uncommon number, those between 60000 and 65535.

Step 2 Point an Internet browser to the wireless router by entering the IP address (for example, "192.168.1.1"). When prompted, enter the Router's administrator password. Click **Applications & Gaming > Port Range Forward** (see Figure 20-39). Enter the chosen port number (from Step 1) in both the Start and End fields. Select **TCP**, and then enter the IP address of the camera, for example, "192.168.1.140." Check mark **Enable**. Click **Save Settings**.

Step 3 While still on the wireless router, click **Status**. Find the Internet IP address (in this example, it's "24.225.91.164"). (See Figure 20-40.) This is the IP address on the Internet to reach your wireless router (and your home network), so write it down.

Figure 20-39 Set Up IP Port Forwarding on the Router

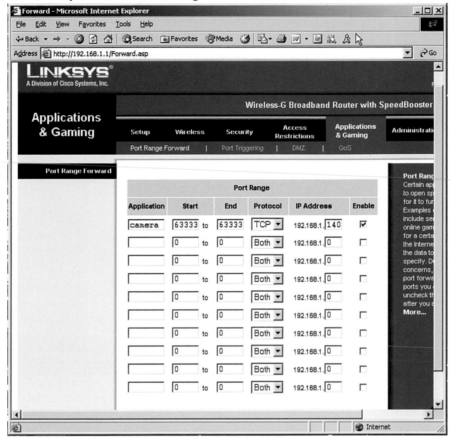

Step 4   Now, when you want to view the video images from a computer outside of your house, you access it in a similar way. Point the Internet browser to the Internet IP address plus the port number we chose, for example, "24.225.91.164:63333." Enter your username and password, and click **View Video**. (See Figure 20-41 for an example of viewing an image over the Internet.)

That solves the majority of the issue, just being able to reach the video camera from outside the home network. (By the way, you have to actually be outside your home network to test these steps.)

NOTE You can also use the Linksys Viewer Client to view video images over the Internet. It has been omitted here to save space. The procedure is very similar to using the Viewer Client from within your home network. The major differences are

■ Click **Internet** instead of **LAN**

■ Specify the Internet IP address

■ Specify the port number (for example, 63333)

Figure 20-40 Finding Your Internet IP Address

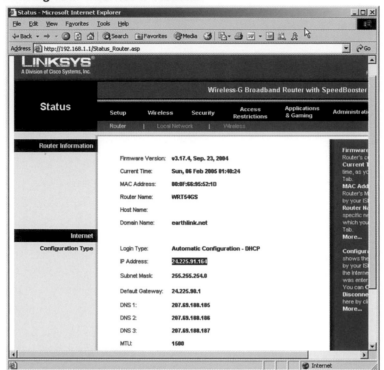

Figure 20-41 Example of Viewing Images Over the Internet

Problems with Viewing Video over the Internet

There is one other potential issue with viewing your video over the Internet. The broadband networks typically assign a dynamic IP address to your broadband service. *Dynamic* means it can change, typically only if you power off and on your broadband modem. This is usually not an issue because, you will be assigned the same IP address for a long period of time.

If the IP address of your broadband modem does get re-assigned, the new address may not match the address you wrote down for the camera. Then when you try to access the camera, you will get an error message from the Internet browser saying "The page cannot be displayed." In this case, you will need to access your wireless router, click on the **Status** function, and write down the new Internet IP address.

If you rely on accessing your camera over the Internet, and the IP address changes too often, here are a couple of solutions:

- Subscribe to a dynamic DNS service that automatically tracks your home network's IP address. Linksys offers a pay service called SoloLink. This service automatically tracks the address used to reach your video camera. (See http://www.linksys.com/sololink/.) (Further detail on dynamic DNS services is beyond the scope of this book.)

- Inquire with your Internet service provider (ISP) about upgrading your broadband subscription to a *static IP address*, which means that you pay a little extra per month, but your address never changes.

Use the Video Camera as a Motion Detector

Another very useful feature of the Linksys wireless Internet video camera products is the ability to act as a motion detector for active surveillance. In other words, it is tedious to watch a video feed for hours waiting for something to happen. Depending on the reason for the video camera, it can be more effective to trigger on motion detected and then perform a notification action. Using the motion detector is pretty easy:

Step 1   Access the video camera using the administrator account as we did before. Click **Setup > Advanced** (see Figure 20-42). Check mark **Send E-Mail Alert when Motion Detected**. Select a length in seconds for a video capture (2–5 seconds). Select the minimum time between e-mail alerts (2–30 minutes).

Step 2   On the same dialog, enter the e-mail account information, including

- Send-to e-mail address

- Show From e-mail address

- Subject

- Outgoing SMTP server (this is from your e-mail provider)

- E-mail login name and password

Click **Apply**.

Figure 20-42 Enabling Motion Detection

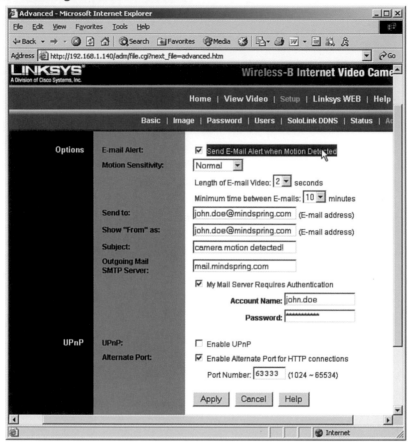

That's all there is to it! A word of caution though: As soon as you enable the motion detector function (and until you shut it off), you will receive a video capture attached to an e-mail as often as you have specified. So take care not to leave it enabled for lengthy periods of time as your e-mail account will promptly fill up!

Figure 20-43 shows an example of an e-mail that was triggered by the settings in this example.

In this example, motion was detected by the video camera. It proceeded to capture 2 seconds of video and e-mailed it to john.doe@mindspring.com. The e-mail attachment in this case (the MPEG4 format video clip) was less than 100 KB of disk space.

 NOTE The Linksys WVC11B model is video only, but the WVC54G model is audio and video. So, the attached clip will contain audio for the latter model.

In the same manner, it's also possible to send alerts to a pager or cell phone. Most cell phones and pagers have an equivalent e-mail address that can be used to send a text message to. Simply supply that e-mail address as the alert address. If the product supports it, you may want to disable the audio/video clip attachment to these types of alerts (the WVC11B does not support disabling, but the WVC54G does).

Figure 20-43 Example Notification E-Mail

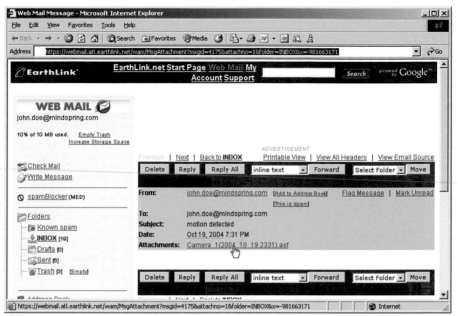

When used properly, alerts based on motion detection can be very effective for verifying that "latchkey" kids have gotten home from school safely, a spouse is home, or perhaps even as a security alarm if motion is detected while on vacation due to a home intruder.

NOTE Here are a few side notes on video cameras and the Internet:

■ Take care where you point your wireless Internet video camera. It may not be a good idea to have an ongoing video feed of the inside of your home being offered up to the Internet. At a minimum, make sure you enable security including pass words to protect access to the camera.

■ Be advised that Internet video cameras normally do not work well in lowlight conditions. This may limit its usefulness as a baby monitor, for example. Conversely, too much light or glare from nearby windows can also spoil images from these cameras.

■ Review the laws in your state with respect to video taping of people without their knowledge. Kids are most likely yours to tape whenever you deem necessary. However, using the video surveillance functions in this chapter to perform surveillance on the activities of an adult (such as a spouse or a babysitter) may be subject to local laws.

GEEK SQUAD Be careful about letting kids get into the web-cam game. You don't necessarily know who is on the other end watching.

Internet Phone Service

One of the more recent benefits of Internet technology is the ability to have voice conversations over an Internet connection. Using the Internet for telephone service in this manner was at first just a cheap work around to long distance phone bills, but the quality of the connection was spotty and, in many cases, unreliable. Recent improvements in technology though have made Internet Protocol (IP) telephony (also known as voice over Internet Protocol [VoIP]) a viable and reliable alternative to a standard telephone connection, or at least a very good option for saving on long distance, especially if you have friends or family living abroad.

As you can see in Figure 21-1, communications systems (including the public telephone system, mobile phone system, Internet, and media providers) are quickly converging.

Figure 21-1   Communications Systems Are Converging

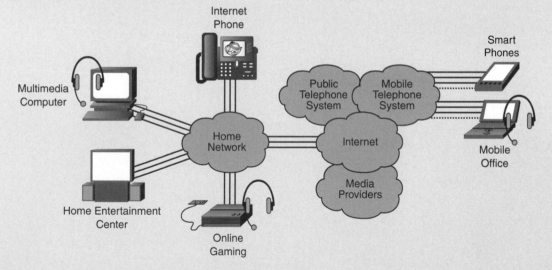

Cell phones have built-in cameras and PDA's (also known as Smart Phones), and PDA's have built-in cell phones. Laptops have built-in wireless, not to mention the capability for multimedia (data, voice, video, music, and so on). The devices we use are becoming smarter and capable of many more things each day.

Since having an Internet phone service, using your home network, is becoming increasingly popular, we thought it appropriate to include in this book.

How IP Telephony Works

VoIP works in a somewhat similar way to the public phone system. An additional step is required to convert the sounds going into your phone into 1's and 0's to allow passage through your home network and across the Internet. The VoIP service provider receives the IP packets containing your voice and forwards them either to another person's Internet phone service or to a gateway to the public telephone system. The gateway acts as a converter between the Internet phone service (IP packets) and the public phone service (analog voice).

All this is, of course, transparent to you. You simply pick up the receiver and dial a phone number, just like you would on a regular phone. There are a few things to know about Internet-based phone services:

- You may experience poor quality from time to time depending on the Internet traffic in and out of your home network.

- If you lose power, your Internet phone will not work (many regular phone lines continue to operate when the power goes out).

- 911 services are not available for every area (you need to contact the phone service to find out), and when they are, you must take a few steps to ensure it is set up with your correct address.

Standard Telephony Versus Voice over IP

Standard Telephony (Analog)

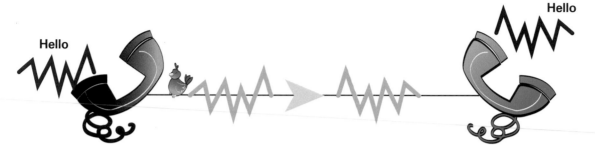

With standard telephony, the speech waveform (produced by your mouth, throat, and voice box) excites a diaphragm in the phone that creates an electric signal. That signal transmits through a copper wire and, on the receiving end, that signal excites another diaphragm that moves a speaker, which re-creates a copy of the original wave form.

Voice over IP (Digital)

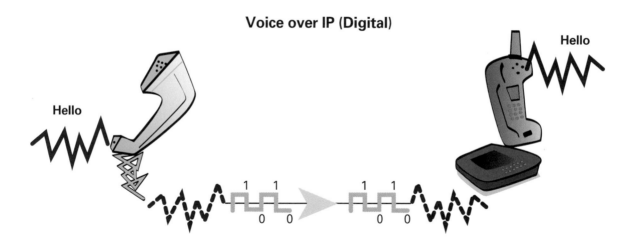

In digital telephony, the speech waveform is measured many thousands of time per second. The measurements are converted into a digital stream of 1s and 0s, which are transmitted down a wire. On the receiving end, the signal is re-created by "connecting the dots," which produces a representation of the original signal.

Broadband Phone Services

Broadband phone services provide an alternative to public telephone service. You can keep your same phone number or get a new number. You can use your existing phones. Your friends and family can call you from their public telephone service (or their broadband phone service). Overall, it looks and feels like your home phone service today. The major difference is, instead of your voice being carried over wires to your local phone company, your voice is carried across the Internet. Figure 21-2 shows the major components of a broadband phone service.

Figure 21-2   Broadband Phone Service Components

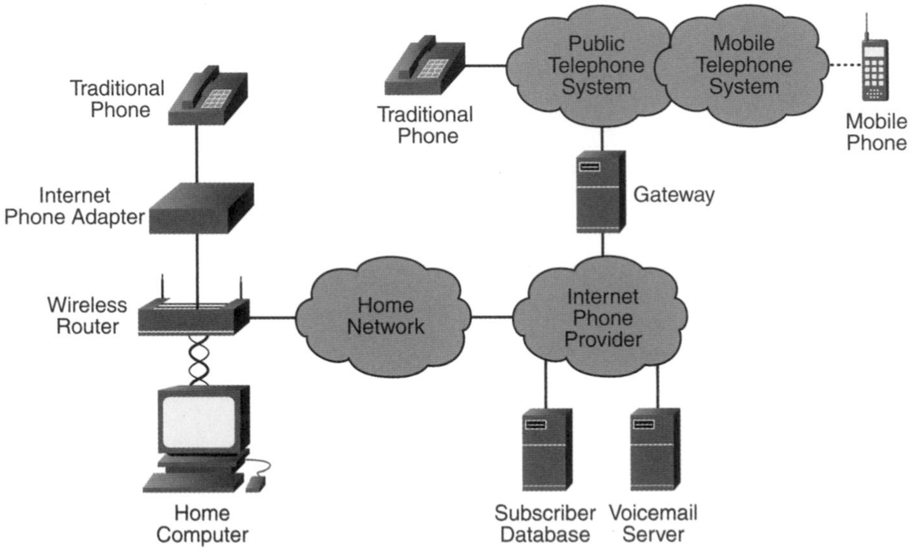

Broadband Phone Providers

There are several important components to be aware of at the broadband phone provider:

- It has a subscriber database that contains your subscription information, phone number, features, billing, and so on.

- A voicemail server will be able to take messages if you don't answer, just like an answering machine.

- The service would not be very useful if you could only call other people on the same service, so a gateway is provided to the public and mobile telephone systems.

To use the service, callers dial a phone number to reach you. To call them, you dial their phone number, just like you do today from your home phone.

Three prominent broadband phone services being offered are

- **AT&T CallVantage**—http://www.usa.att.com/callvantage

- **Verizon VoiceWing**—http://www22.verizon.com/ForYourHome/voip/voiphome.aspx

- **Vonage**—http://www.vonage.com/

There are several advantages to broadband phone services, including

- Typically, they are offered at a substantially lower cost than public telephone services, for example, between $10–30 for unlimited minutes and no domestic long distance charges.

- Due to the integration with the Internet, often many more services are available online to use and manage your service. For example, with Vonage, you can log in to your account online from any computer and listen to your voicemail using your computer.

- Because you are not tied to a physical location for a phone number, you can have a phone number (or several) in whatever area codes you wish (this is available for most area codes in the United States but may not be available elsewhere).

VERY IMPORTANT: Emergency 911 services rely on geographic location to dispatch aid to your home. Internet phone services, because they are accessible virtually anywhere regardless of physical location, require that you register your home address with the provider so that if 911 is dialed from the Internet phone, the call can still be routed to the appropriate local agency.

GEEK SQUAD Internet phone service is good for people who have a lot of long distance calls to make. However, if you make a lot of long distance calls, you are pretty dependent on your phone. So you need to weigh cost with reliability.

Plus, if you have no power in your house, chances are you are not going to have Internet access, which means your Internet phone service is not likely to work either.

Virtual Phone Numbers

Public telephone service (and to a certain extent mobile telephone service) is tied to a geographic location (in the United States and some other countries). Area codes and phone numbers are assigned by geography. Generally, if you move from one location to another, you get assigned a new number (however, this is changing with number portability regulations that started in 2004).

Internet-based phone services are not tied to a geographic location and have complete number portability. Further, you can assign as many phone numbers to your single physical phone as you want. This can be incredibly useful for providing local numbers to callers in a distant city. For example, wouldn't it be cool if your family in another state could reach you on a phone number in their hometown, which means it's a local call for them and they pay no long distance?

Suppose I have my primary residence in Seattle, Washington, which on the public telephone system is area code 206. Now suppose I have friends residing in Oswego, New York (area code 315), and family members living in West Palm Beach (area code 561). With a broadband phone service, I can have a 206 number for my neighbors calling me in Seattle, and for a nominal additional fee (about $5) also have local numbers in 315 and 561 for my friends and family (see Figure 21-3). Now when my family calls me, they incur no long distance charges.

Figure 21-3   Having Virtual Phone Numbers

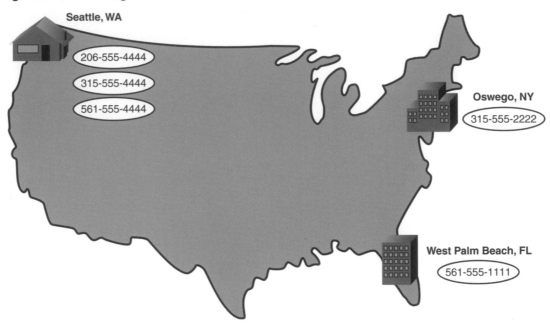

So it's cheaper and far more flexible; sounds too good to be true. Of course, there are limitations to the technology. First, you are using your broadband internet service, so your phone service is only as reliable as your cable or DSL provider. Second, calls are carried over the Internet. There are no quality guarantees like there are in the public telephone system. Services we tested were quite good, but set your expectations at cell phone quality: more than adequate for friends and family, but think it through before taking all customer calls for your business this way.

It comes down to a tradeoff between giving up a little reliability and gaining a lot of flexibility and significant cost savings.

NOTE To be clear, the authors do *not* recommend ripping out your public telephone system line and substituting it with a broadband phone service. We recommend broadband phone service as a supplemental service.

Voice-Chat Services

Voice-chat services are another form of Internet phone service. These services operate similar to instant messaging and chat rooms, but instead of (or sometimes in addition to) sending text back and forth, you can also have a voice conversation. Voice-chat services have some similarities to broadband phone services but also some important differences. Much like a broadband phone service, voice-chat services have a database of subscribers and have a gateway to the public telephone and mobile telephone systems. Figure 21-4 shows the major components of voice-chat services.

Figure 21-4   Major Components of Voice-Chat Services

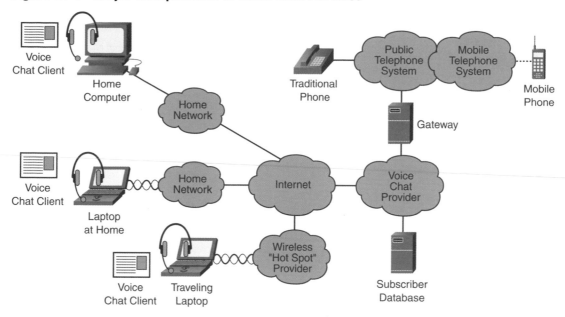

Voice-chat services, however, differ from broadband phone services in these ways:

- Instead of using a traditional telephone handset, all you need is a headset with a microphone and the voice-chat client software that runs on any computer. Your computer is the phone.

- Voice-chat services typically are outside of the telephone system's numbering plan, meaning you do not have a phone number for people to call you. Instead, you create a list of "buddies" much like you would for instant messaging.

- Although broadband phone services typically connect phone calls inside the provider network, voice-chat services are "peer-to-peer," which simply means that they connect directly between your computer and the person you are calling.

- With broadband phone services, people calling you from the public telephone system dial a phone number just like any other person they are calling. Voice-chat services typically have a unidirectional "off-net" gateway, which means you can originate calls from voice-chat service to the public telephone system, but people cannot originate calls to you.

Possible voice-chat services include the following:

- **AOL**—http://www.aol.com/

- **Skype**—http://www.skype.com/

- **Yahoo**—http://messenger.yahoo.com/

How to Build It: Internet Phone Service

There are several types of Internet phone services, but this section focuses on the two most common types:

- Setting up a broadband phone service
- Setting up a voice-chat service (using Skype)

Setting Up a Broadband Phone Service

Setting up a broadband phone service is straightforward. You need to select and buy an Internet phone adapter, and then set it up in your house.

Choosing an Internet Phone Adapter

In your home, instead of plugging your phone into a wall outlet, you purchase an Internet phone adapter (refer to Figure 21-2), which plugs into your wireless router (or it may be integrated with your wireless router), and your existing phone can plug right into it. The Internet phone adapter takes care of these important functions:

- Converts your voice to digital 1's and 0's, chopped up into 10 or 20 millisecond long pieces (10 milliseconds is one hundredth of a second), and places it into packets that are transmitted across the Internet.

- Reassembles the voice packets of the person calling you back into a voice conversation.

- Interprets the signaling between your home and the broadband phone provider (for example, dialing digits are translated into messages, and an incoming-call message is translated into a phone ringing).

Linksys offers a few different Internet phone adapter products, shown in Table 21-1. Often, an Internet phone adapter is specific to the broadband phone service provider, so make sure to check which ones they recommend and support.

Table 21-1   Linksys Internet Phone Adapters

Model	Phone Lines?	Works with Providers	Other Information
PAP2	2	AT&T Verizon Vonage	Standalone Internet Phone Adapter
RT31P2	2	Verizon Vonage	3-port Wired Router + Internet Phone Adapter
RT41P2	2	AT&T	4-port Wired Router + Internet Phone Adapter
WRT54GP2	2	AT&T Vonage	Wireless Router + Internet Phone Adapter

Most of the products allow for up to two independent phone lines to be attached. This means you can have two calls active at the same time.

Depending on the product, you can select a standalone adapter (such as the PAP2), which plugs into your wireless (or wired) router, or you can choose to have the adapter built into the wireless (or wired) router itself. Which you choose is up to you, but it may make more sense to buy the standalone adapter, so that you can easily change your phone provider without having to swap out the entire wireless router, and have to set up your home network again.

NOTE Even though an Internet phone adapter converts an analog phone signal to IP packets, you can still use a fax machine with Internet phone service. The gateway to the public phone system simply converts the IP packets back to an analog signal again that can be understood by the receiving fax machine.

Setting Up the Internet Phone Adapter

Connecting the Internet phone adapter is pretty easy. The steps are shown here (the example shown is for the Linksys PAP2 product):

Step 1 Purchase an Internet phone adapter product, such as the Linksys PAP2 (refer to Table 21-1 and see Figure 21-5). Ask at the store (or online) to sign up for a service, for example Vonage or AT&T CallVantage.

Figure 21-5   Linksys PAP2

Step 2 Depending on the store (or website), the sales associate may log in and perform the online sign-up on your behalf, or you may be instructed to perform it yourself at home.

You are asked for information such as the following:

■ Choose a calling plan

■ Desired phone numbers

- Mailing address

- Credit/debit card information

- User ID/password (for the service)

- MAC address of the Internet phone adapter (for example, Linksys PAP2)

After completing the sign-up process online, you will be e-mailed a confirmation and any relevant subscription information. At any time you can log in to your account, add new features, change settings, and so on.

Step 3   Take the Internet phone adapter home. Connect an Ethernet cable between the PAP2 and the wireless router, as shown in Figure 21-6.

Figure 21-6   Connect the Internet Phone Adapter to the Router

 NOTE The PAP2 must be connected with an Ethernet cable; it does not support a wireless connection. Therefore, it will need to be co-located with your wireless router.

What if you need the Internet phone to be in a different room than your wireless router? Easy. Purchase a wireless game adapter or wireless Ethernet bridge. The steps would be very similar to setting up a wireless game adapter, which is covered in Chapter 22, N etworked Entertainment Systems."

Step 4   Plug any traditional phone into a phone jack on the back of the PAP2 (see Figure 21-7). Both corded and cordless phones will work. Don't forget to plug in the power cord to the PAP2.

Figure 21-7   Connect Home Phone to Internet Phone Adapter

Check to see if, on the front of the Linksys Internet phone adapter, the LAN and Phone LEDs lights are lit. Pick up the phone handset and see if you have a dial tone. If so, that's all there is to it! Congratulations, you just set up an internet phone!

Troubleshooting Tips: Broadband Phone Service

If you do not have a dial tone or if there is some other problem, try the following:

■ If the LAN LED is not lit, check the Ethernet cabling between the Linksys Internet phone adapter and Linksys wireless router.

■ If the Phone LED is not lit, check to make sure the RJ11 phone cable is properly connected to both the Internet phone adapter and the phone handset.

■ Try powering off the Internet phone adapter and turning it back on.

■ Double-check that the correct MAC address of the Linksys Internet phone adapter was typed in online when you or the store sales associate completed the subscription.

■ Read the "Troubleshooting" chapter in the installation manual that came with the Linksys Internet phone adapter.

■ Call the technical support line of the broadband phone service provider.

Setting Up a Voice-Chat Service (Using Skype)

As an example of setting up an Internet voice-chat service, we will set up the Skype service. Here's how:

Step 1 Go to the Skype website at http://www.skype.com/download and download the Skype software client (see Figure 21-8). Make sure to pick the right version for your operating system.

Figure 21-8 Download Skype Software

Step 2 Install the client software (see Figure 21-9). Click **Next** and answer the prompts.

Figure 21-9 Skype Setup Wizard

Step 3 Set up a Skype account (see Figure 21-10). You need to specify a "handle" (much like an instant messaging name or a user ID) that you will be known by on the service.

Some users seem to be following a convention of

firstlastname_state_country

but make up whatever handle suits you. Enter a password containing (you guessed it) random uppercase letters, lowercase letters, and numbers. Enter your e-mail address. It's optional but you can't reset your password if you have not provided one!

Figure 21-10 Create a New Skype Account

Step 4   Skype lets you specify a personal profile so that other people on Skype can know about you (see Figure 21-11). (You can even include a photo if you like.) Specify as much or as little information as you want to. Everything in the profile is optional.

Figure 21-11 Create Your Personal Profile

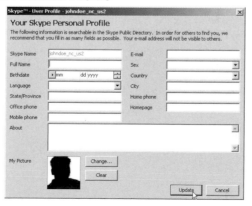

Step 5   The Skype client software will then start up (see Figure 21-12). If you want Skype to start each time you start your PC, click **File > Options > General**. Checkmark the option to start Skype when Windows starts.

Figure 21-12 Skype Is Now Set Up

Now, you need to build a list of friends and family to call, called *contacts*. There are a couple ways to add folks to your contacts list:

- Have your friends and family e-mail you or tell you their Skype name.

- You can search for them based on their e-mail address, city and state, first and last name, and so on. (Keep in mind though that it's up to each person how much personal information appears in the Skype profile, so it may not be possible to find people based on their name or email address. They may list everything about them or nothing.)

Let's look at an example of adding a contact (for this example, we created a user named "johndoe_nc_us1"):

Step 1   At this point, we have no "contacts," so no surprise that the list is empty (see Figure 21-13).

Click the green + icon.

Figure 21-13 Contacts List

Step 2   Enter the Skype user name given to you by a friend or family member who is already on Skype, and click **Next** (see Figure 21-14). If you don't know their Skype name, click **Search for people**.

Figure 21-14 Find a Contact

Step 3   Click **Advanced** tab. Enter the information you know about the person, such as e-mail address, state, city, and so on (see Figure 21-15). Click **Search**. As an example, we searched on a Skype name that starts with "janedoe." We found four possibilities: "jane-doe_nc_us2" is who we are trying to find.

Figure 21-15 Searching for the Contact

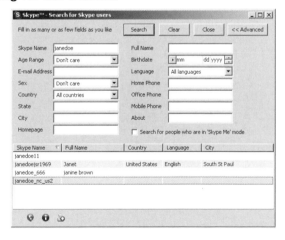

Step 4   Click the user you want to add to your list, and then click the icon on the bottom of the window with the +. Skype requires that the other person must confirm to allow you to see if they are online (see Figure 21-16). Click **OK**.

Figure 21-16 Requesting Permission to Add the Contact

Step 5   After the person accepts the request to let you see if they are online, the contact will
appear in your contacts list (see Figure 21-17). A grey question mark icon means they
have not yet granted you permission to see their online status. A green checkmark icon
means they are online. A grey X icon means they are offline.

Figure 21-17 New Contact Appears in Your Contacts List

After you have some contacts built, you can try placing a call. It's extremely easy. Here's how:

Step 1   Click the **Contacts** tab. Click the person you want to call (see Figure 21-18).

Figure 21-18 Making a Call

Step 2   Click the green phone icon on the bottom of the window.

The computer of person you are calling "rings," meaning their computer will make a sound like a phone ringing (or whatever sound they have programmed to play). (See Figure 21-19.)

Figure 21-19 Waiting for an Answer

Step 3   When the call is answered, you will see the Duration timer start (see Figure 21-20). (This timer does not really matter because it's free!)

Figure 21-20 Call Is Answered

When you are done talking, click the red phone handset icon at the bottom of the window.

That's all there is to it! It's one of the easiest, most straightforward programs that we have seen. Our hats are off to the Skype folks. Nice work!

Note that if you want to place a call to someone who is not on Skype service (such as a regular land line or cell phone), you just click the **Dial** tab, click the numbers to dial, and then click the green phone handset icon (see Figure 21-21). This is called *off-net calling*.

Figure 21-21 Calling a Land Line or Cell Phone

 NOTE Off-net Skype calls (also known as SkypeOut) are *not* free. A per-minute fee will apply depending on where you are calling.

 NOTE As a final note, be aware that an Internet phone service may or may not be secure. For example, the Skype voice-chat service uses a form of encryption to scramble the IP packets carrying the voice conversation. Vonage service is not encrypted.

It would take a highly skilled person with the right access to the network (or to hack it) to gain access to the packets carrying the voice conversation. However, as we have stated several times, where there is a will, there is a way.

Just use common sense when using phone service over the internet.

Networked Entertainment Systems

One of the biggest reasons to put a screaming fast (54 Mbps) wireless router in your house is so that you can watch photo slide shows from any room in your house or play any song from your CD library or Internet radio anywhere in your house. Some new tools even allow you to play movies or digitally recorded TV shows on any television in your house. All this (or most of it, anyway) without stringing wires everywhere.

To view digital pictures on any TV or play music on any stereo, you need a media adapter, which provides you with the wireless equivalent of connecting cables from the back of your computer to a TV or stereo on the other side of the house. The adapter works through a remote control and is pretty simple to use.

A new device now allows you to play movies or recorded TV shows, but it does require a media center PC. Prior to this system the media adapters did not have bandwidth to wirelessly transfer movies throughout a house. This new system makes it possible, allowing you to have full multimedia on any TV in the house.

How to Build It: Networked Entertainment Systems

In this section, we add networking devices to a home entertainment center creating a digital music library and a digital photo library.

Figure 22-1 shows the major components needed to build these two services.

Figure 22-1   Networked Entertainment Center Components

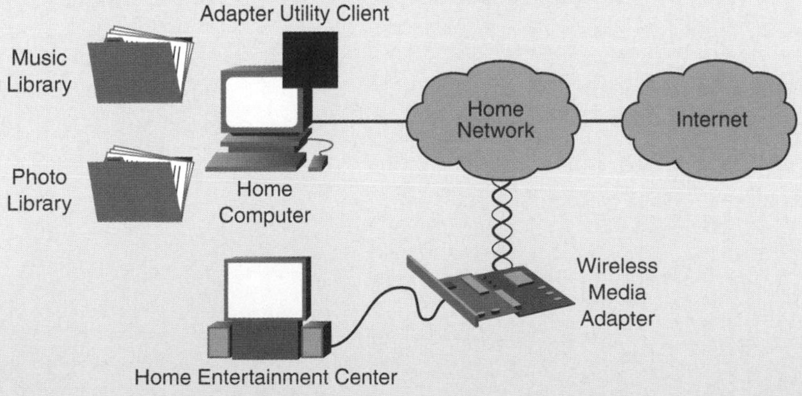

Here is an overview of the steps we will go through in this section:

- Set up the wireless media adapter

- Connect the home entertainment center to the wireless media adapter

- Install the adapter utility client on your home computer

- Play music and view photos

Set Up the Wireless Media Adapter

You must first set up the wireless media adapter (for this example we used the Linksys WMA11B) to communicate within your home network. The adapter and associated Utility Client software program serve up the music and photo content that is requested by the wireless media adapter. Only one Adapter Utility Client can be operating in the home network.

Step 1   Connect the Linksys wireless media adapter to the Linksys wireless router using an Ethernet cable. Plug in the power adapter (see Figure 22-2). The Ethernet LED light on the front should light up.

Figure 22-2   Plug in the Ethernet Cable

Step 2   Put the CD that came with the Linksys wireless media adapter into a computer on the network (a wired computer is preferred). The setup utility should start automatically (see Figure 22-3). If not, use My Computer to browse the CD and double-click **Setup.exe**. Click **Setup** > **Next**.

Figure 22-3   Linksys Wireless Media Adapter Setup Wizard

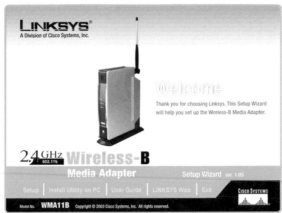

Step 3   The setup utility searches for the new media adapter on the network (see Figure 22-4). If it is not detected, check the cabling and try powering the media adapter off and back on. Then return to Steps 1–2.

Figure 22-4   Searching for the Media Adapter

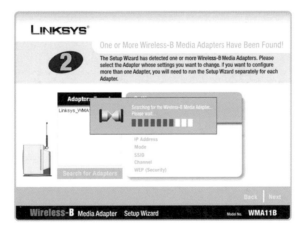

Step 4   If located successfully, the current default settings of the media adapter are displayed (see Figure 22-5). Click **Next**.

Step 5   Checkmark **Wireless network** (see Figure 22-6). Click **Next**.

Figure 22-5   Media Adapter Located

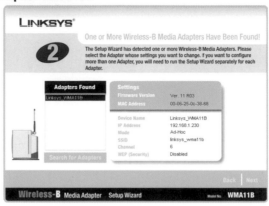

Figure 22-6   Choose Wireless Network

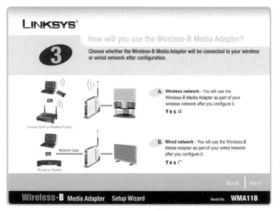

Step 6   Enter a device name for the wireless media adapter (we used "Entertain_Center" for this example) (see Figure 22-7). Select **Automatically** for Network Setting. Click **Next**.

Figure 22-7   Assign a Device Name and Set for Dynamic IP Address

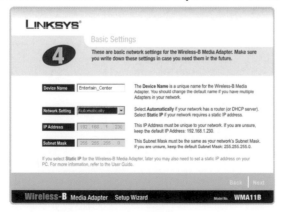

Step 7   Select **Infrastructure** for Mode. Enter the SSID for your wireless network (in this example, we use "J59wgh21MX"). (See Figure 22-8.) Click **Next**.

Figure 22-8   Set the SSID to Your Wireless Network

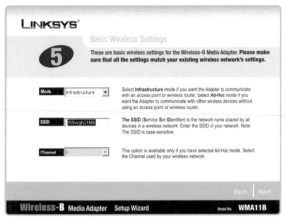

Step 8   Set the wireless security setting to WEP 128-bit keys (or the encryption you are using). Enter the pass-phrase you have been using for your wireless network (in this example, we use "64Gx3prY19fk2"). (See Figure 22-9.) Click **Next**.

Figure 22-9   Enter the Wireless Security Settings

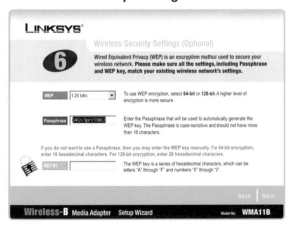

Step 9   Confirm that the settings were entered correctly, and click **Save** (see Figure 22-10).

Figure 22-10 Confirm and Save Your Settings

Step 10   Unplug the Ethernet cable. Power off the wireless media adapter, and then power it back on.

After you complete these steps, the Wireless LED indicator light on the front of the wireless media adapter should be lit (see Figure 22-11). The Ethernet LED will not be lit.

Figure 22-11 Wireless LED Lit

Troubleshooting Tips: Setting Up the Wireless Media Adapter

If the wireless LED indicator light on the front of the wireless media adapter is not lit, try the following:

■   Reconnect the Ethernet cable between the wireless router and the wireless media adapter. Restart the setup utility and repeat Steps 1–10.

Pay close attention to the wireless settings: SSID, WEP key length, and WEP key pass-phrase. They must be entered identically to your wireless network, including uppercase and lowercase letters. You may have to reset the media adapter to the factory settings using the reset procedure in the manual that comes with the media adapter.

■ Check the wireless router to see if the media adapter is getting assigned an address on the home network: Use an Internet browser to access the router; click **Status** > **Local Network** > **DHCP Client Table**. You should see the media adapter with an address on the network (see Figure 22-12).

Figure 22-12 Checking if the Media Adapter Is Receiving an IP Address

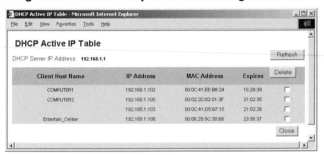

■ If you implemented MAC address locking on your wireless router (see Chapter 11, "Securing Your Wireless Network"), double-check that you permitted the new wireless device's MAC address to access your wireless network.

■ Read the "Troubleshooting" chapter in the installation manual that came with the Linksys wireless media adapter.

Connect the Home Entertainment Center to the Wireless Media Adapter

After you verify that the wireless media adapter is properly communicating with your wireless network, you can begin networking the home entertainment center.

Step 1   Move the wireless media adapter to the location of the home entertainment system.

Step 2   The wireless media adapter has a set of standard audio/video output ports, much like a VCR or DVD player. Using the RCA cable, connect the red, white, and yellow connectors to the same colored ports (see Figure 22-13).

Step 3   Connect the other ends of this cable to your TV, VCR, or however you want the media adapter to use as its input to the home entertainment center. As an alternative to the yellow video cable, a Super Video cable (S-Video) can be used for higher quality pictures. (You still need the red and white cables for audio in this case.)

Figure 22-13 Connecting the Audio/Video Cables

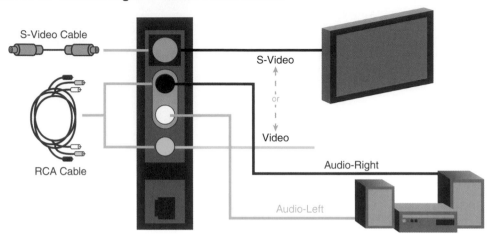

Step 4   Remember to connect the power cable to the wireless media adapter, and push the power-on button.

That's it!

Install the Adapter Utility Client on Your Home Computer

Now that the wireless media adapter is on the network and your home entertainment system is connected, you need to set up the adapter utility client on the home computer where the digital music and photo libraries are stored.

Only one adapter client can be installed on your home network. So you will need to do a little planning at this point as to where your digital photos as well as the music files are stored. If these are on different computers, you could take advantage of file sharing (see Chapter 6, "Sharing Network Resources") to make the photo and music files accessible to the computer where the adapter client will be installed.

One other consideration: The adapter utility client requires a minimum of a 600 MHz Pentium computer running Windows XP. It cannot be installed under Windows 2000 or Windows 98. The software also requires a considerable amount of disk space (150 MB or more, plus the amount you will need to store all your photos and music).

Here are the steps to set up the adapter client:

Step 1   Go to the CD setup wizard that comes with the wireless media adapter (see Figure 22-14). Click **Install Utility on PC**.

Step 2   The setup wizard checks if Microsoft .NET framework software is installed already on the computer (see Figure 22-15). This is a mandatory component. Click **Next**.

Figure 22-14 Linksys Wireless Media Adapter Setup Wizard

Figure 22-15 Setup Utility Searches for Microsoft .NET

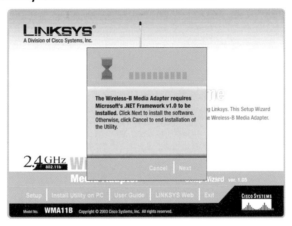

Step 3 If .NET is already installed, skip to Step 5. If it's not already installed, the installer will confirm you want to install Microsoft .NET framework (see Figure 22-16). Click **Yes**.

Figure 22-16 Click Yes to Install Microsoft .NET

Step 4   Follow the installation dialog boxes that come next (see Figure 22-17).

Figure 22-17 .NET Framework Setup Wizard

Step 5   Return to the adapter utility client installer, and click **Next** (see Figure 22-18).

Figure 22-18 Begin Installing the Adapter Client

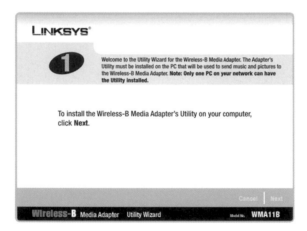

Step 6   The utility guesses where your digital music and photo libraries are stored
(see Figure 22-19). Use **Remove** to take a directory out of the list that does not contain
the photos or music you want to use. Use **Add** to include the directories containing your
photos and music you want to use with the media adapter. When finished, click **Next**.

Figure 22-19 Point the Media Adapter to the Location of Your Music and Photo Libraries

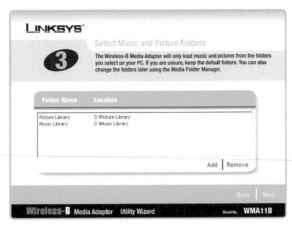

Step 7   Click **Yes** to create a shortcut on the desktop (see Figure 22-20). Click **Exit** on the setup utility.

Figure 22-20 Create a Shortcut for the Media Folder Manager

Congratulations! You have just set up a networked home entertainment center.

Playing Music

Now that everything has been set up, let's test it by listening to some music. (It is assumed that you have uploaded some music files to the library folder(s) you specified in the previous section.) Make sure that the computer hosting the libraries is turned on and connected to the network. The steps are

Step 1   Power on the television and stereo sound system. Select the appropriate channel and inputs to select the inputs from the wireless media adapter.

Step 2   The television screen should show the main menu for the media adapter (see Figure 22-21). Push the **Music** button on the remote control (make sure to put the batteries in it first).

Figure 22-21 Media Adapter's Main Menu

Step 3   Using the remote, navigate through the Music menu to locate a song (see Figure 22-22 and Figure 22-23).

 GEEK SQUAD We recommend *Girl from Ipanema* or some nice Bossa Nova.

Figure 22-22 Choose Music

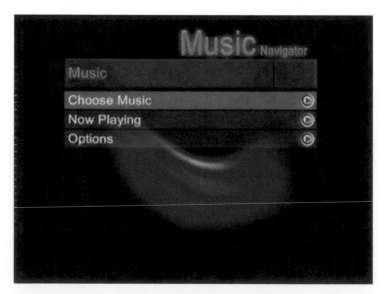

Figure 22-23 Navigating to a Song by Genre

Step 4 Push the **Play** button on the remote control. The song should play through your stereo sound system (see Figure 22-24). (If not, check the red and white cables to make sure they are properly connected.)

Figure 22-24 Song Is Playing

Viewing Photos

Let's try viewing some digital photos. (It is assumed that you have uploaded some photo files to the library folder(s) you specified in the previous section.) The steps are

Step 1   Click the **Pictures** button on the remote control. Using the remote, navigate through the Pictures menu to locate a photo (see Figures 22-25 and 22-26).

Figure 22-25 Choose Photos

Step 2   Push the **Select** button on the remote control. The digital photo should now be displayed on the television screen (see Figure 22-27). (If not, check the yellow cable to make sure it is properly connected.)

Figure 22-26 Navigate to a Photo You Want to View

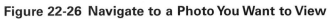

Figure 22-27 Photo Is Now Displayed

We were impressed with the Linksys wireless media adapter. We found it to be easy to set up and use, and the built-in ability to search music by qualifiers such as artist and genre were extremely useful. For photos, the browsing capabilities as well as the ability to create a slideshow were equally impressive.

It is possible to play music and view photos at the same time. Keep in mind that all the digital music and photo libraries always reside on the home computer that is acting as a server (or accessible to that computer via Windows file sharing), so this computer must be booted up and be on the network for the wireless media adapter to function properly.

Also, due to the intensive file transmissions involved, we recommend that the home computer hosting the digital music and photo libraries be connected to the home network via a wired connection. We tested a laptop acting as a server over a wireless connection, and it worked quite well. However, in the long run, you are probably better off with a wired connection for the server.

 GEEK SQUAD If you plan on converting your entire CD collection to MP3 format, you may want to look into a network storage device. These devices make it possible to have a large centralized repository of 120 GB (gigabytes) or more of disk drive space that can be shared by all the computers on your network.

Have fun with it!

Online Gaming

When we were 11 years old or so, we each got an Atari gaming system. We spent the entire summer indoors playing Pitfall Harry, and our mothers were constantly screaming at us to go outside and play like normal kids. In the years since, much has changed. The game systems are out of this world. You can play against people from all over the world, so after you whip everyone in your neighborhood, you can find some dude in Vancouver (or wherever) to play against. Our wives have stepped in for our moms and now they scream at us to turn that darn thing off. Good times.

This chapter walks you through the setup of an online gaming system. Our weapon of choice here is the Microsoft Xbox, which is easy to set up and use online. The online service from Microsoft is called Xbox Live. This system allows you to play one on one against a specific person or join an "open" game to play with or against other people. Some games also allow team play so several people can cooperatively play the same game. Another feature this system has is audio chat, which allows you to speak live (via voice chat) with the other players during the game to strategize or talk smack (whatever the situation calls for). This feature uses the technology we discussed in Chapter 21, "Internet Phone Service."

Gaming Servers

Gaming servers work much like a videoconference bridge in that each individual inputs his or own data, and all parties receive the combined stream of all the individuals. In a gaming server, each person on the server is assigned an entity in the program. This entity could be a car, or a fighter, or a really mean duck. Within the game, you control the actions of this entity, which could affect other entities or the environment, as do all the other players in the game. All the information from all the players is compiled in the server and then sent out to all the players in the game.

A system like this requires a great deal of computing power and speed (both processing speed and connection speed if the players are remote). Fortunately, with dedicated game systems such as Xbox and broadband download speeds, high-end games lose nothing when you play online. Part of the reason for this is that the gaming server sends as little information as possible, just basic instructions to update the game. It's all pretty fascinating, but rather than overanalyze this one, let's set it up and start playing. We, the authors, do not assume liability for any marital or family problems or carpal tunnel syndrome caused by the (excessive) use of this technology.

 GEEK SQUAD As far as gaming goes, online is where it's at. This is the future of gaming.

Online Gaming System

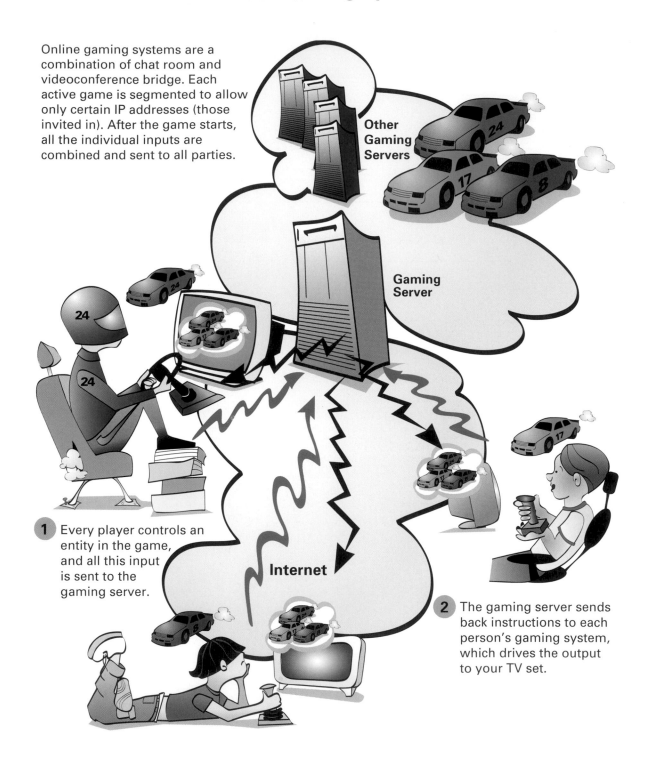

Online gaming systems are a combination of chat room and videoconference bridge. Each active game is segmented to allow only certain IP addresses (those invited in). After the game starts, all the individual inputs are combined and sent to all parties.

Other Gaming Servers

Gaming Server

1 Every player controls an entity in the game, and all this input is sent to the gaming server.

Internet

2 The gaming server sends back instructions to each person's gaming system, which drives the output to your TV set.

Options for Online Gaming

There are a few different options for online game playing, including using a computer or an actual video game console (such as Microsoft Xbox). Table 23-1 compares the options.

Table 23-1   Video Game Options

	NIC	Number of Games	Online Services	Online Play Costs	Voice Chat
Computer	Probable	Hundreds	GameSpy (and others)	Free to $12.95 monthly	Yes
Microsoft Xbox	Built-in	More than 100	Xbox Live	$49.99 annually	Yes
Sony PlayStation 2	Built-in (after Nov 2004)*	More than 100	Various game publishers	Free to $12.95 monthly	Handful
Nintendo GameCube	Add-on for $30–40	Very few	Sega	$8.95 monthly	No

* The new Sony Playstation 2 SCPH-70000 Series released in November 2004 has a built-in NIC; the older SCPH-50000 Series requires an add-on.

 NOTE A computer with video game software installed is certainly an option. There are already hundreds of online games available, some for free and some requiring a fee. A good resource to find out what is available is http://www.gamespy.com. However, this type of online gaming device is not the focus of this chapter.

This chapter focuses on dedicated video game consoles because it takes a bit more work to get these connected, and there appears to be much less information out there about how to do so.

 NOTE If you are truly interested in online gaming, Xbox or PlayStation2 are the leaders in the field. It does not appear that Nintendo is a serious player here yet, in our opinion.

How to Build It: Online Video Gaming

In this section, we look at how to take video game playing to the next level: online.

The first step to online gaming is to have a network-capable video game console. The console can then be connected with an Ethernet cable to the home network, just like any other computer or device. Because it is probable the video game console and television may be in an entirely different room of the house from the Internet connection, a wireless game adapter may also be incredibly useful. This device will allow a video game console to be connected to the wireless network.

So let's get online. It is assumed that you have already installed your home network, have high-speed broadband Internet service, and wireless in your home network. The rest of this section will go through the steps to connect a video game over your home wireless network to an online gaming service.

Here's an overview of the steps we will go through to set up an online gaming system:

- Set up the wireless game adapter

- Connect a video game console to the wireless game adapter

- Connect to an online game provider

- Setting up an online game account

- Steps for troubleshooting

Set Up the Wireless Game Adapter

After you have chosen your gaming console, you will want to connect it to your home network. If the console happens to be in close proximity to the wireless router, you could use an Ethernet cable and just connect it directly. Often, this is not the case, so in this section, we show how to use a wireless game adapter to connect the console from anywhere in our house.

There are a couple of Linksys wireless game adapter products that we can choose from (shown in Table 23-2).

Table 23-2   Linksys Wireless Game Adapters

Model	Works with Wireless Standards	Wireless Encryption Supported
WGA54G	802.11b 802.11g	64-bit WEP 128-bit WEP
WGA11B	802.11b 802.11g	64-bit WEP 128-bit WEP

The steps to connect are as follows (in this example, we use the WGA11B product):

Step 1 Connect the Linksys wireless game adapter to the Linksys wireless router using an Ethernet cable, and plug in the power adapter (see Figure 23-1). Set the X - ‖ switch to ‖. The LAN LED light on the front should light up.

Figure 23-1   Connect the Wireless Game Adapter to the Router

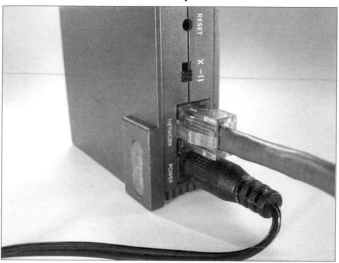

Step 2 Put the CD that came with the Linksys wireless game adapter into a computer on the network (a wired computer is preferred). The setup utility should start automatically (see Figure 23-2). If not, use My Computer to browse the CD and double-click **Setup.exe**. Click **Setup**.

Figure 23-2   Linksys Wireless Game Adapter Setup Utility

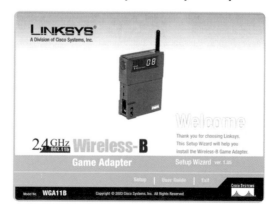

Step 3 The setup utility searches for the new game adapter on the network. If it is not detected, check the cabling and try powering the game adapter off and back on. Then return to Steps 1–2. If the game adapter is located successfully, the current default settings for it are displayed (see Figure 23-3). Click **Next**.

Figure 23-3 Setup Utility Searches for and Finds the Game Adapter

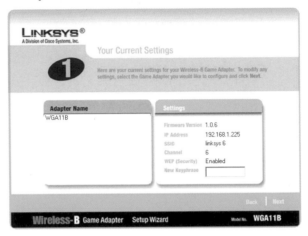

Step 4 Enter the default password **admin** (see Figure 23-4), and press **Enter**.

Figure 23-4 Enter the Default Password

Step 5 Checkmark **Obtain IP Address automatically**. Change the password from the default (admin) to a random series of uppercase letters, lowercase letters, and numbers (see Figure 23-5). Write it down somewhere safe for keeping. Click **Next**.

Figure 23-5   Change the Basic Settings

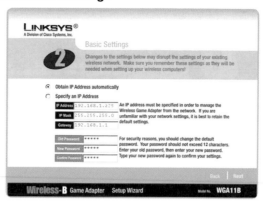

Step 6   Enter the SSID for your wireless network (see Figure 23-6) (in this example, we use "J59wgh21MX"). Set the wireless security setting to "WEP 128-bit Keys" (or the encryption you are using). Enter the pass-phrase you have been using for your wireless network (in this example "64Gx3prY19fk2"). Click **No** to save the settings.

Figure 23-6   Set the Wireless SSID and Security Settings

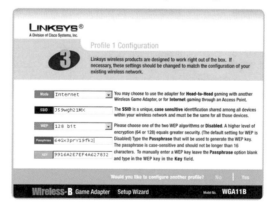

Step 7   Two dialog boxes are then displayed (see Figure 23-7 and Figure 23-8). These are normal—not very graceful, but normal. Click **OK** for both dialog boxes.

Figure 23-7 Not Connected Dialog Box

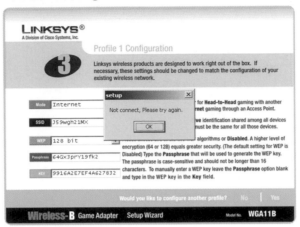

Figure 23-8 Connect Fail Dialog Box

Step 8 Unplug the Ethernet cable connecting the game adapter to the wireless router. Power off the adapter (unplug it), and then power it back on.

Step 9 Press the blue button on the side of the game adapter repeatedly until the display on the front reads P1 (see Figure 23-9). The Wireless Channel LED indicator light on the front of the wireless game adapter should be lit.

Figure 23-9   Select Wireless Profile P1

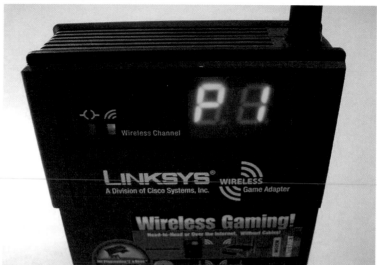

Troubleshooting Tips: Setting Up a Wireless Game Adapter

If the Wireless Channel LED indicator light on the front of the wireless game adapter is *not* lit, try the following:

- There might be a bug in the Linksys Wireless-B game adapter (WGA11B) product, where it cannot acquire a wireless network signal when the SSID broadcast is disabled. Try enabling the SSID broadcast (see Chapter 11) and see if the wireless channel LED light becomes lit.

- Reconnect the Ethernet cable between the wireless router and the wireless game adapter. Restart the setup utility and repeat Steps 1–7. Pay close attention to the wireless settings: SSID, WEP key length, and WEP key pass-phrase. They must be entered identically to your wireless network, including uppercase and lowercase letters! You may have to reset the game adapter to the factory settings using the reset procedure in the manual that came with the game adapter.

- Check on the wireless router to see if the game adapter is getting assigned an address on the home network: Use an Internet browser to access the router, click **Status > Local Network > DHCP Client Table**. You should see the game adapter with an address on the network.

- If you implemented MAC address locking on your wireless router (see Chapter 11, "Securing Your Wireless Network"), double-check that you permitted the new wireless device's MAC address to access your wireless network.

- Read the "Troubleshooting" chapter in the installation manual that came with the Linksys wireless game adapter.

Connect a Video Game Console to the Wireless Game Adapter

After you verify that the wireless game adapter is properly communicating with your wireless network, you can move on with setting up the rest of the online gaming system:

Step 1 Unplug the Ethernet cable to the game adapter (if it's still connected) and move the game adapter to the location in your house where you want the video game console to be. Because it is wireless, it can be placed anywhere there is an electrical outlet (and TV) nearby.

Step 2 Plug one end of an Ethernet cable into the port on the back of the wireless game adapter. Plug the other end into the Ethernet port on the back of the video game console, as shown in Figure 23-10.

Figure 23-10 Connect the Game Console to the Game Adapter

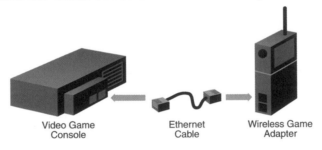

Video Game Console   Ethernet Cable   Wireless Game Adapter

Step 3 Connect the power cable to the wireless game adapter. After connecting the cables to both the game adapter and the video game console, remember to plug in the video game console to the electrical outlet.

Step 4 Turn on the video game console. After it boots, you should see both the LAN and Wireless Channel LED lights on the front of the wireless game adapter light up. If not, check the cabling and try powering off and on the game adapter. Also, try changing the X - ‖ switch setting.

Connect to an Online Game Provider

Now that the wireless game adapter is on the network and your video game console has been connected, you need to set up the online game service. This will vary greatly depending on the particular service. Here's a short example for Xbox Live service. First, we need to set up and verify the network settings:

Step 1 Power on the Xbox. On the main window, scroll using the arrow pad until **Settings** is highlighted, and then press the green **A** button (see Figure 23-11).

Figure 23-11 Xbox Main Menu

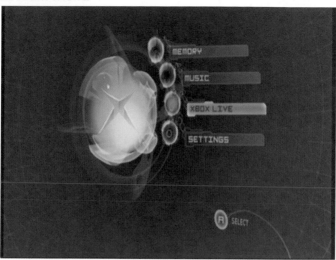

Step 2   Choose **Settings** > **Network Settings** (see Figure 23-12).

Figure 23-12 Xbox Network Settings Menu

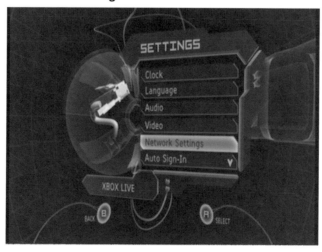

Step 3   There are four network settings sub-menus (see Figure 23-13). Choose **IP Addresses**.

Figure 23-13 Xbox Network Settings Sub-Menus

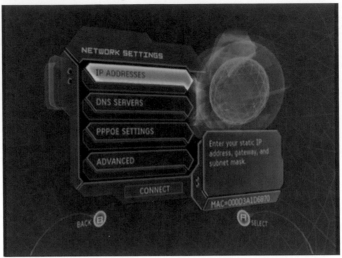

Step 4   Set Configuration to **Automatic** (see Figure 23-14). Click **B** to go back one menu.

Figure 23-14 Setting IP Address to Automatic

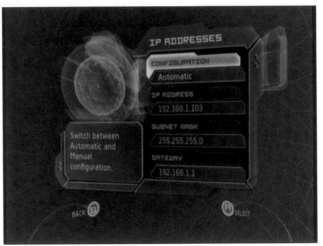

Step 5   Follow similar steps to set

- **DNS Servers** to **Automatic**

- **PPPoE Settings** to **Off**

- **Advanced** to blank

Step 6   After you verify the settings, select and click **Connect** (see Figure 23-15).

Figure 23-15 Test the Connection to Xbox Live

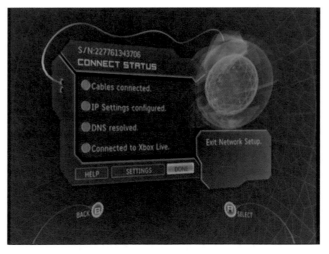

Step 7 The Xbox will test the connection by accessing the Xbox Live server. All four status indicators should appear as green (see Figure 23-16). If not, consult the Help function and see the upcoming section "Detailed Troubleshooting Steps for Online Gaming."

Figure 23-16 Connection Is Successful

Setting Up an Online Game Account

Now that we have set the network settings for the video game console, we can move on to setting up an account with the online gaming provider (we use Xbox Live for this example). Before continuing you will need to purchase a subscription to Xbox Live either from a retail store or online. The subscription will come with a code number that you will need to enter in one of the steps below:

Step 1 On the main window, scroll using the arrow pad until Xbox Live is highlighted, and then press the green A button. Choose **New Account** (see Figure 23-17).

Figure 23-17 Setting Up a New Xbox Live Account

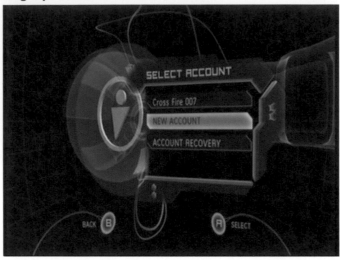

Step 2   Choose **United States** (or the country you are from). Accept the terms and conditions. Create a Gamertag, which is the unique name you want to be known by other Xbox Live players (see Figure 23-18). Enter your date of birth (to verify your age, you must be 18 or older to join). Choose **Continue**.

Figure 23-18 Create a Gamertag

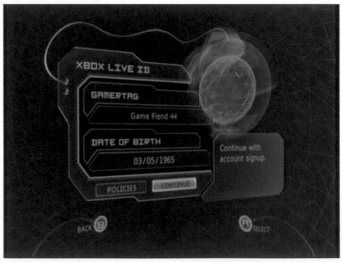

Step 3   You are asked to enter the subscription code for Xbox Live. This is the 25-digit code underneath the scratch-off block from the subscription starter kit you purchased (see Figure 23-19). Enter the code using the keyboard navigation screen, and then choose **Done**.

Figure 23-19 Enter the Xbox Live Subscription Key

Step 4 You are now asked for a valid credit card. You have already paid for the current subscription, but Xbox Live requires a valid credit card to sign up. You will not be billed before renewal. Enter the information and choose **Continue** (see Figure 23-20).

Figure 23-20 Enter Your Credit Card Information

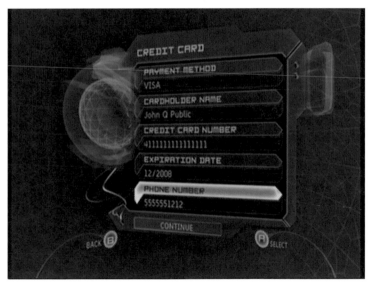

Step 5 You are then asked for your billing address information and an e-mail address. Enter the information and choose **Done** (see Figure 23-21).

Step 6 The new account is created and confirmed. You can then specify whether you want to enable Voice Chat. You also have the option to disable premium purchases (see Figure 23-22).

Figure 23-21 Enter Your Information

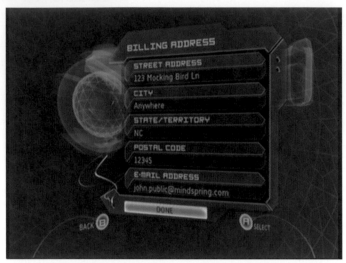

Figure 23-22 Voice Chat and Premium Purchases Settings

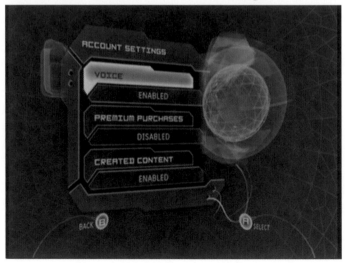

Step 7   You will also create a pass code (like a PIN) using the controller keys to lock the account. Write it down and save it! Click the **A** button.

If you have completed the account setup, congratulations; you have just set up online gaming! Whenever you power-on your Xbox game console, it will automatically connect to the Xbox Live service. Now put in your games and go play!

If something goes wrong, see the next section on troubleshooting.

GEEK SQUAD If you have trouble getting your gaming system online, check your firewalls. You might have to temporarily disable one or more security measures. Just remember to turn them back on when you are done.

Detailed Troubleshooting Steps for Online Gaming

If the Xbox does not connect to the Xbox Live service, the best place to start troubleshooting is with the Connect Status utility built into the Xbox console. To get there from the Xbox main menu, click **Settings > Network Settings > Connect**.

The Connect Status utility performs a series of four tests (see Figure 23-23):

- Checks the Ethernet connection to the home network

- Checks if an IP address is assigned by the home network

- Checks if DNS is assigned by the home network and is accessible

- Checks if the Xbox can reach the Xbox Live server

Figure 23-23 Connect Status Utility

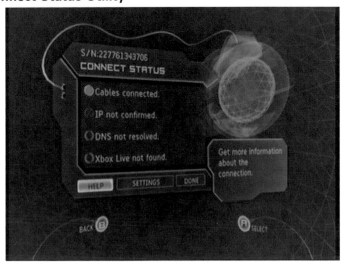

The utility should complete with all four "green" status indicators on the left (see Figure 23-16). If not, where it fails will give a good indication of what is wrong. Table 23-3 shows suggested steps to try that correspond with where the utility indicates there is a problem.

Table 23-3   **Debugging Xbox Live Connectivity**

Test	What "Red" Means	Try
Cables	Ethernet between the Xbox and the game adapter is not working.	Verify cables. Repeat sections on setting up and connecting the wireless game adapter. Try changing the ‖ x switch setting on the wireless game adapter.
IP Settings	Xbox is not getting an IP address assigned by the home network.	Verify IP addresses is set to Automatic. Double-check that the Xbox MAC address is permitted on the wireless network (if you have implemented wireless MAC address locking).
DNS	Xbox is not getting DNS server addresses assigned or DNS servers are not responding.	Verify DNS servers are set to Automatic. Try accessing a web page from the home network to verify your Internet is working.
Xbox Live Service	Xbox is not able to reach the Xbox Live servers.	Try accessing a web page from the home network to verify your Internet is working. Go to http://www.xbox.com and verify that the Xbox Live service is active.

Troubleshooting Tips: Connecting to Online Video Gaming Service

Here are a few other troubleshooting tips:

- Re-verify the steps throughout this chapter. Make sure both the LAN and WLAN LEDs are lit on the wireless game adapter.

- Read the Troubleshooting chapter in the installation manual that came with the Linksys wireless game adapter.

- Contact technical support for the online gaming provider.

From the Geek Squad Files

This section brings us to the deep end of the pool. It shows some pretty cool stuff, but keep in mind that some people who know how to do this can make a living at it (like us, but with less style). Really, though, aside from those who are pretty technically handy, people who want this type of thing typically fall into two camps: People who call us right away, and people who call us eventually. It's worth trying to make these features by yourself, but a professional can save a lot of time and aggravation.

The exception to this is the online gaming. This is big business and the supplies such as XBox or Sony On-Line make it as a simple as possible. If you have a teenager or if there are teenagers in your neighborhood, chances are they are gaming online. If you have not seen this stuff, ask them to show you. It sure beats the heck out of Pong.

A couple of thoughts to leave you with: Some have already been covered, but because we get the last word, it's worth repeating:

- Keep the manufacturer's boxes for 90 days. If you need to return any defective products, having the original boxes can make the process much easier.

- Keep a notepad near your computer and write down all those weird error messages. If you're forced to call a tech support line, your notes could help reduce the amount of time you'll be on the phone.

- Write down your passwords on a single sheet of paper that's kept in a hiding place away from your computer. (It's easier to remember the location of a sheet of paper than numerous passwords for countless websites.)

- If your computer seems slow or isn't obedient, you may need more memory or a bigger hard drive. Spyware has become almost unavoidable, but you can still take some preventative measures. For example, Spy Sweeper is an affordable program that helps find and rid your PC of spyware, and you can set the program to run while you're asleep.

- Be careful of opening e-mails—especially attached files—from unknown sources.

- Play around with your new technology. People learn best when they are playing and having fun, and the gadgets become less intimidating. Balance the need for new technology with being a "heat seeker." This is what we call people who always have to have the latest and greatest in technology, for no good reason, often before the manuals have been translated into English.

- Flip through the manual. You don't need to memorize every detail, but by breezing through, you'll learn things about your gadget that you never even dreamed.

- Back up your data on a USB flash drive. It's the size of a keychain and can be plugged into any PC with a USB port.

- If all else fails or if you're just having trouble and need help, call the Geek Squad or visit us at www.geeksquad.com.

Numerics

128-bit WEP   Wired Equivalent Privacy security algorithm for wireless networks using encryption with 128-bit keys. More secure than 64-bit WEP.

2.4 GHz   Radio frequency spectrum allocated to unlicensed wireless devices, such as wireless networks and cordless phones.

5 GHz   Radio frequency spectrum allocated to unlicensed wireless devices, such as wireless networks and cordless phones.

64-bit WEP   Wired Equivalent Privacy security algorithm for wireless networks using encryption with 64-bit keys. Less secure than 128-bit WEP.

802.11   A family of standards that defines the rules for wireless LAN communications.

802.11a   A variant of the 802.11 standard that operates at 5 GHz and can achieve speeds up to 108 Mbps. This standard is not very popular in home networks but has been adopted in many business networks. 802.11b and 802.11g NICs are not compatible with 802.11a networks.

802.11b   The most common WLAN standard that operates at 2.4 GHz, with speeds up to 11 Mbps. 802.11b NICs also work with 802.11g networks.

802.11g   A standard for WLANs that operates at 2.4 GHz, with speeds up to 108 Mbps. This standard is
compatible with the "b" standard and is growing in popularity. 802.11g NICs also work with 802.11b networks.

A

access point   Term for a wireless base station that provides connections between computers with wireless NICs.

ad-hoc   A type of wireless network that is directly established between two or more computers without the involvement of an intermediate access point. This is convenient, but there are a lot of security risks associated with this type of network.

adware   Small programs that target pop-up advertisements based on the sites you browse on the Internet.

AES (Advanced Encryption Standard)   Cryptography algorithm used to perform encryption of wireless network signals using the WPA2 standard.

anti-spam   Software programs that run on PCs to prevent unwanted spam e-mail from reaching e-mail inboxes.

antivirus   Software programs that run on PCs to prevent and treat infections by computer viruses.

Arpanet   The network that predated the Internet.

ASCII (American Standard Code for Information Interchange)   This code represents each key on a keyboard with a seven-digit binary number.

B

base station   Another term for a wireless access point that provides connections between computers with wireless NICs.

binary   A numbering system based on 1s and 0s. This is the basis for all computer languages.

bit   Short for "binary unit"; this is single digit of information, which is a 1 or 0.

broadband   A term used to describe high-speed Internet service. The term comes from the fact that a broad range of frequencies are used to attain high information exchange rates.

browser   A program used to access content on the Internet.

byte   A standard-size "chunk" of computer language or network information. A byte is made of 8 bits.

C

cable   Can refer to a wire with connectors to connect two devices together, or can also refer to the type of broadband service you get from your cable TV provider.

Cat 5   Category 5 cable is the standard format for Ethernet (computer network) cabling.

CCTV (closed circuit TV)   This usually refers to a video surveillance system that is contained within a building or small area.

CD (compact disk)   Digital disk media itself that is used for audio CDs, data CDs, DVDs, and so on.

CD-ROM (compact disk read-only memory) drive   A CD player that comes with nearly every PC shipped today. Many players are capable of reading DVDs and can now write to blank compact disks.

chat   Instant messaging session where often there are three or more people involved.

cookies   A small text file placed on a PC by a website to track user information and personal setting preferences.

CPU (central processing unit)   The computer's "brain" where nearly all calculations are performed.

D

DHCP (Dynamic Host Configuration Protocol)   This protocol is used by service providers and network equipment to automatically assign random IP addresses from a pool rather than assigning permanent IP addresses to users.

DHCP client   The computer that requests an IP address for use.

DHCP server   The device that receives requests for IP addresses and makes address assignments.

dialup   An Internet connection using a standard modem over a phone line. This type of connection is relatively slower than broadband.

dirty e-mail address   An e-mail address on a free e-mail service, such as Hotmail or Yahoo! Mail, which you use online to register on websites whenever an e-mail address is requested. The object of a "dirty" e-mail address is to provide a location for e-mail solicitations, while your "real" e-mail address stays "clean."

DNS (Domain Name System)   These servers match Internet site names to their actual IP addresses. This system allows websites to be named in English (or most other languages) rather than in numbers.

downlink   The connection and information flow from the service provider to your computer.

DSL (digital subscriber line)   A high-speed Internet connection that uses unused frequencies on phone lines to deliver very high data rates with the use of a specialized modem.

DVD (digital video disk)   Format for storing motion picture video on CD media.

DVD/CD writer   Most PCs today have a built-in DVD player that plays movies and other CDs. Many of these devices also allow you to write onto blank CDs or DVDs.

dynamic IP address   Having an IP address assigned by a device in the Internet service provider's network, which can change each time an address is requested.

E

e-mail   An application used to exchange notes and files between two or more people. An e-mail is identified by the user name and the service provider, such as bob@network.com.

EPROM (erasable programmable read-only memory)   Computer memory not available to the user. This usually contains very basic instructions for the computer's operation.

Ethernet   A protocol that defines the rules for computer communication over certain types of networks. It is the dominant protocol in use for both home and businesses.

expansion card   A printed circuit board that can be inserted for additional functionality.

expansion slot   An opening in the computer for expansion cards.

eyeballs   Measurement for how many people see an advertisement, website, or other facility on the Internet. One eyeball is equivalent to one person seeing the intended material.

F

firewall   A physical device or software program that prevents unwanted access into a private network from an outside location

FireWire   A high-speed cabling standard for devices connecting to a computer. Commonly used for digital still and video cameras.

flames   Angry or insulting e-mails. These are usually sent in response to a breach of web or e-mail etiquette.

floppy disk drive   These are becoming pretty rare, but some PCs still use 3.5" floppy disks for program or data storage.

FTP (File Transfer Protocol)   This protocol is used to copy files between computers over the Internet.

G

gadget porn   Refers to glossy magazine or newspaper advertisements that show many pages of the latest consumer electronics products. Just as likely to max out credit cards as real porn.

Gb (Gigabit)   1.024 billion bits.

GB (Gigabyte)   1.024 billion bytes.

GHz (gigahertz)   Measurement of a radio frequency equating to 1 billion cycles per second.

Google   A website used to search for topics or other sites. Its popularity has made it a verb meaning "to search," such as "I googled Geek Squad."

Granimals   Method during the 1970s using pictures of animals to aid in matching of shirts to pants for the fashion-challenged.

H

hacker   A person who breaks into networks or computers or one who creates virus software.

hard disk drive   This device reads and writes data to hard disk.

hotspot   A wireless network available for use in a public place such as a coffee shop or airport.

HTTP (Hypertext Transfer Protocol)   This is the computer language used to retrieve information from web pages written in certain "mark up" languages.

hub   A "dumb" device that provides the minimum features needed to connect computers for basic networks.

I

IM (instant messaging)   IM is quickly becoming one of the most popular forms of communication over the Internet and cell phone networks.

IMAP (Internet Message Access Protocol)   A standard protocol for accessing e-mail from a mail server.

infrastructure   A type of wireless network where all endpoints (computers) connect to the LAN through a central device.

interface   A device that connects two pieces of equipment (a mouse and computer, for example).

Internet   This is the worldwide system of computer networks. Although many private networks connect to it, the Internet is public, cooperative, and self-sustaining.

Internet phone adapter   Device that allows you to plug in a typical home phone and converts it to use the Internet instead of the PSTN.

IP (Internet Protocol)   Defines the communication rules for devices on the Internet. Communication within this protocol is based on the assignment of IP addresses.

IP address Numerical address by which computers, web servers, and devices are known by on the Internet. IP addresses have little bearing on geographic location.

IP telephony Telephone service provided over a data network.

IR (infrared) A wireless communication technology that uses frequencies in the non-visible light spectrum (not as high as radio frequencies).

ISP (Internet service provider) A company that provides access to the Internet for residential or business use.

J–K–L

JPEG Also referred to as jpg, this is a standard digital image format.

Kilobit (Kb) 1024 bits. This is a standard transmission rate unit for dialup modems when referred to over a portion of time such as Kbps or kilobits per second.

Kilobyte (KB) 1024 bytes.

LAN (local-area network) This is small network within a house, department, or business.

LED (light emitting diode) These are the green, red, and amber (or other color) status indicator lights on computers and networking gear.

M

MAC (Media Access Control) address The unique physical serial number given by the manufacturer to every networking device used for network communication.

Megabit (Mb) 1.024 million bits. When measured over time, this is the standard transmission rate unit for high-speed modems.

Megabyte (MB) 1.024 million bytes.

media The physical path that signals take across a network.

memory Temporary data storage within a computer.

microprocessor A silicon chip that contains a CPU.

modem (modulator demodulator) Devices that translate computer language for transmission over a network media (see media) and back again.

motherboard The main circuit board of the computer. Everything else in a computer plugs into the motherboard and is controlled by it.

MP3 A standard technology and format for compression of audio (music).

N

NAT (Network Address Translation) A method of translating private IP addresses, such as a home network, to an outside network, such as the Internet. NAT conserves IP addresses and offers some level of security.

network interface card (NIC) A circuit board either added or included in a computer that provides network access.

P

parallel port An interface that communicates more than one bit of information at a time. Usually used to connect devices such as printers.

parental control Software programs or security settings that allow parents to control and limit access by children to computer usage, websites, and chat rooms.

PCB (printed circuit board) A thin plate on which integrated circuits are placed.

PCI (Peripheral Component Interconnect) A local bus standard used by the motherboard of most PCs to communicate between components, such as cards.

PCMCIA (Personal Computer Memory Card International Association) card Also referred to as a PC card, this card fits into an expansion slot on a laptop. Many different PCMCIA cards can be purchased for different functions including, but not limited to, extra storage (hard drive), NICs, and cellular modems.

PDA (personal digital assistant) This is a term for small handheld computers such as Palm Pilots.

peer-to-peer Another term for ad-hoc wireless networking, whereby two computers establish a connection directly to each other without a wireless access point.

phishing A rip-off scheme where scam artists fool people into sharing account numbers by e-mailing official looking notes from credit card companies or e-commerce web sites, which request account verification. When a person responds with their personal information, the thieves rack up credit charges.

pimpware Free software that you download which requires you to continually view advertisements, respond to surveys, or some other action each time you use it.

ping Utility program on most PCs that can be used to test a network connection.

POP (point of presence) This refers to the location of Internet access, typically with reference to a service provider.

POP3 (Post Office Protocol 3) This is one of the standard protocols used for retrieving e-mails from a server.

pop-up Advertisements that appears spontaneously in Internet browser windows.

pop-up blocker Software program that runs on PCs to prevent pop-up advertisements from appearing.

PPPoE (Point-to-Point Protocol over Ethernet) Commonly used communication protocol for DSL connections.

PSTN (Public Switched Telephony Network) The standard phone network we all know and love.

R

RAM (random-access memory)   A temporary storage place for data while programs are in use. If the computer loses power, all data in RAM that was not saved is lost.

RF (radio frequency)   The range of frequencies that are easily transmitted over the air.

ROM (read-only memory)   Prerecorded or "startup" memory.

router   A networking device that makes "intelligent" decisions regarding how traffic is moved across or through a network.

S

satellite   In the context of home networking, this is an emerging type of broadband Internet access.

scam blocker   Software program that runs on PCs and prevents scams such as phishing from being successful.

serial port   An interface that can communicate 1 bit at a time; usually used to connect external drives and modems.

signal strength   Measurement of the quality of a wireless network signal received by a wireless NIC, similar to the "bars" of service on a cell phone.

Skype   Popular free Internet-based voice chat service.

SMS (short message service)   A protocol used in cellular networks to send instant messages between cellphone users.

SMTP (Simple Mail Transfer Protocol)   A protocol used in sending and receiving e-mail.

socket   A connector for expansion cards.

spam   Unwanted commercial e-mail sent out to millions of random addresses.

SpeedBooster   Linksys proprietary extension to the 802.11g wireless network standard to allow speeds up to 72 Mbps.

SPI (stateful protocol inspection)   Firewall programs or devices that are able to perform inspection of the communication protocols, such as TCP/IP and HTTP, to ensure that the actions are appropriate to prevent hacker attacks.

spyware   Software placed on your computer by programs or websites that track what Internet sites you visit for commercial or illegal use.

spyware/adware blocker   Software programs that run on PCs and prevent spyware and adware programs from installing themselves on your computer.

SSID   Service set identifier. A term used for the name wireless network identifies itself in order to recognize one wireless network from another.

static IP address   Having an IP address assigned by the Internet service provider, which does not change.

STP (shielded twisted-pair)   A type of media used in networking; STP is composed of pairs of twisted wires that are then covered with a material that prevents signal interference.

switch   A network device that moves traffic through a local network. This device uses simple rules to make "decisions," and is not as intelligent as a router.

T

TCP (Transmission Control Protocol)   A subset Internet Protocol (IP) set of rules to send data in the form of message units between computers over the Internet.

Trojan horse   A program hidden inside of another (carrier) program by a hacker. When the carrier program is opened, the hidden program is launched, giving the hacker control of the infected computer or
sending him or her personal information.

U

uplink   Refers to the data flow from the computer to the service provider (and then to the Internet).

URL (uniform resource locator)   Commonly known as a web link, an address to a location on the Internet.

USB (Universal Serial Bus)   An interface that allows other devices to be connected and disconnected without resetting the system. Also a serial communication standard that allows high-speed data communication to many devices.

UTP (unshielded twisted-pair)   A type of media used in networking; UTP is composed of pairs of twisted (intertwined) wires. With UTP, no additional material is added.

V

virus   A program that attaches itself to (or really within) another program (the host) so that it can replicate itself when the host program is run or executed.

virus scan   A thorough search of the computer's memory, hard drive, and boot-up code for the presence of computer viruses.

voice chat   Using the Internet for voice conversations and phone calls, where there is typically no number to call, but you reach others through their "handle," much like instant messaging. Online gaming systems, such as Xbox Live, often provide a voice chat feature for players to communicate during games.

VoIP (voice over IP)   A protocol for transporting voice conversations across a data network. Also known as IP telephony.

Vonage   A company that provides residential IP telephony service over a high-speed Internet connection.

VPN (Virtual Private Network)   Refers to secure private connections between two endpoints over an otherwise public network.

W–Z

WAN (wide-area network)   Large-scale networks that connect smaller networks together.

war driver   A person who travels around looking for open wireless networks to gain free Internet access.

WEP (Wired Equivalent Privacy)   A security protocol designed to provide basic security for wireless LANs.

Wi-Fi (wireless fidelity)   Used to describe a WLAN that uses 802.11 protocols.

Windows 98/Me   Windows 98/ME are widely installed products in Microsoft's evolution of the Windows operating system for personal computers.

Windows XP   The latest version of the Windows desktop operating system for the PC.

Wireless A   Another term for a wireless network using the 802.11a standard.

Wireless B   Another term for a wireless network using the 802.11b standard.

Wireless G   Another term for a wireless network using the 802.11g standard.

WLAN (wireless LAN)   A LAN that is connected using wireless technologies instead of wire cables.

worm   Similar to viruses in that their defining characteristic is self replication usually over networks and computers. Unlike viruses, however, a worm does not alter or remove files from computers.

WWW (World Wide Web)   Refers to all the resources and users on the Internet that are using the Hypertext Transfer Protocol (HTTP).

WPA (Wi-Fi Protected Access)   Wireless network security standard, considered a more secure successor to WEP.

WPA2 (Wi-Fi Protected Access version 2)   Wireless network security standard, considered a more secure successor to WEP, and security improvements beyond WPA.

Xbox Live   Online game playing service for Microsoft Xbox video games.

ZoneAlarm   Common software personal firewall program for PC's.

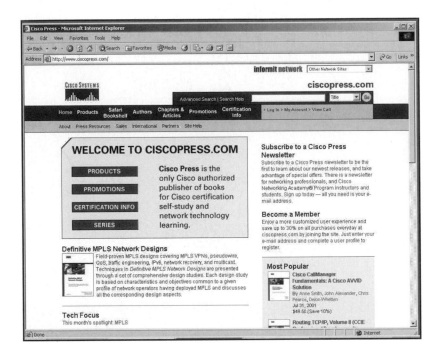
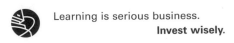